REACHING CHINESE WORLDWIDE

G. Wright Doyle

With Laura Mason

Torchflame Books
An imprint of Light Messages

Reaching Chinese Worldwide
G. Wright Doyle
civirginia@nexet.net
www.chinainst.org

Printed in the United States of America
Light Messages Publishers
Durham, North Carolina

ISBN: 978-1-61153-067-4

This book is thankfully dedicated to my life-long companion and indispensable co-worker,

Dori,

without whose constant counsel and prayers I would have made far more, and worse, mistakes than I have. You are definitely God's gift to me!

Acknowledgements

Though I composed the text of Reaching Chinese Worldwide, my editorial assistant, Laura Philbrick Mason, has performed the very difficult but essential task of turning a jumble of disconnected thoughts into a relatively coherent whole. Anything that remains unclear can be ascribed to me, not her. She tried her best!

TABLE OF CONTENTS

CHAPTER ONE
PILGRIMAGE IN MISSION

In 2005, I began writing a series of newsletters on the subject of "Reaching Chinese Worldwide." These short articles outlined and explored various ways in which people who desire to see Chinese blessed by the gospel of Jesus Christ might share this Good News effectively with them.

Of course, there are more than a billion Chinese people, and they live not only in Mainland China, but also in Taiwan, South East Asia, Europe, Latin America, Africa, and North America. This geographical variety is matched by similar differences in sub-culture, religion, age, economic status, and spiritual condition. Furthermore, those who eagerly long to see God's love and truth manifested among the Chinese themselves represent a mosaic of countries and cultures, beliefs and traditions, personalities and abilities, passions and fears. Thus, the opinions that follow must necessarily be circumscribed by my own knowledge and experience, which I shall describe briefly below. To take you beyond my limited understanding, however, there is an abundance of resources on both China and ministry among Chinese, and a short list of these will be given at the end of book, so that you can follow up each topic in greater detail.

EARLY LIFE AND EDUCATION

My father was a Naval officer, so we lived in a variety of places when I was growing up, including Bermuda, Puerto Rico, and Taiwan. Our stay in Taiwan lasted one year, July 1957 to August, 1958, when I was thirteen years old. I spent many happy and adventurous hours wandering around the countryside, climbing mountains, traversing rice paddies, fording streams, and exploring Chinese neighborhoods. This was back before Taiwan's great leap into modernization, when water buffaloes pulled wooden plows through knee-deep water in terraced fields and we rode around Taipei in three-wheeled pedicabs.

As a student at Taipei American School, I learned a smattering of Mandarin. A visit to the National Art Museum, still in a warehouse in Taichung, impressed me with the beauty and wealth of China's artistic heritage, while banquets put on for my parents by Chinese colleagues left an indelible impression of Chinese cuisine. All in all, the experience created in me a great respect for Chinese people and their culture, although I never expected to return.

In college, I majored in Latin and took three years of Greek, thus beginning to gain some knowledge of Classical culture. I attended a liberal seminary, where there was no mention of cross-cultural missions, but I did receive an introduction to non-evangelical theology. After seminary, I served as pastor for three small Episcopal churches in rural eastern North Carolina. That was truly a cross-cultural experience for both my wife, Dori, and me! In 1991, I returned to the University of North Carolina at Chapel Hill for a PhD program in Classics, which further deepened my knowledge of the Greco-Roman world. Since then, I have seen those years of studying Greek and Latin literature, philosophy, and religion as excellent preparation for gaining additional perspective on Chinese culture, which shares many similarities with Classical civilization.

FIRST STEPS IN MISSIONS

My "pilgrimage in missions"[1] actually began in 1973 while I was in graduate school. Dori and I attended the Chapel Hill Bible Church, where I was elected as an elder (we were all very young!). Since each elder had to be responsible for one of the ministries of the church, I was given oversight of the Missions Committee. I knew absolutely nothing about cross-cultural missions, so I did what graduate students do: I gathered a group of men who were interested in missions, and we met monthly, discussing a different book about missions each time. At the end of that year, Dori and I attended Urbana '73, the triennial Student Missions Conference sponsored by Inter-Varsity Christian Fellowship.

At that conference, we sensed strongly that God was leading us to spend our lives serving as missionaries to people of another culture, and started looking for an appropriate sending agency. We finally applied to, and were accepted by, Overseas Missionary Fellowship (OMF), the successor organization to the China Inland Mission (CIM), founded by J. Hudson Taylor in the nineteenth century. As part of our orientation to OMF, we read a short biography of Hudson Taylor, which immediately captured

---

1   This phrase is taken from a regular feature of the *International Bulletin of Missionary Research* (*IBMR*), in which long-time participants in mission work share their life story. I have changed the word "mission" to "missions," however. "Mission" often refers to the totality of God's saving work among mankind, while I am using "missions" to denote intentional cross-cultural witness, often involving extended time spent living in another culture.

my heart and inspired me to imitate his example, though I could not be like him in every way.

At first, we did not know where in Asia we would be assigned. OMF leaders suggested several possible Bible schools and seminaries to me, but none of them seemed to fit what I wanted to do. For months, we prayed for guidance. Then one day, as I was having my daily quiet time in the Bible and in prayer, I "saw" my first—and only—vision: a map of mainland China, and Taiwan, with the West Coast of the United States off the to right. Then I "heard" a "voice" in my mind, saying, "I want you in Asia." By "Asia," Greater China was obviously meant.

But was this from God, or my sub-conscious? Previously, I had had no thought of ministering among Chinese, having almost forgotten my wonderful year in Taiwan as a teenage boy. This "voice" seemed to come from nowhere, just out of the blue. Over a period of three days, in a variety of ways I tested it to see whether it really was God's will for us to serve among Chinese in Asia. I finally concluded that it was, and told Dori, who immediately accepted it as the Lord's leading. (This was not the first or last time that she has expressed her love for me and faith in God by following my sense of his guidance.) We told OMF, and they acted accordingly.

MISSIONARY TRAINING AND MINISTRY IN SINGAPORE AND TAIWAN

In 1975, Dori and I went to Singapore as new members of OMF (now called OMF International). Our exposure to ministry among Chinese began with living and teaching at the Discipleship Training Centre (DTC), which was founded by the late David Adeney, who went to China as a missionary with the CIM in 1934. Under his tutelage, we learned a great deal about how to understand and relate to Chinese from all parts of Asia, as well as people from South and Southeast Asia, since DTC's student body was quite diverse. Watching him and his wife, Ruth, we saw veteran and well-beloved missionaries at work in a variety of roles. In our weekly times together, David (as he insisted I call him) answered my questions and opened up his mind and heart to me. I shall always be grateful to him. Of course, the Chinese and other Asian students and faculty at DTC also taught Dori and me a great deal, always with respect and gentleness. While in Singapore, we attended an English-speaking Chinese Anglican church.

After several months at DTC, we entered OMF's ten-week orientation, where we were instructed in all aspects of missionary life and work, including the necessity of gaining historical, cultural, and religious knowledge and understanding of the people among whom we would serve. That was followed by two years of full-time language study in Taichung, Taiwan. Every day of the week, we attended three hours of class, with each student having only one teacher; each new class period brought a different teacher, so we had to stay alert. In the afternoons, we listened to tapes and pored over the textbooks, seeking to gain an elementary grasp of this ancient, beautiful, and difficult language. Weekly OMF prayer meetings put us into close contact with missionaries with decades of experience, who freely shared their wisdom with us. As new workers with OMF, we were also treated to special classes and lectures on how best to serve the Chinese; these events supplemented the special lectures given at the annual field meeting. Our leaders also encouraged us to read as much as we could, to make at least one Chinese friend, and to observe our Chinese neighbors as closely as possible.

We also attended a Chinese church, where we were warmly welcomed despite our almost total inability to communicate. I am not sure I understood more than a dozen words during the first six months of Sundays, but comprehension improved with time, and by the end of our two years in Taichung we could make out much of the sermon and service. Dori even sang in the choir. Our lack of facility in Mandarin compelled us to watch, listen, and receive, though we were eager to speak out! Several of the church members befriended us; we maintain close relationships with three of them to this day.

In 1978, cumulative illnesses and mild depression, aggravated by a back injury, forced me to return to the United States with Dori. Almost as soon as we arrived in Chapel Hill, whence we had been sent as missionaries by the Chapel Hill Bible Church less than three years previously, we found out about a Chinese Bible study group that was meeting in a small room in a local Baptist church. We invited them to larger premises at the Bible Church, and began what has been a most happy association with a fellowship that has grown and matured over the past several decades. Whenever we return to Chapel Hill, I am invited to preach to special evangelistic meetings that they hold; "Come hear a foreigner speak Chinese" seems to be the drawing card.

In 1980, I received an invitation from Dr. James H. Taylor, III, the founder and President of China Evangelical Seminary in Taipei, who was departing for Singapore to assume the position of General Director for OMF. He wanted me to take his place as Greek instructor. I was reluctant to return to the scene of so much pain, but sensed God's leading. That commenced a total of seven very enjoyable years at CES. In addition to teaching New Testament and Greek, I served with Dori as advisor to a group of students, worked with the young adults group at our church, and participated in the leadership training program of Campus Evangelical Fellowship, a sister organization to Inter-Varsity Christian Fellowship. The pastor of Friendship Presbyterian Church was gracious to meet with me almost weekly; from him I learned a great deal about Chinese church life, as Dori did from his gracious wife. Dori and I also hosted a small group in our home. Over these years, countless hours spent in seminary faculty meetings, church services and informal gatherings, OMF prayer meetings, and private conversations broadened our understanding and appreciation for Chinese Christians and the cultural heritage they bring to bear on their walk with Christ. We saw, too, the suffering of those without Christ, the folly of worshiping idols, and the pressures of modern urban living. Gradually, our facility with the Chinese language improved to the point where I could preach and teach in Chinese and we could both counsel individuals in their mother tongue.

I was given an introduction to the challenging task of effective missions administration by election to the OMF Taiwan Field Council, a group of senior missionaries who meet quarterly to advise the Director. We wrestled with personnel issues, mostly, but also with matters of strategy, relationships with Chinese Christians and church leaders, and finance. Until you have worked for at least a year as a missionary in a foreign country, it is quite hard to imagine just how complex and difficult this sort of life can be. And until I served on the Field Council, I did not appreciate the arduous task that faces administrators of missionary organizations. You can believe that I was much less critical of our leaders after this experience![2]

TRANSLATION

More than one observer has noted that the essence of cross-cultural missionary work is "translation," in both the narrower and the broader senses.[3] Over the years, I have also been involved in the arduous process of translation in a number of ways. When I began to teach Greek at Chinese Evangelical Seminary, though we had a grammar book that had been translated into Chinese, there was no modern Greek-Chinese

2   Perhaps I am here gently reminding historians and others to temper their sometimes harsh criticisms of the foreign missionary enterprise with a little bit of humility and understanding.

3   See, for example, Lamin Sanneh, *Translating the Message.*

lexicon. I formed a team of my students to translate the standard work, Gingrich and Danker's Greek-English Lexicon of the New Testament, into Chinese. The translation was done by my students, with my supervision. In the course of this work, I discovered even more just how difficult it is to render biblical Greek into modern Chinese, but I also found that it is possible. Naturally, teaching classes on the Greek New Testament also involved translation, since I had to help my students learn how to turn the Greek text into acceptable Chinese, despite the vast differences in vocabulary and grammar. That was an ongoing education for me as a missionary translator.

Later, as I composed books in English for Chinese readers, I frequently worked with helpers to check the translations of my original into Chinese. As English Editor of the Biographical Dictionary of Chinese Christianity, I have translated some of the articles by our Chinese editor, Dr. Yading Li, into English. My biggest translation challenge came in 2011–2012, when I translated A Critique of Indigenous Theology by Lit-sen Chang (Zhang Lisheng) into English. I am most thankful to several Chinese for enabling me to understand the very complex writing style and finish the work. Over the years, I have occasionally also done simultaneous interpretation into either English or Chinese for preachers. When preaching or speaking to Chinese audiences, I either work from an English outline or from the Chinese Bible. Although I am sure that all my translations have been riddled with errors, I have done enough of it to know both its difficulty and its possibility.

MINISTRY TO CHINESE IN THE U.S.: CHINA INSTITUTE

We returned from Taiwan to the United States in 1988; the next year, we moved to Charlottesville, Virginia, where we have lived since then. OMF did not at that time have a ministry to Chinese living in North America, so we were encouraged by our church to start our own organization for that purpose. I am not gifted in administration, but had no choice other than to establish a nonprofit ministry, China Institute. From the beginning, I had two goals: to minister directly to Chinese and to mobilize others to share Christ with them. Our focus has been upon educated Chinese, not out of prejudice towards others, but because these are the ones whom God has brought in large numbers for higher education in the West. The University of Virginia is a premier state university, and hosts hundreds of Chinese scholars and, recently, undergraduates.

In 1989, we began a Bible study that grew from one man meeting weekly with me to as many as fifty, with an average of about twenty-five, that gathered each week until 2002. Consisting mostly of people from the

People's Republic of China, this group introduced us to a whole new world, far different from Taiwan, which maintains total religious and political freedom. God's Spirit has been moving in marvelous ways among the Chinese since the 1970s, with a new wave of interest and conversions among college graduates after June 1989, when the Tiananmen incident broke their faith in the goodness of man and the benevolence of the Communist Party. Through friendships and groups like this Bible study, we have come to know a bit about the complex and ever-changing society of mainland China. During the dozen years we met, more than two dozen people asked for baptism, though I never pressured anyone to do so. I taught about the necessity of repentance, faith, and baptism as a sign of commitment, and waited for them to come to me. In the Lord's providence, two Chinese couples were led to start a new fellowship just when most of our members had moved away. I began to serve as their informal advisor.

Meanwhile, in 1993, a member of the Chinese Bible study group, who was studying at UVA, founded an English-speaking fellowship of undergraduate ethnic Chinese studying at the university. That fellowship grew within seven years to about seventy students, then returned to its previous number of about twenty in attendance weekly. The students continue to lead this Chinese Christian Fellowship, and Dori and I have served as advisors. She meets with the women in leadership, and I with the men. Dori also has hosted their annual Christmas party in our home and provides some of the food for other events. For a while, I also led a small group of men in studying my book, Jesus: The Complete Man. Increasingly, I agree with those who affirm the vital strategic importance of student work, and I am thrilled that Dori and I have been part of that endeavor.

In 1996, in order to provide a smaller English-speaking worship service for Chinese, I started International Christian Fellowship with two other men. We met for ten years, with attendance varying from ten to seventy. I did most of the preaching, while others helped lead the service. For most of those years, more American-born Chinese came than did those from overseas, though there were always a few from China or Taiwan. God worked among us, and about twenty-five people were baptized. In the end, dwindling numbers led us to believe that God was not going to turn this into a sustainable church, though that had been our dream. Accepting this "failure" wasn't easy, but we did, and terminated the weekly meetings in 2006 after advising people to attend one of the Chinese-language congregations in Charlottesville or the English-speaking church to which we belong. Though we did not succeed in our original plan, the entire experience taught me a great deal about the difficulties of planting churches.

Most of the members of International Christian Fellowship chose to come with us to our church, where we had been meeting for more than a year. A couple of years later, we asked the pastor whether we could start a Mandarin Sunday school class for the Chinese-speaking people who attended the worship services. He kindly offered the use of his own office, which provided a very warm and cozy setting for our class. We continue to meet every Sunday to discuss the sermon for the day. Our pastors always preach exegetical sermons, so that discussion is at the same time a Bible study. Along the way, however, we answer the many questions that come up about the Bible, theology, church liturgy and practices, and the Christian life. When baptisms take place, we explain the meaning of that ordinance; we also teach about the Lord's Supper, which is celebrated weekly. If one of the historic Creeds has been recited, we briefly go over it to remind the believers and instruct the newcomers. We spend a lot of time talking about how to apply the teaching of the Bible to daily life, including marriage, family, and work, with a special focus on what it means to live as a Chinese Christian. At the end of the hour, we pray for each other. A steady stream of fresh arrivals keep this class growing, so much so that we have recently had to re-locate to an adult education classroom to accommodate the increased numbers, who include young people attending the local Christian school and living with Christian families, students at the University, and mature scholars and their spouses.

Realizing that people who were brought up in China come with a unique background, worldview, and questions, our church has decided to provide them with their own baptism preparation class in Mandarin. Currently, we are going through the Apostles' Creed, supplemented by the Nicene Creed and the Westminster (or Baptist) Confession of Faith from the seventeenth century. We find this to be a helpful outline for introducing basic Christian doctrines, and we try to apply each one to our daily life. At the end of each class, people are given a chance to share their response in groups of two or three. Questions are always welcome, of course. When this course is completed, each person desiring baptism will be interviewed to see whether he has a clear knowledge of the gospel; agrees with the fundamentals of the faith; has repented of sin and trusted entirely in Christ for salvation; and has experienced a radical change in life direction. If these conditions appear to be met, we shall recommend them to the elders of the church, who will again interview them.

MISSIONS MOBILIZATION

For four years, from 1991 to 1995, I served as part-time Director of Missions for our church in Charlottesville. Though I was at first reluctant to divert time from exclusive ministry among Chinese, I soon found that exposure to a variety of Christian works among cultures of all sorts gave me a different perspective on what God is doing among the Chinese. I saw both similarities and differences between Chinese culture and other cultures, and between Christianity in China and its manifestations in other societies. My understanding of cross-cultural missions was broadened by attending conferences, reading journals and books, and coordinating and participating in the Perspectives on the World Christian Movement course. Taking others through the massive Perspectives Reader three times was a most edifying experience. Overall, though I later decided to return to full-time work among Chinese, I profited greatly from that brief tenure as Director of Missions. For one thing, I saw from the inside the possibilities and challenges of mobilizing a church for cross-cultural ministry. For a number of years, I also served on the church's World Missions Team.

In 2004, two young people who attended our church and were about to graduate from the University of Virginia indicated to us that they sensed God's leading to serve among the Chinese. Rather than advising them to go to a seminary, I created a two-year internship for them. They read Integrative Theology, a very comprehensive book that combines historical, biblical, and systematic theology with apologetics, Christian living, and ministry. Books on Chinese history and culture, Christianity in China, and the Perspectives Reader rounded out their intellectual preparation. Dori and I met with each of them separately each week; the man participated in a men's group led by one of church's pastors; and they helped with Chinese Christian Fellowship. They both also held part-time jobs. In time, the class grew to include several others, who with them became a small and very close fellowship of like-minded people. This couple left for Taiwan in 2005, and immediately began intensive language study, which lasted for three years; after that, the husband enrolled in China Evangelical Seminary. Upon graduation in 2010, he began working in an English-language church in Taiwan, first as intern, and then as Associate Pastor.

They joined others on the China Institute team: a couple who live and serve in Cambridge, England and an American graduate of China Evangelical Seminary who was working on his PhD in Chinese History (he has since graduated and will start teaching at an American university). Others have become China Institute Partners since then; they now include three Chinese couples and three American couples, including Dori and me. Financially, we follow Hudson Taylor's practice of relying on God, through prayer, to move people to give funds for this ministry, though of course we do our best to keep our prayer supporters informed of what God is doing through us.

In other words, I have become a mini-missions administrator, which has forced me to learn yet another set of skills, some of which do not come easily to me. I am conscious of serious failures, but grateful that God has placed me in a position to provide a platform of ministry for others.

A few years ago, our church decided to make ministry to ethnic Chinese a major focus of the church's cross-cultural outreach. For a while, I belonged to the Ethnic Chinese Ministry Team that was formed to oversee this "focus ministry." They are charged with caring for the Global Partners who work with our church among Chinese around the world, including Taiwan and Charlottesville (the church has no "missionaries" in mainland China), and with crafting an overall strategy for tapping the considerable resources of the congregation for Christian witness among the Chinese. Among other things, they also help work with the team responsible for ministry to international students as they seek to encourage our members to serve as friendship partners with Chinese students. The Chinese leader of the Mandarin Sunday school class belongs to the team also, and keeps it up-to-date on developments in that group. The team carefully designs and leads short-term visits to China to have the most impact, and makes plans for the growth of this work.

GLOBAL CHINA CENTER

In 2004, Dr. Carol Lee Hamrin and I sensed God's leading to initiate a new kind of outreach to Chinese. Since there are so many Chinese scholars studying Christianity as an academic subject, opportunities to interact with them abound. Some are committed Christians, while others are simply interested in Christianity as a social or religious phenomenon. In any case, they are eager to engage scholars from outside China in discussions about the nature of Christianity, its relationship to Western culture, and its possible role in twenty-first century Chinese society. Global China Center was started as a vehicle for building relationships and disseminating information and analysis among, and about, this group of intellectuals.

Since then, GCC has launched two websites: globalchinacenter.org posts book reviews and articles about Chinese history, culture, and society, including religion, and especially Christianity in China. This site has become a trusted source of information and analysis for thousands of readers, both Chinese and Western, around the world. The Biographical Dictionary of Chinese Christianity (bdcconline.net) features brief biographies, in Chinese and in English, of Chinese and Western Christians who have played a part in the building of today's Chinese church. There are several hundred of these stories on the site, with more being added constantly.

GCC Associates have made presentations at international academic conferences in Beijing, Shanghai, Hong Kong, London, Washington, D.C., and elsewhere, and have lectured in universities in mainland China, Taiwan, and the West. Participation in these events has widened my own perspective considerably. Having a number of Chinese scholars visit us in Charlottesville has done the same.

Thus, without really planning to, I have become the leader of two ministries—China Institute and Global China Center—with different emphases and strategies for sharing the Good News of Jesus Christ with Chinese around the world.

LEARNING THROUGH TRAVEL

Since 1988, when we made our first trip to China, I have made about twenty trips back to Taiwan, and have visited mainland China about ten times. In my role as a missionary with China Institute, I have taught short seminary courses, preached in Chinese churches, and visited a dozen major cities in North America; Cambrige, England; Hong Kong; and Taipei, Taichung, Tainan, and Kaohsiung in Taiwan. My association with Global China Center has taken me to academic conferences and special briefings in Oxford, and London, England; and Shanghai, Beijing, and Shantou, China. Starting in Singapore in 1975, by listening to hundreds of Chinese believers—both those who stand in the pulpit and those who sit in the pews—and non-Chinese who seek to minister among them, I have gained a little bit of perspective on the state of Christianity in Chinese society. People with far more experience and knowledge than I possess have shared their insights, which have been supplemented by my own reading, as well as attendance at China ministry conferences sponsored by ChinaSource and other organizations and churches.

READING AND CONFERENCES

In addition to the books we read the year that I led the Missions Committee of the Chapel Hill Bible Church, my early exposure to Missiology[4]

---

4   Missiology is the study of missions (or "mission," as some would prefer to say).

included most of the chapters from the compendium of the 1972 First International Congress on World Evangelization held at Lausanne, Switzerland, and several compendia from Urbana Student Missions Conferences. These laid the foundation later studies in this fascinating field, one that combines biblical studies, theology, history, anthropology, sociology, and several other disciplines. In the early 1990s, I coordinated a Perspectives on the World Christian Movement course and worked through the Workbook and Reader for the course. Leading students through that large volume twice more after that has been of great benefit to me. Our Overseas Missionary Fellowship Orientation Course in Singapore in 1976 included readings in many fields, including missionary anthropology. I was very stimulated by Louis Luzbetak's Church and Cultures: An Applied Anthropology for the Religion Worker. It opened my eyes to the need for careful observation and sympathetic understanding of the culture and customs of the people whom we want to serve.

Journals offer a wealth of information and insight. For a number of years I have regularly read the Evangelical Missions Quarterly, Missiology, and the International Bulletin of Missionary Research, as well as more China-specific periodicals. Biographies put flesh and blood onto the skeleton of general history and theoretical works. The collection of missionary biographies in Mission Legacies, and in the Biographical Dictionary of Christian Mission, both edited by Gerald Anderson and others, along with a few dozen book-length biographies, have greatly deepened my knowledge of the great leaders in missions theory and practice over the past two hundred years.

Many, though not all, of the major influences on my views about cross-cultural ministry, including specific work among the Chinese, are named at the end of this book in the Resources section This short list of some of the printed works that have partly informed my views on ministry among Chinese has obvious gaps. I emphasize that I am not a trained, professional missiologist, but a practitioner who has tried to avoid total ignorance of the essential theological and theoretical work of scholars in the field. I am aware that my reading is quite limited; I only hope that my own ideas are not too far from what the Bible teaches, and invite correction from readers with far more learning than I possess.

Conferences, too, have broadened my perspective. In addition to Urbana '73, Dori and I also went to Urbana' 79, this time with two years of cross-cultural living behind us. Hearing and speaking with missionaries from all over the world opened our eyes to the scope of what God's people are doing to obey the Great Commission. The sheer variety has helped to prevent myopia and narrow-mindedness. Various church missions conferences, China ministry consultations, and academic meetings have further widened my horizons.

PHYSICAL AND EMOTIONAL WEAKNESSES

Not long after we arrived in Taiwan in 1976, I began to suffer from a series of minor ailments. In 1977, I re-activated an old injury to my back, and was almost incapacitated for a while. On the advice of Chinese Christian friends, I went to a Christian practitioner of acupuncture, which was a real education. His ministrations brought only temporary relief, however. Finally, the missionary doctor who had seen me often in the previous two years, after looking at my chart, which took more than two pages of fine print, asked, "Have you ever considered going home for a rest?" That led to our first furlough (now called home assignment), after which I returned to Taiwan in good health. After seven more years of very fulfilling life in Taiwan, however, I began to experience chronic aches and pains, though I ignored these because I was enjoying myself so much. When we came home in 1988, the discomfort increased, until finally, in 2001, I had a sort of minor breakdown. My doctors said I had mild depression and something like fibromyalgia syndrome, though technically I lacked some of the distinguishing symptoms of FMS.

Several months of spiritual counseling by several pastors, rest, exercise, and greater attention to diet brought some improvement, but I was resigned to a life of almost constant discomfort. In 2004, however, the Lord miraculously worked in my body, and I was largely freed from the aches, pains, brain fog, and other discomforts. As I learned to trust God to forgive my sins and provide all that I needed each day, as well as to forgive those who offended me, my mild depression also went away. For a few years, I enjoyed a new burst of energy, but I apparently over-did myself, and in the past few years I have struggled with chronic fatigue, though I remain free from the other symptoms that once plagued me.

In other words, for much of my pilgrimage in missions, poor health and limited strength have been constant companions, challenging my faith in God's presence, power, and promises. He has remained faithful, however, even though I am still greatly hindered by fatigue.

FAMILY MAN

For more than forty years, Dori has been my other constant companion, counselor, colleague, and friend. As wife to me and mother of our daughter, Sarah, she has focused her time and attention on her family and her home. Like a true missionary wife, however, she has entered into our ministry among Chinese with all the extra energy she has, especially after Sarah left home for college. Dozens, perhaps hundreds, of Chinese have benefited from her wisdom and kindness. Who knows what has been effected by her daily morning prayers? The number of meals she has served to Chinese and Western guests cannot be counted, nor the number of nights she has welcomed guests into our home.

Of course, marriage to me has not been easy. After all, I am only a guy! We have been helped along the way by marriage counseling and the prayers of our friends, and all this has further equipped us for ministry to Chinese and those who want to serve them`. We are not the only ones who have not found family life a smooth, problem-free existence!

Sarah was born in Taiwan and lived there until she was six years old. At one time, she was fluent in Mandarin; she still remembers a bit of that difficult language. Bringing up a child in a foreign culture poses its own peculiar challenges, as does trying to balance ministry to others and ministry to our own child. Meanwhile, our Chinese friends have been watching us to see what a "Christian" family looks like. We thank God for his preserving grace.

All of this is to say that I am first a family man, and then a witness of Christ among the Chinese. Though I have often failed at preserving this priority, I have constantly tried.

A CHILD OF GOD

Finally, of course, my pilgrimage in missions cannot be severed from my pilgrimage as a follower of Christ. Multiple failures have thrown me upon God for consolation, and even more, my sin has driven me constantly to the Cross and the Risen Lord for forgiveness and grace to go on, assured of the Father's love to me in the Son. Without frequent reliance on the Holy Spirit by prayer during each day, and without the prayers of many who have faithfully brought our needs before the Throne of Grace, we would have accomplished nothing. Increasingly, I realize that God is more interested in who I am than in what I do, and I am trying to learn how to rest in his love for me, even as I seek greater conformity to the likeness of Christ, who was sent by the Father into this world as the supreme Missionary. To him be all the glory.

CONCLUSION

You can see that God has been teaching me through a wide variety of experiences: living in another country and trying to acquire a working knowledge of its language and culture; participation in Chinese churches; teaching in Chinese-language seminaries and other training programs;

counseling and mentoring others; family life; participation in missions leadership; working as a missions mobilizer in two American congregations; reaching out to Chinese students and scholars in the West; trying to plant a church; serving an international team of missionaries and scholars; attending conferences and reading what the experts have to say. All have contributed to what I shall be sharing with you in this brief introduction to ministry among Chinese worldwide.

I offer the suggestions in this book in the hope that they will further the conversation about how best to declare the glory of God among this ancient and intelligent, but spiritually very needy, people. The volume could been expanded with hundreds of stories and examples from my experience and reading, but I have tried to keep it simple and unencumbered, though obviously potentially less interesting, by limiting the content to the presentation of a few principles. Likewise, I have resisted the temptation to document every statement with a biblical reference or citation of some authoritative book. This is not an academic work, though you may find a number of weighty tomes that have influenced my thinking in the Resources section. On the other hand, there is a bit of repetition, partly because I want to emphasize a few key themes, and partly because I know some readers will only dip into the parts that interest them, and I want to increase the odds that they will encounter these major emphases. At least to some degree aware of my poverty of knowledge and experience, I am confident that the pages that follow contain many egregious errors and are marred by major omissions. Please forgive what is amiss, feel free to contact me with suggestions for any future edition, and consult the experts whose books are named in the Resources section.

G. Wright Doyle
April, 2013

CHAPTER TWO
PRELIMINARIES

BIBLICAL FOUNDATIONS

Before we can talk about how to reach Chinese with the gospel of Christ, or even why we should focus on Chinese, we need to be clear about what we are doing.

The Gospel

What is the gospel that we need to share with our Chinese friends and neighbors? What is the rationale for sharing this gospel with them? What promises do we have, and what power can we rely on in our efforts to introduce them to the light, liberty, and love of God in Christ?

Much confusion surrounds the mission of God's church today. Some say we should work for political reform, social justice, and economic opportunity for the poor. Others maintain that we must concentrate upon proclamation of the simple message that we are saved through faith in Christ. There are those who see all religions as valid paths to knowing "God" and being "saved" from our spiritual troubles. Should we tell folks that God loves them and has a wonderful plan for their lives, if only they say a simple prayer to receive Christ? Or should we announce that healing and prosperity come to those who merely believe? Traditionally, Chinese have hoped that Christianity would make their nation strong and wealthy. Quite a few think that Christians should seek to promote democracy and freedom as the solution to China's problems. In the next few pages, I shall briefly state the convictions that inform the strategy and tactics outlined in this little book.[5]

We must begin with God, as the Bible does. "In the beginning, God created the heavens and the earth" (Gen 1:1). He made all that we see and all

---

5   Trained students of missions may consider this brief exposition of my guiding principles, and the pages which follow, as "missiology lite," since I do not interact with some major writers in this field, nor do I do treat any subject in the detail which it deserves. I ask their indulgence, since this book is meant as an introduction only, and is really an exercise in applied missiology as I understand it.

that we do not see, including the world of angels. Men and women were created in the image of God and given commands to exercise dominion over the earth and to "be fruitful and multiply." Placed in a paradise, they were supplied with all that they needed and told to take care of the Garden. Additionally, they were warned not to eat of the Tree of the Knowledge of Good and Evil, lest they die. When they believed the deceptions of the serpent (Satan), their relationships with God, each other, their own bodies, and the world around them were drastically shattered. Expelled from the Garden, they were condemned to toilsome work, painful child-bearing, marital strife, and waiting for physical death.

Ever since then, each person born into this world has been "conceived in sin," that is, sinful from the moment of conception (Ps 51:5). We are all "dead in trespasses and sins," slaves to the influences of the world, and servants of the devil (Eph 2:1–2; John 8:44). Dead people and slaves cannot deliver themselves. They are caught in their condition. In biblical terms, before they are born again, people are "darkened in their under-standing," (Eph 4:18). Non-Jews are also "strangers to the covenants of promise…without God and without hope in this world" (Eph 2:12). As a result of our sin, we are alienated from the life of God; as "sons of dis-obedience," we are also "children of wrath" (Eph 2:2–3); that is, we are doomed to eternal death in hell, far from the presence of God, suffering endless torment (Matt 25:41).[6]

We must be clear about this awful reality: Unless we are saved by God's grace, we are utterly lost. In this life, we are without God and without hope, as we have seen. Not only so, but all our relationships are shat-tered by sin and its effects. To one degree or another, we are alienated from others, even those closest to us, by fear, envy, greed, lust, pride, resentment, and all the selfishness that expresses itself in manifold forms but essentially keeps us from intimacy and harmony. You can see this in your own family, even if it is marked by an unusual degree of love and respect. Just reading the newspaper or watching the news on TV should

---

6   See also Isa 30:33; Matt 3:12; 529; 7:13; 8:11–12; 10:28; 13:30–42, 49–50; 18:8; 22:13; 25:41, 46; Mark 9:43–44; Luke 3:17; 16:23–25; 2 Thess 1:9; 2 Pet 2:4; Jude 6, 23; Rev 9:1–2; 14:10–11; 19:20; 20:10, 15; 21:8. For concise statements of the biblical teaching on the eternal punishment of unrepentant sinners, see the articles on Hell in A. Scott Moreau, ed., *Evangelical Dictionary of World Missions* and William A. Dyrness and Veli-Matt Kaarkkainen, *Global Dictionary of Theology*. To the philosophical (not biblical) argument that punishment of infinite duration by an infinite God upon finite beings is unjust, the answer is that sin against an infinite Being of infinite goodness and holiness deserves a punishment of infinite duration.

be enough to convince us that the profound problems facing each society find their root and source in individual sin. Until people are filled with God's love for them, they cannot truly love others; instead, they will live for themselves and use others.

In former times, before the June Fourth Incident in 1989, this Christian doctrine of "original sin" found little welcome in the minds of Chinese, but since that tragedy, and since the immense degradation of interpersonal relations that started in the Cultural Revolution (1966–1976) and has only been intensified during the period of opening and reform, Chinese people have come to realize that human nature is flawed at the core. For this reason, the Christian message is most definitely not one that highlights material prosperity, physical health, or national strength. These things may result from biblically-based faith, hope, and love, but they are only byproducts.[7] In our attempts to bless Chinese, we must meet their fundamental crisis head-on with a gospel that offers hope of forgiveness, reconciliation with God, and a transformed life that will inevitably lead to less conflict with others and more productive social interactions, and finally result in eternal bliss with all of redeemed humanity and creation in the presence of the Triune God.

So how does the gospel offer hope? We read in the Bible, beginning in Genesis 3:15, that God would not let the people whom he had made in his image remain forever in bondage to the sin and guilt that their disobedience had brought upon them. He promised a Deliverer who would crush the head of Satan, and repeated that promise through prophecies, types, and historical previews of his final saving acts in and through Christ. In the New Testament, we read that this Deliverer was God's eternal Son, his personal Word, who was equal with the Father in every respect, and who came down to this earth to be born as a little baby in Bethlehem. After he had come to adulthood, he commenced a ministry of preaching, teaching, healing, and exorcism that expressed his unique deity and revelation of God's own character and the power of the Holy Spirit.

Supremely, Jesus demonstrated God's love for us by dying on the Cross as a substitutionary sacrifice, a propitiatory offering, for our sins. He rose again on the third day, proving that he was indeed God's appointed Savior for the world, and ascended into heaven forty days later. There he sits at God's right hand, pouring out his Spirit upon all who truly

---

7   My books, *The Lord's Healing Words* and *Christianity in America: Triumph and Tragedy*, which are also available in Chinese, point out how the gospel can transform individuals and even nations, but these changes are partial in this life.

repent of their sins and trust in Christ alone for forgiveness and reconciliation to the Father, and incorporating them into the Body of Christ,
the family of God. At the end of the age, he will return to establish a
New Heaven and New Earth, where righteousness dwells, and where his
followers will live and rule with him, clothed in glorified bodies that will
never again see suffering, sorrow, or death. That final state of everlasting
fellowship with God and all those who are saved through Christ is the
hope of all believers. Meanwhile, we are to live for God's glory as his
beloved children and as disciples of Christ, doing our utmost to trust our
heavenly Father in all things and imitate Jesus throughout the day, by the
power of the indwelling Holy Spirit.

How does God reconcile individuals to himself and begin to re-fashion
them into the original image of holiness and love? He uses truth combined
with love, spoken and lived out by people of faith whose hope is set upon
the grace that will be revealed to them when Jesus returns. As the full
gospel goes out, people are convicted of sin; they repent of their wrong-
doing; they trust in Christ alone as Savior; and they commit themselves
wholly to his kingdom. They do this by the work of the Holy Spirit, who
empowers his people to communicate the Word of God, to pray, and to
live as becomes followers of Christ, and who alone can grant profound
repentance, sincere faith, and a new heart to sinners. In God's economy,
human action is usually essential for outsiders to be brought into the fold.
The gospel must be preached by people who live by its light in communities of truth and love.

In all of this, God's grace and his sovereignty are evident. Some receive
the message humbly and gratefully, while others remain cold and hard,
even to their dying breath. Those who have come to know God always
affirm that their salvation was not of themselves; it was the gift of God.
The Lord uses his Word and his Spirit to convict us of sin and convince
us to trust in Christ; his Spirit gives us faith and moves us to dedicate ourselves to his cause and kingdom; that same Spirit creates in us a profound
sense of being loved, so that we cry out, "Abba! Father!" No human
eloquence can work this miraculous change in our hearts; only God can
bestow the new heart. Why some believe and some do not remains an
impenetrable mystery, impervious to our attempts to explain it.

On the one hand, contemplation of God's sovereign grace evokes gratitude for his mercy to us; on the other, it impels us to share the wonderful
news of Christ with all around us. We want others to experience the love,
joy, peace, and hope that have been poured into our hearts and lives. We
can't stand the idea that anyone should be ignorant of this astounding

news, which we know is the only fountain of life, liberty, and love for this sad and broken world. That is why we dedicate ourselves to the task of evangelism of unbelievers and edification of Christians. We seek the glory of God and the good of our neighbors.

Until the Lord's return, we live in a world that is defiled by sin, corrupted by lust, and darkened by ignorance and willful rejection of God's truth. No amount of social reform, political revolution, or economic growth will change the hearts of men and women who do not know God. Our best efforts in those areas will be temporary and partial, and doomed to frustration and even failure.

It is true that the Holy Spirit, who now dwells in the hearts of true followers of Christ, daily transforms their minds, their affections, and their decisions, so that they increasingly resemble their Lord and Master, Jesus Christ. That same Spirit causes them to be born again as children of God into a new family of people from every race and nation, where real love can be tasted and shared. Communities of these people—especially small ones—can so reflect the love and beauty of God that people around them take notice and are drawn to the light and the life of this new society. As they live faithfully in the world, these believers and these little communities (churches) become "salt and light," whose influence, though gradual and often hidden, eventually impacts all of society.

The Fruits of the Gospel

Jesus summarized God's commands in two: We are to love the Lord our God with all our heart, soul, mind, and strength; and we are to love our neighbors as ourselves. Loving God includes praising him, delighting in him, thanking him, worshiping him, adoring him; listening to his Word daily; gathering with his people regularly; relying on his power to obey his revealed will; and doing our utmost to keep his commands. Loving our neighbors includes, at least, praying for them, setting them a good example, and assisting them whenever we can. Our "neighbors" are, first, other Christians (Gal 6:10) and then all those around us, or those whom we are able to help. We also love our neighbors when we fulfill our family responsibilities, do our jobs well, keep the laws of the land, and participate in activities that promote harmony and justice in society.

Just before he left his disciples to ascend to heaven, Jesus issued the Great Commission. Found in five places in the Bible, it tells Christians what we should be doing until he returns (Matt 28:18–20; Mark 16:15; Luke 24:46–48; John 20:21; Acts 1:8). Love for God now includes declaring his name and fame throughout the world; spreading the gospel of repentance and forgiveness of sins through faith in Jesus Christ; praying for and announcing the coming of the King and his kingdom; and living as befits those who have received a gracious calling.

Actually, fulfilling the Great Commission is also now an essential aspect of loving our neighbors. Not only for God's glory, but also for their good, we announce that they can be reconciled to God through faith in Jesus Christ. How can we say that we love them if we withhold from them the only information that will enable them to escape everlasting punishment and enter into eternal life? When we call them to repentance and faith in Christ, we are pointing them to the sole source of personal renewal, relational restoration, and social transformation. Only those who have known the love of God in Christ can truly love others in the home, at work or school, and in the nation. Only they can pray with faith, work with love, and labor in hope, and only they can submit to the providence of an Almighty God when facing poverty, disaster, or oppression. Profound peace and inner tranquility come only to those who rest in the love of God, and only those who are at peace with God can become peacemakers among men.

Those who know God are brought into his family, the Body of Christ, the Church universal. They belong to local congregations where God's truth is proclaimed and his love is lived out among people who are gradually being changed into the likeness of Christ. Within this Body, there are various members with different gifts and responsibilities. Some will concentrate upon the ministry of the Word and prayer; others will minister to the physical needs of the group. But all must be witnesses of Christ by word and deed in this dark and lonely world. The same is true of cross-cultural mission work. Some will dedicate themselves to evangelism and teaching, while others will devote their time and energy to works of mercy and social construction as housewives and nannies; teachers, physicians, and nurses; helpers in orphanages; artists and entertainers; or productive business people. All, however, must be quick to declare the love of God in Christ Jesus verbally, and all must be ready to offer a helping hand when it is needed and they are able.

Obedience to the Great Command and the Great Commission must result from the life-giving and life-transforming power of the Holy Spirit, who fills our hearts with love for God and for others, enables us to "put to death the evil deeds of the body" (Rom 8:13), and impels us to take the gospel to the ends of the earth.[8] God the Father grants the gift of the

---

8   For the central role of the Spirit in missions, see Luke 24:49; John 20:21–22; Acts 1:8.

Spirit to all who truly trust in Jesus the Son of God as Savior and Lord. Indeed, the entire work of redemption, and therefore all of our witness as followers of Christ, issues from God, and is therefore often now called the "mission of God" (missio Dei).[9] This God, however, is revealed to us as Triune, with Father, Son, and Holy Spirit equally divine and equally, though distinctly, involved in the "mission" of saving the world from the ravages of sin and restoring it to a condition that will even excel the pristine beauty of Eden. Missions, therefore, are conducted as a response to, and by the presence and power of, the Triune God and his "mission" to glorify himself in and through his redeemed people.[10]

The gospel carries implications for personal health and happiness.[11] More than that, when Christians follow the example of Christ and proclaim his truth in all arenas of society, changes take place that can transform entire nations. For several centuries, the United States of America served as an example—albeit an imperfect one—of what can happen when Christian ideals and ideas are woven into the fabric of a nation's laws, education, literature, family, work, and government. Just as the gospel has affected nations, so there are triumphs in individual lives, churches, and corporate life when those who trust in Christ seek to obey his commands and communicate his truth. But there are also tragedies, especially when Christians succumb to pride, worldliness, and ungodly ambition, particularly utopian visions of societal and political reform and renewal.[12] We must work for the total welfare of those around us, but we must not imagine that our efforts will Bring about heaven on earth; that must await the return of Christ.

These convictions are, I believe, derived from the Bible, which has been

---

9   A recent example is Christopher J.H. Wright, *The Mission of God: Unlocking the Bible's Grand Narrative*. Though I have not read this magisterial work in its entirety, extensive sampling leads me to believe that it has considerable merit as a work of biblical theology, though Wright seems to focus a great deal on deliverance from earthly ills, including oppression, with virtually no mention of deliverance from eternal punishment.

10   Many works on Missiology now explicitly speak of the Trinitarian nature of Christian missions. See, for example, Samuel Escobar, "Evangelical Missiology: Peering into the Future at the Turn of the Century," in William D. Taylor, ed., *Global Missiology for the 21st Century*, 114–120, and all of Part Three of that volume (189–258).

11   See my book, *The Lord's Healing Words*, available also in Chinese.

12   This view of American Christian history has been explained in detail in my book, *Christianity in America: Triumph and Tragedy*, and earlier version of which was published in Chinese under the title, *Hope Deferred*.

traditionally and properly considered by Christians to be the inspired Word of God in written form. As such, the Scriptures are infallible (they will not lead us astray) and they are inerrant (they do not contain errors).[13] They thus carry divine authority, and are unique in the literature of the world. Other books sometimes considered sacred, such as the Buddhist Scriptures and works by great sages like Confucius and Mencius, contain a great deal of truth, but they are incomplete at best and filled with serious errors at worst. In any case, they do not tell us how to be reconciled with God through faith in Jesus Christ and the regenerating work of the Holy Spirit. While Christians respect the wisdom of non-believers, they give supreme allegiance to the revelation of God in the Bible as the standard by which all other belief systems are evaluated. These biblical foundations underlie all that follows in these pages. I believe that in order to "reach Chinese worldwide" with the life-giving message of the gospel, we must be clear about the true state of men and women and the only truth that can save us.

WHY REACH OUT TO CHINESE?

In 1986, at the Chinese Congress on Evangelization held in Taiwan, I heard a speech by the late Dr. Jonathan Chao that has lodged in my mind ever since. He claimed that the evangelization of China is, and ought to be, the main priority for the church around the world. Though I do not remember the specifics of his argument, the overall force of his presentation convinced me at the time and still determines my own ministry.

That is not to say that we should not be engaged in vigorous, determined, and intentional evangelism of all other parts and peoples of the world, in Europe, Africa, Asia, the Middle East, Central Asia, Latin America, and North America. Jesus' command to take the gospel to all the world remains in force. Perhaps we should not even say that reaching Chinese with the gospel should stand at the top of the list of priorities for all churches everywhere, for conditions and situations vary, and God leads different congregations in different ways, according to his unique plan for them. At the same time, Dr. Chao issued a challenge that should at least capture our attention and cause us to think: Why, indeed, is reaching China and the Chinese people worldwide so important?

First, the Han Chinese, who comprise ninety-five percent of China's population, remain the largest unevangelized people group in the world. Yes, a strong and growing church exists among this people, and Chinese

---

13   For a persuasive case for the authority of the Scriptures, see Carl F. H. Henry, *God, Revelation, and Authority*.

Christians are working hard to introduce the saving truth of Christ to their fellow countrymen. The fact remains, however, that more than 1.2 billion Han Chinese do not know Christ; most of these have never heard the gospel; and most cannot hear unless someone goes to a great deal of trouble to tell them.[14]

Second, the Chinese church itself suffers from a number of serious weaknesses that greatly reduce its ability to bear effective witness to God's redemption in Christ. Many church leaders lack biblical and theological training, so their lives tend to diverge significantly from biblical standards, not to mention the lives of church members. Their inadequate teaching results in a huge lack of biblical knowledge, causing sects and heresies to abound, and a focus on the supposed material benefits of trusting in Jesus. Very few Christian intellectuals are attending to the relationships between Christianity and other Chinese belief systems; those who are engaged in this vital enterprise often tend towards accommodation and even syncretism. Liberalism heavily influences the official church, and freedom to evangelize is strictly circumscribed by the government. I will talk about this in greater detail, but these examples should suffice to demonstrate the limited capacity of the Christian church in China. Christians in China need help, not only to spread the gospel, but also to instruct their own people, including their pastors, elders, and evangelists, in the "whole counsel of God."

Third, the potential of the Chinese church almost defies imagination. With the rise of China to superpower status, Chinese believers have openings to take the gospel around the world. The existing networks of overseas Chinese Christians provide exciting opportunities for Christians from China to build upon; meanwhile, they are creating new avenues and building new relationships, such as those formed by enterprising business people from Wenzhou. Is there any other group of Christians with the same access to so many places? I doubt it. Adding value to their numbers is the current lack of resentment towards the Chinese that hampers evangelistic work by Americans, who are resented and often even hated in various parts of the world, especially in Muslim nations.

We should reach out to Chinese, then, because they are created in the image of God and must hear about salvation by faith through Christ; millions of Chinese believers need more solid instruction in the Bible and

---

14   There are dozens of minority groups in China, some of them with populations more than one million; they are also important for all who take the Great commission seriously. In this work, however, I shall focus on the Han.

good examples of mature Christian living; there are serious theological needs that must be addressed; and the Chinese church has the potential to take the gospel to the whole world in a way that no one else can.

CHINA RISING?

China's dramatic rise as an economic, political, and military force, and its transformation in other sectors of society, has stunned the world and given Chinese immense pride in their nation. Shanghai is surely one of the most amazing cities in the history of the world. Never have so many buildings been erected in such a short period of time (less than twenty years), and nowhere else can you find so many skyscrapers. New York looks small, and short, in comparison. There are shiny new subways and trains; high-rise malls full of stores, restaurants, and Starbucks coffee shops; even a Shanghai development model that proves that this metropolis has only begun to grow.

In Beijing, futuristic buildings such as the Bird's Nest and the Cube were erected for the 2008 Olympics. People form lines when waiting for buses and trains, evident fruit of the government's strenuous efforts to promote "civilized" behavior. Even the historic buildings feature beautiful new faces, as the process of restoring China's glorious past rushes into the future. The Forbidden City, Great Wall, and Temple of Heaven are more imposing than ever, and remind us of the weight of imperial splendor.

Fields Ready to Harvest

Chinese Christians, too, have reason for confidence and hope. Their numbers continue to expand, with student groups and churches seeing increased numbers in recent years. The government allows public lectures on the Bible at college campuses. Students respond with excellent, informed questions, some of them evincing strong faith in Christ. A state-sponsored church is full well before the service begins. Those coming "late" fill the annex, and then the courtyard, where they sit on little stools. Leaders of house churches struggle to keep up with high interest and rapid growth. One group has rented a whole floor, where they hold multiple services for about 600 people. Others choose to keep their meetings small, to avoid attention. A high percentage of common people indicate strong interest in Christianity when presented with the gospel.

Clouds on the Horizon

On the other hand, not all is well in the Middle Kingdom these days. The rich get richer and the poor get poorer, with one of the widest income gaps in the world. The pollution is so thick in most cities that you wouldn't want to run for exercise. The Party and government leaders openly address the crisis of endemic corruption, which eats away at the government's legitimacy, and seems to be ineradicable. While some praise Mao Zedong, many speak bitterly of his bloody legacy, which the current regime refuses to repudiate. Most Christians can worship freely, but the police sometimes visit pastors whose churches grow too large. Some groups don't dare to sing; they simply hum along to a recording. How can Christians in the West minister to these people, who are now stepping into the center of the world's stage?

Western Decline

At the same time, the West is declining dramatically, especially America. Europe has been morally bankrupt for a century, and now faces the prospect of multiple sovereign debt defaults. The United States has lost its former prestige in almost every field, except perhaps entertainment. Senior economists predict the default of many states and municipalities, and no longer rule out the virtual default of the U.S. government, which is already technically bankrupt. Some analysts are even warning that wild creation of money out of thin air makes hyperinflation very likely, perhaps inevitable. With a devalued currency, America would lose not only financial power, but military capacity as well. Despite some encouraging signs recently, not all foresee economic recovery; the opposite is now being widely predicted.

What are some implications of these rapid changes? If American influence is indeed dwindling, this is no time for relying on the U.S. Government to support Christians in China—if, indeed, that was ever called for. China-bashing of any sort, along with beating the drum for political freedom, especially if these are done in the name of Christianity, will be even more counterproductive than in the past. Faced with economic hardship, those who support Christian ministries will have fewer resources. Expensive operations may simply have to be curtailed, perhaps even eliminated. If there was ever a time for careful stewardship of limited funds, it is now.

OBSTACLES

Though China's millions continue to demonstrate widespread openness to the gospel, a number of obstacles make effective ministry to them difficult.

Distance

Most Chinese live in China! Only a few foreigners can go there for any length of time.

Government Restrictions

The fierce crackdown on house church Christians of previous years has abated markedly, but there are still many restrictions upon religious activity. For one thing, foreign Christians in China face closer scrutiny from a government fearful of their influence. A few have been sent home for open religious activity. All feel the pressure of keeping a low profile.

Some leaders in the government wrongly see the growth in the number of believers as a threat. Though the constitution of China guarantees religious freedom, many in the government harbor a particular loathing for Americans who seek to "infect" their people with Christian doctrine. In general, direct proclamation of the Christian faith by foreigners is not allowed, and any attempt to work with "house churches" is illegal. Too many government officials simply do not believe that neither Chinese nor overseas Christians have any intention to challenge their authority. Their ignorance and prejudice have blinded their eyes to the many benefits of the Christian religion, and made them paranoid.

Language

Though many Chinese university students can understand and even speak English, that is not their "heart" language. In order for the truth to penetrate their minds and become rooted in their own culture, it must be expressed in Chinese.

Culture

Even then, however, massive cultural barriers make it hard for Chinese people to assimilate the faith into the depths of their value system and ways of thinking and acting. To give only two examples: How do you help a Chinese person overcome the pull of family obligation and the pressure to "save face," unless you are aware of the long history and profound influence of those values in Chinese culture?

Our Own Culture

Westerners approach Chinese people with our own assumptions and values, which may not necessarily come straight from the Bible. For instance, Chinese friends of ours have often indicated that they consider our focus on individual rights and freedom a bit overdone. They think we have too little regard for one's obligations to the group.

Nationalism

Though Chinese tend to treat foreigners with great courtesy, and often enjoy their friendship, we must not be ignorant of underlying tensions.

Western criticism of China's human rights policy runs head-on into the intense national pride that its people had in hosting the 2008 Games and the Shanghai Expo in 2010, and in the dramatic growth in prosperity and ensuing economic, diplomatic, and military power now enjoyed by their nation after a "century of humiliation."

CHINESE CHURCHES IN CRISIS

Especially among intellectuals, the gospel continues to make rapid progress. Many highly-qualified Chinese are offering themselves for full-time ministry in the church; many more seek greater understanding of the Bible in order to serve more effectively in the church and in the world. Foreign Christians employ an extensive array of methods both in China and in their own countries to reach out to Chinese, and have seen some fruit result.

Crisis of Faith

On the other hand, dark clouds are appearing on the horizon, causing great concern. Millions of Chinese who profess faith in Christ hardly know the essential elements of the gospel. All too often, they have been presented with a message that says, "Believe in Jesus and you will gain benefits." Their faith is more a "baptized" form of their own traditional religion that promises worldly rewards for those who worship a particular god than it is conviction that God saves sinners through the work of Jesus Christ. So-called "prosperity theology" long ago captured the stage in churches outside of Mainland China; now it has been widely proclaimed there as well. As a result, one article claimed that "Millions of Chinese are only one unanswered prayer away from deserting the faith."

Instead of Christ and him crucified, some preachers focus on signs, wonders, and healing. In many congregations, people look for emotional "highs" and know little of the way of the cross, steady discipleship, or solid Bible study. Even in evangelical churches and seminaries, preachers and teachers distract their hearers with interesting information about Bible backgrounds, psychology, cute stories—anything but the core of the gospel itself. Even worse, all too many have drunk deeply from the wells of modern critical scholarship, and assert that the Bible contains mistakes, or that the Reformers were wrong about the atonement. This lack of biblical understanding is also fertile ground for the proliferation of heresies and cults, some of which have had disastrous impact.

Crisis of Practice

Both because of poor teaching, and because Chinese church leaders tend to emphasize quantity over quality, Christians often do not practice what they profess. Most church leaders imitate the "imperial" style of traditional Chinese leadership. Deep devotional life is rare. Leaders are exhausted, and their health and families suffer from neglect. The same goes for common believers. Marriages are in disarray; children follow the idols of success and pleasure, and the name of Christ is dishonored among the Gentiles. In other words—they are beginning to look like us!

If Chinese believers do not understand and live out the fundamentals of the Christian faith, how can they share it with their neighbors? In the pulpit, the classroom, and in writing the focus must be on the core message of the Cross. We must seek to convey the old, old story, and to defend the gospel against modern errors.

OVERCOMING OBSTACLES

Should we give up our efforts to bring the life, love, and light of Christ to the world's largest population? Of course not! But we must be careful not to cause unnecessary offense and especially not to compromise the safety of our brothers and sisters in China. It's time to reevaluate our methods, and perhaps adjust our plans, for reaching the Chinese with the gospel. We must concentrate our efforts on those forms of outreach that promise the greatest return on our investment. Here is a brief outline of a number of possible steps we can take.

Prayer

Only God can change men, including leaders, but he surely can! Prayer knows no boundaries, waits for no visa, costs no money, and fears no police. As we intercede for the government and people of China, God will work in their hearts. Our intercessions for Christians there, and particularly for preachers of the gospel, will be used by God to build his church in truth and in love (Eph 6:18–20).

Understanding the Chinese

Without taking time to study the history, culture, and society of China, the story and current condition of Christianity in China, and fundamental principles and practices of effective ministry among Chinese, we shall run the risk of failing to address their deepest convictions, fears, values, aspirations, and assumptions. Our gospel will penetrate only the surface of their lives, not its core.

Relationships

Aside from prayer, the next most effective way of impacting Chinese for the gospel is to forge lasting friendships with them. This will require time and perseverance; there is no quick shortcut to building bonds of trust, respect, and affection that earn us the right to be heard.

Befriending Chinese Living Overseas

Several million Chinese dwell as aliens throughout the world. Outside China, they are free to explore the claims of Christ, and a high proportion of them come to faith. Though many of us live in the West, we have ready access to Chinese who have come here for further study and work. Hundreds, perhaps thousands, of churches and organizations have vigorous programs of outreach to Chinese. Their potential for reaching China is vast, and they deserve our best attention and prayers. Instructing them in the faith pays rich dividends.

Non-threatening Activity by Foreigners Living in China

Serious study of Chinese language and culture wins respect and deepens our understanding of the people we seek to serve (Jas 1:19). Long-term residence in Asia by foreigners who truly seek to listen and learn, and who have a viable, sustainable position in society, such as in education, medicine, care for orphans, community development, or business, can also foster relationships that lead to effective witness without proselytizing. Obeying Chinese regulations about religious activity by foreigners is essential for sustainable witness there.

Academic Exchange and the Arts

For almost thirty years now, Chinese intellectuals have been unusually open to Christianity. Furthermore, the relative freedom enjoyed by the academic community in China, and the frequent travel of Chinese scholars overseas, make academic exchange an especially potent tool in God's hands. Christians who can relate to Chinese academics as peers and discuss the gospel with them on a relatively deep level have amazing opportunities. Likewise, in this era of globalization, artists of all sorts can gain a hearing in China.

Short-term Visits

Short-term visits to China by tourists, business people, scholars, and those simply wanting to know more about China, can initiate long-term friendships and inform our prayers. Quickie "mission trips," however, are exorbitantly expensive, and may not lead to lasting results. They can be of some value, however, if they are attended by well-prepared people with some specialty to offer, strictly monitored to prevent hasty and ill-informed evangelism, and coordinated with long-term residents who can follow up.

Internet, Radio, and Literature

Media also leap over walls, despite government attempts to block them. From far away, words of truth and life bring hope and change to desperate people deep within China. Solid Bible teaching builds lives and equips leaders in the church (Eph. 2:20; 4:15–6), without the need for any personal presence. When rightly used, these materials also transcend the language limitations of foreigners seeking to communicate the gospel to their Chinese friends. Since Chinese, like most people, enjoy stories, using books and other media to portray the lives of Chinese and Foreign Christians who have made a contribution to Chinese society is particularly effective.

Points of Contact

Christians can exploit "points of contact" between the gospel and Chinese society today. Although only a few will be discussed in this volume; they are meant to serve as examples of doors through which entrance to the minds and hearts of Chinese can be gained.

Equipping and Mobilizing Westerners

There are too many non-Christian Chinese for any one person or group to reach them all. This task will require a team effort by members of the entire Christian community. Not just specialists, but "ordinary" believers in the West can serve as powerful witnesses to Christ among the Chinese. For this, they need instruction and motivation. Helping them to become more capable of sharing God's truth is thus a major "method" of reaching Chinese worldwide.

Training, Mentoring, and Counseling Chinese Believers

In addition to widespread proclamation of the gospel through a variety of media, we must take time to train and mentor a few people with leadership potential. Chinese society is changing at a breakneck pace, and individuals and families are crumbling in this process. Small group Bible studies and counseling by skilled and loving Christians is an urgent necessity.

The Church

Quite a variety of groups seek to reach out to Chinese with the gospel, but not all of them place a high priority on the church. Not surprisingly, neglect of the church usually results in ephemeral "decisions for Christ" and shallow discipleship. In particular, I believe that we need to recover the New Testament emphasis upon congregations based in homes.

Witness by Chinese Christians from Taiwan, Hong Kong, and Overseas

Speaking the language and looking "normal," these believers exert a huge influence by their personal example and verbal testimony (1 Pet 3:15–16). We must also spend time equipping Chinese believers, who have none of the liabilities we do, to share the Good News with their own people. Since hundreds of thousands of Taiwanese live and travel in China, the evangelization and equipping of Taiwan constitutes a very high priority for the church (Eph 4:11–13).

We will explore each of these methods in more detail, as we seek with others to develop an overall strategy for sharing with Chinese around the world the healing blessings of Christ.

"For with God nothing will Be impossible." (Luke 1:37)

CHAPTER THREE
PREPARATION

PRAYER
The most effective form of service that we can render to the growth of the church among Chinese is prayer. Why? Only God can raise those who are dead in sin; give sight to eyes that are spiritually blind; soften hard hearts; cause the self-righteous to repent and confess their sins; Change minds; and create faith (Eph 2:1–10). In his wisdom, the Lord is pleased to use the preaching of the gospel, the performance of good deeds, and the prayers of his people in saving sinners and causing them to grow into maturity (Eph 1:13; 2:10; 3:14–21; 4:15).

Our only hope is in God, who is still on his throne, and fully capable of advancing his kingdom against all opposition. We can come to him with humble supplications for "all the saints," for preachers of the Word, those in prison, Chinese government leaders, and all who seek China's welfare, that wisdom, peace, and gentleness would prevail (Eph 6:18–20; 1 Tim 2:1–2; Heb 13:3). In all our intercessions, we must not forget to thank God for the wonderful works he is already doing among his people, and this is especially true of the stunning advance of his kingdom among the Chinese.

A "NEW" PARADIGM: LIFELONG LEARNING

The "Old" Approach: Does it "Work"?

In the past, and up to the present, Western Christians have sought to evangelize China by proclaiming the message of salvation. The early missionaries learned enough Chinese to convey the basic truths of the faith, and then plunged into evangelism, preaching, and teaching, greatly assisted by Chinese converts. God blessed their efforts, as many did respond to their proclamation with repentance and true faith.

The same is true today, when thousands of zealous Americans (and others) travel to China for a few weeks, a summer, or even a couple of years, eager to see many Chinese brought to Christ. With little or no ability in Mandarin, they take advantage of the current interest that young people have in things western, including Christianity. Communication in English seems to demolish the language barrier. Once again, God has done great things, as thousands of people have come to Christ and even formed churches.

On the Other Hand...

Nagging questions about this approach to China ministry remain. Although we do not for a moment wish to disparage the wonderful results of service in English, some question whether it can go as deep as necessary for long-term transformation. A recent book recounts how the author discovered that even Ph.D. students in America, after living here and being discipled in English, had huge gaps in their comprehension of the gospel. That led him to go to China to learn Mandarin, so he could communicate with people in their mother tongue.[15]

When we probe a bit, we find that ignorance of Chinese language and culture inhibits understanding of the people whom we are trying to persuade to change their entire way of living. Working "in the dark," so to speak, we say and do things that seem normal to us, but baffle our Chinese friends. We answer questions that they are not asking, or respond before understanding what they are really saying. I could give many examples from my own experience. Another problem is that we often transmit a Western brand of Christianity that cannot thrive in Chinese soil.

Discipleship in Depth

Furthermore, unless we can read and explain the Bible in Chinese, and in the context of their religious and cultural background, it's very hard to "make disciples" of even the sincerest converts. Our goal must not be just a "profession of faith," but discipleship in depth, which allows the truth of God to penetrate into all departments of thought and action. We must seek to build life-transforming relationships, leading to changed lives at home, school, work, and all domains of society. That takes time, patience, and considerable understanding.

A "New" Way?

In order for this to take place, we need to pursue a path of lifelong learning: years of hard study of Chinese language and culture, as well as of Christianity in China. Especially for the first few years, we should assume the role of students, not teachers, asking our Chinese friends

---

15   See Mike Falkenstine, *The Chinese Puzzle.*

to instruct us, which they are happy to do! There is no substitute for learning the Chinese language. Even though many Chinese understand and speak English, those who wish to get to the heart and the basic mental assumptions of these intelligent people will have to humble themselves to acquire a high level of ability in the language, as well as more than a superficial knowledge of their culture. As one expert has said, "We are aiming to communicate complex concepts in a difficult language to a highly-cultured people, and we cannot do this without advanced facility in their language."

At a gathering of Chinese and Western scholars recently, I noted how our Chinese partners, who are fluent in English (both have PhDs from Western schools), eagerly switched to Chinese when they could, particularly when they wanted to express what was on their hearts. If we want to communicate the whole counsel of God in terms that are comprehensible and persuasive, we must plan to spend several years in full-time language study, as well as a lifetime in careful reading and observation of the many dimensions of traditional and modern Chinese culture. In particular, it's essential that we learn "Christian" Chinese, for the Bible has its own vocabulary (think "redemption," "reconciliation," etc.) and Christians have their own sub-culture with its peculiar lingo. We do not have to speak the way they do when conversing with non-believers, but we should at least know how to communicate with Chinese believers.

Actually, the nineteenth century Protestant missionaries also set themselves to study the language and culture of China. The China Inland Mission (CIM) required its new workers to attain a level of proficiency that few Westerners today (including me) could match. Some missionaries even became superb Sinologists. Though they did not agree with Roman Catholic doctrine, they were following the example of the early Jesuits, who acquired amazing knowledge of the literature, religion, and history of China, and were adept at following the etiquette of their hosts.

To earn the right to be heard, we must first listen. "Listening" encompasses language study, reading, asking questions, observing, and associating with those whom we wish to serve. After all, isn't that what Jesus did? He didn't preach his first sermon until after thirty years of earthly "education"—and he was the Word of God! Anyone who has tasted even a bit of Chinese language and culture, or read about Chinese Christianity, knows that this is a banquet with many delights. But being invited to the feast, and conversing with our hosts, requires many years of persistent effort.

RESEARCH

You might think it strange that I should consider "research" a means of reaching Chinese with the gospel. After all, aren't we supposed to be sharing the Good News with everyone we meet, day and night, in season and out of season, spreading the Word as widely as possible? Of course. Why should we spend precious time reading books and articles about Chinese culture, society, and church life, including Chinese church history? The Bible is clear enough, and relevant to all people everywhere; what need do we have to divert energy to apparently non-productive activities like research and writing?

Well, let me ask a few questions. What if companies like Apple and Microsoft had no research and development divisions? How long would they continue to hold and expand their share of the market? Why do the U.S., China, Russia, and other great powers spend so much money on intelligence? What experience lies behind the carpenter's dictum: "Measure twice, cut once"? Why do you think the Bible contains this statement: "He who answers a matter before he hears it, it is folly and shame to him" (Prov 18:13)?

The Need for Research

In fact, several hard facts point to the need for solid, sustained study of Chinese history, culture, and society, including Chinese Christianity.

China possesses a long history, a rich culture, and a highly-sophisticated civilization, one of which the Chinese are justly proud. What message do we send if we barge in, without any serious study, and push "our" views upon them? Confucianism, Daoism, Buddhism, and popular Chinese religion have staged a colossal comeback in recent years, not only posing powerful rivals to Christianity but also influencing the way people hear and respond to the gospel. Ignorance of these faiths represents folly and almost guarantees failure. Chinese intellectuals have imbibed a variety of philosophies and world views, especially in the past three decades. Unless we are aware of what they think, we shall not only have little credibility with them, but we will also be in danger of completely missing the mark in evangelism.

Chinese young people may wear Nike shoes and depend on the iPad to communicate, but they are not only buffeted by various waves of Western popular culture, but are also deeply impacted by their own heritage. How can we reach them if we don't understand them? Chinese families are falling apart. Some reasons for this match the same crisis in the West, but others are distinctly Chinese. Wise counseling will take these factors into consideration.

Chinese churches, and those who lead them, are to some extent products of their culture and society. Without an awareness of Chinese cultural assumptions and pressures, our efforts to teach and build Christians will be shallow, at best. Absent serious study, we won't understand why so many Chinese respond so quickly to the gospel, or why so many leave the church almost as rapidly as they enter it. Chinese Christians are eager to serve God, but are largely ignorant of the marvelous history of believers and missionaries whose lives shaped today's Chinese church. We can help them by sharing the thrilling stories of Christians on whose shoulders they stand.

At the very least, by studying the history of Christianity in China, we can perhaps avoid repeating errors made by well-intentioned folks who nevertheless caused unnecessary damage, such as when they allowed themselves to be associated with foreign governments, dressed the faith in "Western" garb, or made Chinese believers dependent upon funds from overseas.

AWARE OF THE PAST: CHINESE HISTORY

Before we can effectively communicate the Christian message to Chinese, we need to know something about the history of this great and ancient civilization. More than many peoples, the Chinese cherish their past and live in its afterglow—or shadow. Even in casual conversation, they may refer to persons and events from previous ages in a way that few Westerners will. For them, many things that took place long ago really happened "yesterday."

Chinese history furnishes more than material for conversation, however; it permeates Chinese culture and consciousness. Think of the opening ceremonies of the 2008 Beijing Olympics. Can you remember any other similar Olympic presentation, saturated as it was with images and concepts from China's rich cultural heritage? Even the recent anti-Japanese furor finds its source in the horrible suffering from an aggressive Japan in the twentieth century, before most people in China were even born.

Chinese patterns of leadership, likewise, reflect attitudes and customs going back thousands of years. I remember sitting in a class on the imperial administration of the Shang dynasty a few years ago, and commenting to the professor afterwards, "'You just described the president of the seminary where I used to teach!" More often than not, governance at every level in Chinese society, including the Christian church, resembles the hierarchical structure that Chinese have always known.

In short, we simply cannot hope to comprehend the passions, aspirations, fears, and assumptions of Chinese people without pondering their long history. Put another way, if we want to connect with our Chinese friends, we need to study their past. When they see that we have taken the trouble to familiarize ourselves with both the triumphs and tragedies of China's long and complex story, they will likely respect and trust us more than they otherwise would.

How can Westerners, who usually know little about Chinese history, make up for this deficit? In my opinion, there is no substitute for reading. As it happens, there is a plethora of books that narrate the flow of wars, dynasties, literature, philosophy, and outstanding personages of the Middle Kingdom.

AWARE OF THE PAST: CHINESE CHRISTIAN HISTORY

The zealous Christian who arrives in China with the hope of bringing the gospel to its spiritually lost millions needs to know that he is not the first to do so. Depending on your definition of "Christianity," some form of "Christianity" has been known in China on and off since the seventh century, when missionaries from the Syrian Church of the East (often called Nestorians) arrived at the imperial court with a "luminous doctrine" that was warmly welcomed by the emperor of the glorious Tang dynasty.

After being suppressed in a general anti-religious campaign, "Nestorianism" revived again under the Mongol rulers, when emissaries from the Roman Catholic Pope also arrived and began to establish churches in China. Both groups were forced to leave when the Mongol (Yuan) dynasty was toppled by the Ming. Later, in the sixteenth century, Jesuit missionaries led by Matteo Ricci arrived as part of the general expansion of European powers through maritime explorations and conquest. They made converts among the elites, while Franciscan and Dominican monks who came after them worked among the uneducated people. A fierce controversy between the Jesuits and the others over whether it was permissible for Chinese Christians to participate in ancestor worship ceremonies finally led to a judgment by the Pope against the more tolerant position of the Jesuits. That, in turn, provoked an angry reaction from the emperor, who proscribed Christianity and expelled all but a few missionaries from China.

The Roman Catholics from Europe worked "underground" for more than a century, and were still at it when the first Protestant missionary, Robert Morrison, arrived in Canton (now Guangzhou) in 1807. Morrison was followed by others, mostly from Britain and the United States but also some from Germany, who laid the foundation for today's large Protestant church by translating the Bible and other key Christian literature; preaching the gospel widely and gaining some converts; training some of those to share the faith with their countrymen; engaging in medical missionary service; and planting a fledgling church in a few port cities. The "unequal treaties" referred to above gradually opened all of China to travel and residence by Westerners, including missionaries, and soon the entire length and breadth of the Celestial Empire were traversed by intrepid preachers of Christ. By the end of the nineteenth century, they had established churches and mission stations, as well as clinics, hospitals, schools, and even colleges. The Bible and other Christian books and tracts were published and widely sold, while key concepts from Western science, engineering, government, and law were also introduced through translated works.

The Boxer Rebellion wreaked havoc for a few months, killing hundreds of missionaries and thousands of Chinese Christians, but it could not stop the advance of the gospel. More missionaries came, and more Chinese accepted this "foreign religion." After the overthrow of the Manchu dynasty in 1911 and the establishment of the Republic of China, full freedom of religion allowed for further expansion of Christianity in all sectors of society. Christian colleges trained thousands of young people and gave them some knowledge of Christian truth. Enterprising Chinese Christians began to form their own congregations, independent of foreign mission control. As the twentieth century developed, so did Chinese Christianity, which was becoming a truly indigenous religion.

The Japanese invasion in 1937 curtailed the work of missionaries, but did not stop the spread of the gospel, taken now by Chinese themselves to war-ravaged people whose lives had been uprooted and devastated. A more severe blow came around 1950, when the new Communist regime forced all missionaries to leave China, brought the churches under strict government control, and mobilized the entire nation to promote an atheistic vision of building a perfect society by human effort alone. During the Great Cultural Revolution (1966–1976), even the "official" Three-Self Patriotic Movement churches were closed, their clergy being forced to take secular jobs or even thrown into jail, and all religious activity banned and harshly punished.

Outside observers sometimes wondered whether Christianity had completely died out in China, but the opposite was true: In the fires of persecution, Christians were being refined, strengthened, and even used to bring encouragement to non-believers who were also suffering from the general chaos and violence. When the doors to China once again "opened" in the late 1970s, the truly amazing story of God's work among the Chinese began to startle Western observers. All of a sudden, it seemed, Christianity had exploded into a major movement, starting in the countryside but quickly taking root also in the cities among intellectuals and professional people. Now we know that there are tens of millions of people in China who name the name of Christ and gather in Protestant congregations of various sorts, and that Roman Catholicism survives as well.

The current situation is quite complex, and reflects the diversity of China itself. Both Roman Catholics and Protestants gather in "official," "Patriotic" associations that are carefully controlled by the government. The Protestant one is called the Three-Self Patriotic Movement (TSPM)/ China Christian Council, sometimes referred to as "the two organizations." Within bounds, however, people can worship God and preach the gospel with a great deal of freedom, though evangelism is still illegal. Many more Protestants worship in unregistered congregations, sometimes called "house" churches because many trace their origins in home meetings. The TSPM congregations sometimes try to obstruct growth among unregistered groups, and sometimes they cooperate; it depends upon the area and the people in charge. Urban intellectuals have formed their own Bible study groups, many of which have grown into full-fledged churches, some of which meet quite openly in rented premises under a watchful but mostly tolerant government eye. "Christian" sects and even heresies further confuse the scene, while Buddhism and traditional Chinese religious temples are once again flourishing as well.

In other words, though regulations forbid preaching and making converts by foreigners, and congregations that grow too large or influential can be shut down by the officials, in general, persecution is no longer a major problem for Chinese Protestants. Church leaders worry more about materialism, greed, worldliness, insufficient knowledge of the Bible and vulnerability to false teaching, and the huge distractions of the mad rush for money that has gripped the population. The restrictions upon activity by foreigners are quite strict, however, and those who would circumvent them must realize that they will be watched (there are no real secrets in China), and that those who associate with them could face real trouble. Do they really want to expose their Chinese friends to such a risk? For the very real historical reasons that I have briefly outlined above, joining with foreigners, especially Americans, can arouse government suspicion of being a traitor to the country and a tool of foreign imperialists.

Finally, let me say that the more you know about the history of the spread of the gospel in China, the less likely is it that you will commit the same mistakes that caused so much trouble in the past. These include confusing the biblical message with some form of foreign culture (such as democracy or modernization); interfering with normal growth, and arousing government suspicion, by supplying foreign funds to Chinese Christians; failing to understand the social and cultural environment in which the Chinese live and thus being unaware of what preconceptions they bring to their ideas about Christianity; assuming that a profession of faith indicates real conversion and commitment; working in competition with others; failing to connect biblical doctrine with Chinese concepts and customs; blindness to cultural habits that distort the gospel and its application to Chinese church life; and, perhaps worst of all, giving Chinese officials reason to believe that they are working for the United States government.

Equally, a wide and deep knowledge of Chinese Christian history can provide us with a wealth of positive examples and reveal what practices yield lasting fruit. These include: learning the language and culture, living among the people, respecting their customs whenever possible, identifying with their aspirations, sympathizing with their fears and false values, training them to think biblically and to apply the truth of Christ to all sectors of life and society, helping them form indigenous congregations under forms of leadership that reflect Scriptural principles, providing practical help with no motive other than to glorify God and benefit people made in his image, and persevering in hard work over a long time. All these and more have fed what is now a very large, growing, and vigorous church, and how foreigners and Chinese from overseas can play a small but important part in this great work of God.

AWARE OF THE PRESENT: CHINESE CULTURE AND SOCIETY

Those who desire to share the truth and love of God in Christ with Chinese need to know something of their background, including their society. Otherwise, how can we hope to understand their hopes and dreams, their struggles, their pressures, their values, or their ways of doing things? Chinese society, like all societies, is immensely complex and complicated. A lifetime of study and observation would not suffice to understand it all. The basic features may be outlined, however.

Complexity

Everything is complex in China; nothing is simple or straightforward. Communication can be indirect, subtle, and confusing. Relationships are defined and constrained by multiple levels of obligation, starting with the nuclear family and moving outwards. American-style individualism, though increasingly evident among the young, can be exercised only so far before it collides with the collective mentality of Chinese culture. Decisions must take many others into consideration. It seems that nothing is ever done without some pragmatic purpose. You are never talking just to one person; behind him is a whole web of relationships that influence this individual in a variety of ways.

Pressure

All of this produces pressure—pressure to conform, to fulfill others' expectations, to avoid others' censure, to comply with group standards. For most of their history, and even today, most Chinese have also faced an enormous pressure just to survive. Millions still live in poverty, not only in the countryside, where life remains hard, but in the growing cities, where it's "big fish eat little fish; little fish eat shrimp." If you don't like your job, ten or twenty or a hundred others are eager to take it, and your boss knows that. Competition to enter college drives millions of high school students, and their parents, to anxiety and even despair. Hours are long, recreation is hard to come by.

Hope

For the first time in a long while, younger Chinese, at least those in the cities, have hope. Their parents have seen conditions improve enormously since the late 1970s, as living standards have risen dramatically for the growing middle class and China itself has become a part of the modern world. Ubiquitous cranes and the pounding of jack-hammers represent the energy and vitality of a nation on the move. China has emerged from "the century of humiliation" to a place of power and prestige in the world, and expresses its sense of national, even imperial, destiny with greater and greater confidence and abrasiveness.

Competence

We must assume that the Chinese whom we meet, especially the educated elite who come to our universities here or attend out English classes there, are good at what they do. They work long and hard to excel academically and in business. Their scientists are making impressive breakthroughs, while their engineers have already built so many marvels that people have ceased counting them. As always, they produce beautiful books, art, and music, but now they are also making world-class movies. Expect them to dominate one field of human endeavor after another—from sports, media, science, and technology, to economics and military power—for the foreseeable future.

Corruption

At the same time, expect to find shoddy work, cut corners, false labeling, fake credentials, cheap or even toxic ingredients, poorly built bridges, highways, and train tracks, plagiarized papers and cheating on exams, and transactions based on bribes or nepotism. The rot is endemic, and it is crippling China's progress, but there is nothing short of a non-violent, gradual, Christian "cultural revolution" that can hope to change this sorry state of affairs. The corruption affects everything, and shows up in rampant sexual immorality, rising rates of adultery and divorce, vulgar language, and entertainment that would plunge the depths of Western depravity if the censors did not step in.

Heart-hunger

Like everyone else, the Chinese are created in the image of God. They long for beauty, truth, and goodness as much as we do, and respond to genuine love like thirsty travelers in a parched desert. They have seldom known real, unconditional love. True, the only-child policy has spawned a generation of immature, spoiled, pampered, and self-centered youth, but genuine love, expressed by unconditional acceptance balanced by firm adherence to standards, remains rare. Above all, Chinese tradition has no notion of real transcendence, for which all of us long, so when they encounter God, they can be at first incredulous, and then overwhelmed.

Caution

At the same time, they have been lied to so often, and for so long, especially by those in authority, that they are slow to trust people who only speak beautiful words. They want to wait and see what you are really like. Do you mean what you say? Do you live according to your stated convictions? They are watching and observing more than you can ever imagine and they are very sensitive to non-verbal communication. Actions speak much louder than words. Most of them also want to test the truth claims of Christianity for quite a while before committing themselves to another idealist ideology. Pragmatic to the core, they want to know whether Christianity will "work" for them in the real world.

Fear

With all its openness and unprecedented (at least in recent times) freedom, China is still not a free country. You never know when someone might betray you in order to advance himself. Nor do you know when the government will suddenly change direction and re-impose more restrictions, controls, and sanctions. How long will the economy keep growing? How will I pay for my parents' medical care? Will my spouse be faithful? What happens if I get sick? What awaits me beyond the grave?

Loneliness

People are moving so incredibly fast that few have time to slow down and listen (except, perhaps, close classmates during college years). The elderly are increasingly left to themselves, their children being too caught up in the rat race to care for them. Women and children are left behind when the men go off to the towns for better-paying jobs. Life in the huge cities leaves millions living isolated existences. Even romantic relationships, which at first seemed to offer intimacy, turn into contests where the men exploit the women and the women try to gain love through manipulation. Children feel that their parents only care about their academic performance, with no time for their hopes, dreams, and fears. When these people find true community in the church, their hearts come alive with joy.

Much, much more could be said. Chinese society is in a state of immense transformation at dizzying speed, and both the people and the government are having a hard time adjusting. It is a good time for Christians to step in with the message of a God who never changes and who has promised his people that he will never leave them or forsake them (Heb 13:5).

AWARE OF THE PRESENT: CHINESE CHRISTIANITY

Anyone wanting to serve effectively among Chinese needs to know something about the present state of Christianity in China and among overseas Chinese. First of all, we must be cognizant of the immense diversity among Christians in China. There are Protestants and Roman Catholics. Each of these is further split into those who belong to an official "Patriotic" association sponsored and, to some degree at least, controlled by the government, and unofficial, unregistered, or "underground" congregations and networks of churches.

Roman Catholics

For Roman Catholics, there is the Catholic Patriotic Association, whose bishops are consecrated in China without the participation of the Pope in Rome, and the "underground" Catholics who only recognize bishops and priests whose consecration comes from Rome. Both groups refuse to cooperate with each other, at least in theory, but there is some collaboration on the ground in various places, and some bishops have a "dual" consecration.

The Three Self Patriotic Movement/China Christian Council

Protestant churches are supposed to belong to the Three Self Patriotic Movement/China Christian Council ("two organizations") in order to be considered legal. These organizations are under the direct supervision of the Religious Affairs Bureau of the government, and operate under restrictions, including the so-called "three designates": meetings must take place in designated places, at designated times, and under the leadership of designated personnel who have been vetted by the government. Children under the age of 18 should not be instructed or baptized. In fact, the TSPM churches can and do stretch these limits, depending upon locality. Chinese citizens are free to worship in these churches with no penalty or hindrance and the preachers can generally speak freely. Their numbers are estimated at 25 million. Most who attend seem sincere; most students at seminaries and Bible colleges hold to biblical faith.

On the other hand, pastors must be approved by the government; the curriculum for seminaries is strictly prescribed by the TSPM, and contains a great deal of political material; the church is supposed to serve the interests of socialism and of the government generally; and the TSPM/CCC is adamant that only they represent Protestant Christianity in China. In the past, and not too long ago at all, the TSPM worked with the government to persecute Christians belonging to unregistered (often called "house") churches; bitter memories of that persecution linger and make cooperation difficult. On the other hand, younger leaders don't hold onto the past, and many TSPM/CCC pastors happily cooperate with and even assist unregistered groups.

Unregistered Churches

Unregistered churches account for the vast majority of Protestant Christians in China today. Estimates as to their number vary widely, from 40 million to 100 million. No one really knows, but all admit that there has been explosive growth of these groups over the past three decades, starting in the countryside and now gaining momentum in the cities, especially the major metropolises. Within unregistered Protestantism, there are Charismatics, Pentecostals, Arminians, Reformed, Presbyterian, Baptist, and Seventh Day Adventist, as well as adherents of independent Chinese denominations such as the Little Flock, the Local Church, and the True Jesus Church.

For a number of years, unregistered churches have enjoyed considerable freedom of action, particularly in urban areas. Some meet in homes, while other congregations number in the hundreds or even more, and gather in large, even elaborate buildings, or semi-public places like office buildings and restaurants. They conduct a full range of ministries, and even publish much of their news on websites. They were largely left alone by both local and central government officials, and with occasional exceptions, even cooperating with Western and other foreign Christians seemed to be tolerated.

Many of these unregistered churches are entirely independent, but others, especially in rural areas and among those that were started by people from Wenzhou, belong to vast "networks" numbering in the hundreds of thousands or even millions. They run their own training programs, some of them quite sophisticated. Often, present or promising leaders are sent to Hong Kong, Taiwan, or the West for advanced theological education; many gain further theological knowledge through Internet programs. Recently, the major networks and urban congregations have been connected with each other through the Lausanne Movement, a development that greatly worries the government. Many student groups have been started by overseas campus ministries, which are also under close scrutiny by the government.

At the time of this writing, depending on the area, unregistered Protestant Christians are almost always allowed to gather and to operate almost without persecution, though they labor under restrictions: they are not allowed to purchase property in their corporate name, for example. They may be "visited" by the police at any time and questioned extensively about their membership and finances. The government particularly fears and loathes any connection with foreign organizations, especially those based in America. The days of violent persecution have passed, however, at least for now, so that church leaders are more concerned about materialism, worldliness, and biblical illiteracy than they are about government oppression.

Overseas Chinese Christians

Furthermore, Chinese Christians living outside China in Hong Kong, Taiwan, Singapore, Southeast Asia, and the West may number a million believers or more. They belong to a wide variety of denominations and independent congregations, though they generally adhere to conservative and evangelical theology. They run dozens of seminaries, publishing houses, broadcasting networks, camps, conferences, and other ministries, many of which reach into mainland China. No description of Christianity in China is complete without taking full notice of the huge impact that these overseas Chinese Christians have upon Protestants in China proper. For one thing, they have produced thousands of Christian books, some translated and others written by Chinese, with many being of very high quality.

Sects, Cults, and Heresies

Particularly in the countryside, but now also in cities, all sorts of sects, cults, and heresies confuse the Christian scene in China. Some are relatively harmless, though they mislead people, but others are highly dangerous, and resort to kidnapping, seduction, torture, and even death to lure people from more orthodox churches. A few of them have millennial expectations that border on messianic and revolutionary tendencies, and of these the government is most justly afraid. One of the worst is the "Eastern Lightning" movement, which claims that Christ returned as a female, and employs violent tactics, including kidnapping, torture, seduction, and even murder to coerce Christians into its orbit. Others are The Disciples' Society, also known as the Narrow Gate in the Wilderness; the "Established King" movement and the "Lord God Sect."

Some groups were accused of being heretical or even cults (xiejiao) by other Christians or the government, such as the Shouters, who were connected with the Local Church started by Li Changshou; the Weepers, begun by Xu Yongze; and the Three Grades of Servants, whose founder was Xu Shuangfu. These have all received vigorous defense by themselves and others, however. At the very least, it can be said that some of their ritual practices and phrases, such as loud shouting or weeping as signs of true zeal or repentance, go beyond the bounds of Scriptural teaching. Some of the top leaders have been charged with fostering undue allegiance to themselves, and a few have indulged in extravagant living. Whether these groups are actually "heretical" by historical standards continues to be a matter of debate.[16]

In the 1990s, several of the largest house church networks, under the tutelage of the late Jonathan Chao, drew up a common statement of faith in order to express what they believed and thus show the government that they stood within historic Christian orthodoxy and were not to be considered "evil cults" and thus liable to legal action. Urban house church pastors have also come together in recent years to affirm traditional biblical Christianity. Both seek to refute claims by the TSPM that only it guards true Christianity. In fact, the TSPM has, in recent years, even purged evangelical teachers from its seminaries and its own official

---

16   For more on these groups, see Lian Xi, *Redeemed by Fire*, 204–232.

statements have included Ding Guangxun's controversial "justification by love" doctrine; how long that will persist remains to be seen, since most TSPM pastors are evangelical in their convictions.

Recent Government Restrictions

Urban churches are composed mostly of younger professionals, highly educated and confident. Though most are not at all anti-government or eager for political power, they have, in effect, defied government regulations, largely with impunity. Many of the leaders of these churches have created informal networks with their peers within metropolitan areas and even across the nation. Experienced leaders were saying that the age of "red persecution" (suffering for the faith) had been replaced by "white persecution" (the temptations of rampant secularism in a postmodern society), though in some rural areas, house churches were subject to harassment from officials.

When two hundred unregistered Chinese Christian leaders attempted to attend the Lausanne Congress in Cape Town in 2010, they were prohibited from leaving the country, and the earlier optimism took a blow. It seemed that both the political rulers of China and the leaders of the Three-Self Patriotic Movement (TSPM) just could not countenance the possibility of so many unregistered church leaders forming even closer connections with a worldwide movement.

Then the leaders of Shouwang Church in Beijing were told that they could no longer meet in the restaurant where they had been gathering as they waited, vainly, for the keys to the space they had purchased in a large office complex. Rather than returning to the small-group format with which they had started, the top leaders, in a highly controversial move, decided to take their Sunday worship outdoors to a pedestrian area near a large shopping center. The police then prevented their members from gathering and the five pastors and elders were placed under house arrest. Other unregistered church pastors came out publicly in support of Shouwang, and even sent a petition to the National People's Congress calling for re-examination of religious regulations.

Meanwhile, a few other church leaders who had tried to go to the Lausanne Congress were arrested, and there were reports of foreign Christians' visas being denied or not renewed. As part of a wider crackdown, academic and cultural conferences involving Westerners were cancelled. Nonprofit organizations, including charities, were under close scrutiny, especially those with foreign connections.

Government organs insisted that they would enforce the regulations that call for all Protestants to meet under the auspices of the TSPM, and angrily denounced all expressions of support from the West. Most believe that these actions were connected with official paranoia about the possible spread of the turmoil in the Middle East to the Middle Kingdom, and with the run-up to the major leadership change in 2012. There have been reports in the press of an intense struggle between hard-left Maoists and more moderate elements in the Party. When the new leaders were announced in November, 2012, it seemed that the more control-oriented faction had defeated the more reform-minded faction. However, unregistered churches that are not part of the group that tried to attend the Lausanne Congress and smaller groups meeting in homes seem to be left alone for the time being.

Protestant Christians in China are young and old, male and female (though there are more women than men); rich and poor; educated and illiterate; simple and sophisticated; urban and rural; "official" and unregistered, even "underground." The one thing they seem to have in common is a great hunger for the Word of God and a great zeal to propagate the faith that has saved them.

CHAPTER FOUR
PRESENCE

Although strict regulations prohibit open Christian ministry by foreigners in mainland China, there is a wide array of options for foreign Christians to advance the kingdom of God among the Chinese. In many countries, the presence of Chinese in our midst provides immense openings to demonstrate the love of God and to share the gospel, as long as we are prayerful, patient, and wise. Nearer to mainland China, Taiwan and Hong Kong enjoy complete religious freedom. The church is strong in each place, but Christians comprise only a fraction of the population, so foreigners can augment local witness in a variety of ways, including direct Christian ministry. In mainland China, people who are engaged in teaching, business, medicine, and other legitimate professions, as well as tourists, are still welcome.

CHINA AT YOUR DOORSTEP

For centuries, Chinese have left their motherland to seek a better life overseas. Beginning with South East Asia, they have scattered to East Asia, Africa, Latin America, Australia and New Zealand, Europe, and North America. You can find them not only in the huge Chinatowns of large cities, but in small towns all across the globe. Among them are shopkeepers, cooks, and busboys, but also graduate students, professors, and professional people at the highest levels of their field.

At present, hundreds of thousands of students from China, Taiwan, and Hong Kong seek higher education in the United States alone. In 2010, the number of Chinese students in the United States reached 128,000, a 30% increase over the previous year, and has climbed since then. The number in the United Kingdom is only slightly less. Increasingly, this group includes undergraduates. These people represent China's "best and brightest," who would not be in the West unless they were smart, well-connected, and ambitious. Many will return to China to exercise positions of great influence in their society; the rest will retain links with their homeland while living abroad. Even if they don't go back for many years, they are in constant contact with their family and friends at home, and often either make short visits or have their parents stay with them for as long as a year. In other words, they form a bridge to China even while living overseas.

For a variety of reasons, the presence of these students and scholars represents the most important arena for outreach to Chinese worldwide. Aside from prayer, reaching these people with the whole counsel of God is perhaps the most strategic thing we can do in spreading the gospel. They present Christians in the West with a marvelous opportunity to reach the future leaders of that great nation, "influencers" who will set the pace for a changing society and culture.

Showing Them Love

"Love the sojourner, therefore, for you were sojourners in Egypt" (Deuteronomy 10:19).

For Christians, the presence of these strangers in our midst presents an obligation to welcome them and demonstrate to them the truth and love of God by word and deed. Just as the Old Testament Hebrews were commanded to care for the aliens among them, because they were once aliens in Egypt, so we must open our hearts to people a long way from home.

They represent a vast field that is often ripe for harvest. Curious about their host country and freed from restraining influences, some even come with an intention to learn more about Christianity. Their alert, curious minds are eager to wrestle with fresh ways of looking at life. Uprooted from their native land, they are, especially at first, missing their family and friends, struggling to adapt to a new language and culture, and sometimes very anxious and afraid. How can we not treat them as our neighbors with a claim on our love?

Principles for Effective Ministry: How Should We Serve Them?

There is no one way to reach these people, of course. A variety of options exist for reaching out to them. Let's review some general principles for effective witness to these bright folks.

Long-term relationships must form the basis of all outreach to Chinese. Genuine friendships, with no hidden agenda, will remove pressure to make the person a "project" who turns into a "product"—a number to report. Maybe the most valuable gift we can give is genuine interest in them, expressed by sincere questions about their country, culture, family, and reactions to their host culture.

Exposure to Christian living will enable Chinese to see how the gospel "works" in the life of the believer. Actions speak louder than words, and have their own persuasive power. They also teach people with no Christian background how to live out the faith in a variety of contexts, especially family and work.

As Christians, we know that what people need most is a saving relationship with God as Father through the Lord Jesus Christ, and we want to share our faith with them, we may now know how. Make it known that you are a Christian and that you go to church. Invite your friend to attend one service with you, as a cultural experience, then to lunch afterwards. Before the service, explain what is about to happen, perhaps going through the order of worship and reading the passage of the Bible for the day. Afterwards, ask for an honest reaction.

The most obvious route is to open our doors to people from China. You can register with your local university to be a "host" to Chinese students, or simply make friends with the ones you meet at work or school. You don't have to invite them to live with you, or eat dinner with you once a week! Monthly contacts will suffice, especially since your new friend is probably even busier than you are. Away from home, they would love to be part of your family, not just for meals, but on outings and during holidays. A little bit of your time will go a long way. They are especially touched by sincere expressions of love, making hospitality and friendship towards them particularly effective if done from a genuine concern to help the newcomer and to get to know him as a person.

The careful use of literature in Chinese can overcome the language barrier. Since most non-Chinese can't speak Mandarin, their ability to express Christian truths is limited. Though many Chinese speak good English, it's not their heart language. Much of the time, our Chinese friends only seem to understand what we are saying. Furthermore, they may be hesitant to talk about religious topics with you at first. For this reason, bilingual Bibles and apologetic booklets written especially for intellectuals can be very effective. Present these, one or two at a time, as gifts, and ask them to tell you what they think.

Cooperation with Others

Over the past few decades, the potency—even necessity—of teamwork has been repeatedly proved. Cooperative efforts will help to overcome the limitations of ministry exclusively by Chinese or Western Christians. Both have their contribution to make, and need to work together for maximum impact. It often takes a team to weave a tapestry of loving influence.

Cooperate with your local church and perhaps with a nearby Chinese church. There are also organizations that do this sort of thing well: English-speaking international ministries, such as International Students Inc., Inter-Varsity Christian Fellowship, and Reformed University Fellowship International; Chinese-speaking ministries, such as Ambassadors for Christ, Overseas Campus, and China Outreach Ministries; and others such as Overseas Missionary Fellowship International and the Navigators.

Some Chinese like to attend Christian meetings in English, but most really enjoy getting together with their countrymen in a Chinese-language setting. That's why it it's so important to join hands with a local Chinese church. Most university towns and all big cities have at least a Chinese Bible study, if not one or more active churches. By working with them, we can create a web of care and concern that helps to replace the supportive communities that have been left behind in Asia. In fact, more than one person from China has observed that he found more love here than he ever knew back home.

Students

"Moving without Mom is hard!" The newly-arrived student from China was standing amidst her luggage, confronting the challenge of adjusting to life in a strange place. "I don't understand. It wasn't this difficult when I went off to college in China," she went on. Like many others, she had thought that it would be easy to continue her studies in America; only the place would be different. Especially for the first few weeks of their sojourn, these young people are in need of our help, particularly practical assistance with settling in to a new place. Coming to a strange country, they long to have a "native" friend. Sadly, most will return without ever having entered a local home. Instead, they will just spend most of their time with other Chinese.

Befriending these students can make a difference. Organizations like International Students Inc. have programs for connecting people with international students. Invest at least a few hours each month (preferably more) in just getting to know each other. When studies consume their time, ongoing friendship, including meals in our homes, outings with the family, and trips to historic sites can make them feel cared for. Let them see your life as it is. They will be watching, and your Christian manner of going through the day will impress them deeply. With the use of materials provided by organizations like International Students Inc. and Inter-Varsity Christian Fellowship, as well as partnership with the local church, they gain insights into cross-cultural sharing of the love of God.

"And just who is my neighbor?"

"The Chinese at your doorstep."[17]

GIVING CHRISTMAS AWAY

We often say that Christmas is a time for giving, but the fact is that we usually end up spending huge amounts of time and money on ourselves, and very little on others. My daughter, Sarah, once worked for the Salvation Army's Angel Tree project, and was dramatically affected by what she has learned about the state of poor people in her area. It's opened her eyes to the privileges she has always enjoyed, in contrast to the poverty in which millions around us live. Without drawing your attention from the materially poor among us, may I also suggest that we also consider the needs of the gospel poor?

Christmas: For Chinese Too?

In Mainland China and Taiwan, Christmas has become a major holiday. As with us, the focus is largely upon giving and receiving gifts and cards, and has become almost totally commercialized. Christians in those places see things differently, however. They grasp this rare opportunity to share the gospel with their friends and neighbors, especially through special Christmas events in their churches. In China, these meetings are packed out, usually with overflow crowds spilling into the streets, most of whom are young people who are curious to know more about Christianity.

Wise Men Seek Him Still

Here in the West, tens of thousands of Chinese students, scholars, and their families continue to express openness to the gospel. You can compare them to the "wise men from the East," who travelled a long distance to find the Babe about whom they had heard in their homeland. Generally, they are willing to listen to an intelligent presentation of the truth, if it is wrapped in love and care for them. Sadly, most of them never see the inside of an American home, except perhaps at an annual departmental Christmas party where the alcohol flows freely and the conversation touches upon everything but God.

No Room in the Inn?

We Christians have a splendid opportunity at this time to demonstrate the difference that Christ makes. Motivated by the love of God, who gave his only Son so that we might have life, we can extend this love to the

---

17   Title inspired by *China At Your Doorstep* by Stacey Bieler, published by InterVarsity Press.

strangers in our midst. Unless, that is, we seek to lock up our homes and our hearts, jealous of our privacy, perhaps a bit ashamed of our self-indulgence, and maybe fearful that an outsider will somehow spoil it all for us. After all, we are so busy, and have so little time for our own family; why spread our emotional resources even thinner?

More Blessed to Give Than to Receive

On the other hand, we can imitate God and re-define "family" to embrace those whom God leads us to love as we do ourselves. My older siblings tell me that when our father was off at war, our mother would send them to the USO center to find soldiers and sailors to invite home for Thanksgiving and Christmas dinner. When I was growing up, I don't think we ever celebrated a major holiday with just family. My whole family treasures this heritage of hospitality.

Giving Christmas Away

You don't have to neglect your family to reach out to Chinese nearby. Include Chinese and other foreigners in your Christmas parties, making sure that the Story is celebrated in word and song. Invite Chinese to special musical presentations and Christmas services, then for dessert or even supper afterwards to discuss what they heard and saw. Present them with a Christian book, perhaps a Chinese-English Bible or another book. You might even consider having one or more Chinese in your home for Christmas dinner or even for a couple of days. We have all been bombarded with requests for donations in this poor economy. Perhaps we should ponder the possibility of spending less on ourselves and more on others, especially Christian churches and ministries.

FELLOWSHIP WITH CHINESE CHRISTIANS

In all we do, let us remember that true Christian growth cannot take place in isolation from frequent fellowship with other believers. Though Westerners can perform a vital service by introducing newcomers to the Christian faith and even to an English-speaking church, that is not enough. Sooner rather than later, inquirers and new believers must be introduced also to other Chinese Christians. Only then can they begin to learn to "do" Christianity as Chinese. Only other Chinese will know their background, peculiar difficulties, cultural biases and temptations, and unique questions, and can address these in a way that Westerners simply cannot.

They may object, however, and say that they prefer to remain only with Western Christians. Many causes may generate this reluctance to join

Chinese. Some, especially those form wealthier families, may fear embarrassment by those who are "fresh off the boat" and don't speak English as well as they do, or dress as fashionably. If their parents are government officials, they may be afraid of exposure and the possible difficulties this may bring to their father and mother. Others just think it's "cool" to hang out with Westerners. Maybe it's just a desire to practice English.

In any case, we must slowly but firmly nudge them towards integration with Chinese believers, at least as a condition for baptism. If they settle in their adopted country, then of course they may want to join a local English-speaking church; that is their right. There is always the possibility that they will return to Asia, however. Meanwhile, they need the tools to share their faith with their family and friends back home. For all these reasons, we should do all we can to get them into a fellowship composed largely of Chinese.

FOREIGNERS LIVING IN CHINA

The Challenge

The Chinese government knows that thousands of Christians go to China for the express purpose of winning converts to Christ. Within their own narrow mental framework, for at least three reasons, such people are threats to the social order. First, they come from overseas, especially the West, and particularly America. Communists view them as agents of foreign powers seeking to de-stabilize China and even overthrow the regime. We know that is untrue, but they believe the myths and slander about nineteenth-century missionaries, and tar modern emissaries of Christ with the same brush. Second, they know that faith in God poses a fundamental challenge to Communism's atheist assumptions. If God exists, then their ideology is basically wrong. Finally, they remember the prominent role that Christians played in the fall of Communist governments in Eastern Europe, and especially Romania, formerly their close ally. All foreigners in China receive close scrutiny; members of Christian organizations are watched even more closely, as are their Chinese friends. Serious consequences may befall those who engage in, or are the recipients of, explicit Christian outreach.

The Opportunity

On the other hand, foreign Christians living in China report remarkable openings. In today's climate of globalization and intellectual ferment, new ideas from the outside find a ready welcome, and there is a receptivity to the gospel rarely seen in Chinese history. If foreign believers can demonstrate integrity in their daily lives; respect the laws of the land; evince a humble desire to learn and to serve; rely on prayer and the Holy Spirit; and build friendships based on mutual respect, patient listening, and genuine love—then they can have a profound impact on the Chinese who get to know them.

As I have said before, in my opinion, the best way to demonstrate real concern is to learn Chinese language and culture. We must not use language study as a mere cover for proselytizing in China, nor should we give answers before we know the questions in the hearts of the Chinese. But if foreigners truly seek to learn, they can build relationships that allow Chinese to see their transformed lives and ask questions. Over a period of several years, they will prove that they really seek to understand and, to some degree, they will begin to comprehend enough to know how the gospel speaks to the deepest yearnings of the Chinese people. Hard work, discipline, and prayer will also bring a growing skill in speaking the gospel in a way that their friends can understand and apply to their lives. There are other reasons for learning the language and culture of China, including China's rising prominence in the world, but surely Christians have the strongest motivation to spend several years as humble listeners and eager learners.

ACADEMIC EXCHANGE

Open Minds and Hearts

For a variety of reasons, academic exchange presents one of the most effective ways of reaching Chinese with the Good News of Christ. The growing number of Chinese intellectuals who display an unprecedented openness to the gospel represents a fertile field for effective Christian witness. Ever since their confidence in the goodness of human nature was shattered by the Tiananmen Square incident in 1989, they have seen the Christian view of man's fallen nature as plausible. The general collapse of Communist ideology has further prepared the way for another total world-and-life view, which biblical Christianity offers.

Unusual Influence

Chinese intellectuals play a role in their society that is far out of proportion to their numbers. Partly because of the Confucian tradition of the scholar-official, those with advanced education are often called upon to give advice to the government on policy issues. Those without contact with the government dominate education, the arts, and the media, exercising indirect influence as teachers, writers, and conversation partners with key thought and culture shapers. It behooves us to engage them in critical examination of their culture and the potential role of Christians within it, and to develop relationships with them. They are, after all, people like us, and their personal lives are fraught with stress, uncertainty, and frustration—suitable soil for a message of light and love.

Open Doors

Hundreds of thousands of China's best academics and students travel to other countries annually, bringing them into contact with Western Christians, opening their eyes to a totally different way of looking at life, and introducing them to real love. Many more remain at home to pursue truth, and increasingly they are pondering the value of Christianity for themselves and their society.

Although the Chinese government has sometimes cracked down harshly on house churches in some places, has stepped up its promotion of atheistic socialism (under various names), and sometimes discourages explicit religious inquiry and expression in the academy, many open doors await those with the right resumes and relationships. Indirect approaches can often bear much fruit. Chinese are eager to learn from scholars in other countries, including the United States and Britain. More and more, they also have something of value to contribute to academic dialogue. Conferences, scholarly colloquia, and personal interchange between peers offer ready access to people who are eager for both information and friendship.

More direct openings are also available, for over the past two decades, more and more Chinese scholars have begun to investigate the role that Christianity has played in Western society, especially in America, as well as the contribution that Christians—both foreign and Chinese—have made to their own nation. As a result, they have become aware of the immense contribution that Christians make as "salt and light" in any society, and they want to know more. Research into Christianity has become an accepted academic subject all over China. Academic conferences and publications have multiplied, with Chinese scholars sharing their findings with an ever-widening circle of interested colleagues. Some believe that Christianity might have something to offer their nation, which is in the midst of a crisis of faith and culture now.

Necessary Preparation

These sorts of openings do not come as a matter of course. Only if we expend a great deal of time and energy in hard study will invitations be extended to us. Without years of concentrated, consistent, and careful reading, reflection, and writing, doors to influential academic arenas will remain closed to us.

Is It Worth It?

As Mark Noll pointed out in The Scandal of the Evangelical Mind, and as James D. Hunter has brilliantly demonstrated in his book, To Change the World, evangelicals have, by and large, neglected the life of the mind. As a consequence, at least in America, they have "lost" the "culture wars" to those who have put resources into shaping thought and culture. Sadly, many engaged in service to the Chinese likewise go for quick, shallow results. They invest in short projects with numerical-ly-measurable "outcomes" or they concentrate all their attention on the very real needs for pastors and leaders of the Chinese church.

But what will happen if the current generation of Chinese intellectuals is neglected at this crucial time in their history? The growing urban church in China is led by people who look to their educated peers for theological and philosophical direction. What if they end up receiving the wrong kind of "help"? We envision a time when Christian ideas permeate this huge nation; when Christian leaders, both clergy and lay, are equipped to answer hard questions and to propose better solutions to society's pressing needs.

Your Part

So what can you do to share Christianity with Chinese intellectuals? Anyone living in a university town can find a Chinese student or family to encourage with your friendship. If you are in the academy, as a teacher or a student, we urge you to ask God to lead you into fruitful relationships with Chinese whom he has prepared to investigate the claims of Christ. Consider going to Greater China for a short time to exchange ideas— and share the love of God—with your colleagues across the ocean. Remember, too, that we are talking about real "exchange." We have a lot to learn from the Chinese, especially the heroic believers.

THE ARTS

In the past few decades, China's growing economy has fueled a resurgence in not only popular entertainment but also "high-brow" art. Galleries feature paintings, sculpture, and other art work from a rising generation of very talented artists, whose works fetch high prices in an increasingly globalized market. Orchestras perform Western and Chinese classics before crowds of well-dressed people who can afford pricey tickets. In this climate, Christians with either talent or interest in the fine arts can make a significant contribution to the dissemination of God's truth through performance and among practitioners and patrons of the arts. The possibilities are as many as there are people with creativity to recognize and grasp emerging opportunities.

For example, a ballet school run by a large church sends its best students to a ballet school in China for a week of joint practices, lessons, and finally a performance. Each contributes its best offerings—classical ballet by the Americans and modern dance by the Chinese. During the week, they eat and converse with each other. Acquaintances are formed that could lead to friendships later. The Chinese notice that there is something different about these young American girls. More than one asks, "Why do you dance? Why do you seem to have so much joy? We do this as a job, but you seem to like what you are doing. Our life is grim and gray; yours seems full of sunshine. Please tell us your secret." Naturally, the foreigners know better than to give a full-fledged presentation of the gospel. That would embarrass the sponsoring organizations. There is nothing to stop them from saying, however, that God is the source of their joy, and the love of God the reason for their energy and peace.

In the same city a year later, a world-famous Japanese painter who lives in America attends an exposition of his work and gives lectures on his philosophy of art, during which he also talks about reconciliation between Japanese and Chinese who still remember the atrocities of World War 2, a reconciliation that he thinks can only come through Christ. His stature as an artist makes this sort of explicit testimony possible.

In another city, Christians have opened an art gallery that features the work of local artists in several media. Some of these are Christians, who are invited to talk about their life as artists at gatherings attended by both believers and non-believers. The private venue gives them space to share their Christian worldview openly. The gallery hosts concerts by local musicians with no Christian affiliation, with refreshments and conversation afterwards. More than one person has noticed the different "atmosphere" in this gallery and has been willing to meet later for Bible study.

A Christian film critic gives lectures on the deeper message and assumptions of Academy award films, and expresses his own conviction that there is something other than nihilism available to those searching for meaning in life. Private meetings later with Christian film directors open the door for him to show ways in which Christians can communicate the good, the true, and the beautiful through film, without being "preachy" or shallow.

Performances of sacred music such as Handel's Messiah are obvious opportunities of exposing people to the gospel without a "sermon," but even music without Christian lyrics can furnish a platform for discussion of the fundamental issues of life. Imagine a lecture, or a whole course, on American folk music? Or a series of discussions of films with Christian themes, or novels expressing Christian values and assumptions?

We must assume, of course, that Christians hoping to gain access to Chinese people through the arts will be knowledgeable, talented, and subtle. There is no place for anything shabby or trite. But the tradition of Christian excellence in the arts goes back many centuries in the West, and there are many Chinese who are more than eager to learn more about what sort of culture produced Bach, Beethoven, Michaelangelo, Rembrandt, and a host of others whose art moves and inspires us to this day. From Francis Schaeffer's How Should We Then Live? to the more scholarly Modern Art and The Death of a Culture by H.R. Rookmaaker, Christian reflections on art and Christianity can stimulate discussions with thoughtful Chinese who are in search of God or are desiring to glorify God through the arts.

SHORT-TERM TRIPS

The Challenge

Despite their immense popularity over the past two decades, short-term trips to China have been sharply criticized as both ineffective and too expensive. By "short-term" I mean anything less than two years. I realize most people would consider a year or more as "long-term" service, but this is not the case, for you can't learn the language, acquire cultural sensitivity, and build deep relationships in that little time.

Because of those limitations, "short-term" ministry in China faces tremendous challenges. How can you understand the real needs of someone if you don't know their language? Without a profound knowledge of culture—customs, values, thought patterns, world view—how can you share the gospel in a way that penetrates the mind and the heart and leads to lasting transformation? In China, as in many similar "high-context" societies, relationships are crucial. With five decades of mutual mistrust and suspicion behind them, Chinese will not quickly entrust themselves to a stranger. (There are exceptions, of course.) Furthermore, in order to help a person apprehend God's truth and apply it to the burning issues of life, you usually need to earn the right to be heard over many years of faithful friendship and loving listening. That's all the more case in China.

Alas, most people who go to China for a week or two, and even those who serve longer, just don't have the opportunity to hear before they speak. As a consequence, many so-called "conversions" turn out to be shallow, or even insincere. Chinese tend to be courteous folk, who will tell you what you want to hear in order to give you face. Add the current widespread eagerness for something to fill the aching voids of life in China, and you have fertile soil for quick "decisions for Christ" that look good in letters back home but don't necessarily reflect a work of the Holy Spirit.

Then there's the expense. Travel, lodging, tuition for language study that is meant only as a "cover"—all these cost a great deal. You could support a long-term worker with facility in Chinese for a year on the amount spent on one two-week trip by a few people.

The Opportunity

On the other hand, short-term visits, even only for a few days, have been used by God to make a lasting influence upon people in China and Taiwan. Even those without the language can promote the gospel among Chinese if they build on existing relationships, increase their knowledge and the knowledge of others, contribute something useful, and lead others to pray.

How can you make the most of a short-term trip? Learn as much as you can before you go. Do not expect to convert anyone in a few days or a few weeks. Even though that occasionally happens, it's usually the result of years of seed-sowing by someone else. Do expect to listen, to learn, to pray, to evince the character of Christ. Seek to understand and to help others back home know more about Chinese culture and current conditions. Discreetly share literature with interested people, such as materials provided by OMF International and Ambassadors for Christ.

Meet a real need. There are many requests for medical work; practical assistance in orphanages; and teaching, including English, business, and other subjects. Serving in these ways demonstrates God's love and opens doors for lasting friendships. Follow up with prayer, communication, and sharing the vision with others back home.

Work with a team. As the Chinese see us relating to each other in a Christian way, they get a taste of social relationships based on love (John 13:34–35). Go with an organization that has close ties to Chinese Christians. In this way, you can help to strengthen existing relationships and be assured that you are playing a truly supportive role.

Serve with experienced groups. Some organizations have been in China and Taiwan for many years, and know how to make the most of short-termers.

Even if you can't go, your prayers and gifts can enable others to participate in vision trips.

I believe that short-term visits are by far the least effective way to communicate the gospel effectively, but that does not mean that they have no value. Properly done, brief trips to China can be part of an overall strategy of discipling China's millions.

FRIENDSHIP

At the 1910 Edinburgh World Missionary Conference, Indian church leader V.S. Azariah cried out, "You have given your goods to feed the poor. You have given your bodies to be burned. We also ask for love. Give us FRIENDS!" In the 1920s, China's C.Y. Cheng wrote, "He who comes to us with the spirit of a friend through and through will ultimately win our hearts… We believe it is this friendship, which is another word for Christian love, which will solve many of our mission problems, and will lead the work to a more successful issue."

A Rich Tradition

Like many peoples, the Chinese have a long and rich tradition of friendship. The second line of the Analects of Confucius says: "To have friends coming from afar—is this not a delight?" Throughout the centuries, Chinese people have valued deep, lasting friendships with one or two, or at most a few, loyal and like-minded peers.

Lin Yutang, in My Country and My People, wrote that China is a more "feminine" culture compared to the "masculine" cultures of the West. We may take the Chinese emphasis upon personal relationships as an example of this difference. As we all know, Westerners are relatively more goal oriented, eager to get down to business and conclude deals right away, without much personal interaction, whereas Chinese prefer to get to know each other, establish trust, and then "do business" based on a solid relationship. In profound contrast to the Americans' breezy use of the word "friend," taken to extremes by today's social networking media, Chinese emphasize relationships that last a long time and manifest trust, frankness, and commitment. This concept of friendship was almost shattered during the Great Cultural Revolution (1966–1976), and comes under constant pressure in a society where all children are taught that they must be "Number One," but it has not died.

Friendship and Mission

In an important article, Dr. Dana Robert traces the transition from a focus by missionaries upon friendship in the early twentieth century to the current call for partnership.[18] The former is individual and personal, the latter is corporate and institutional. Without denying the role of institutional partnerships, she reminds us of the primary role of friendships in effective cross-cultural ministry. Dr. Robert points out that cross-cultural friendship requires several essential ingredients: "Long-term commitment to particular persons and places, major efforts to understand and to respect another culture or religion, and living with and putting themselves in the service of others." This friendship must be unconditional, not based on the expectation that the other will become a believer in Christ.

While Westerners often focus on rapid, mechanical (even impersonal), short-term, "measurable results," the Chinese value slower, warmer, personal, longer-range, and lasting relationships. The first approach seems, at least at first, more efficient and, applied to Christian ministry, does yield the all-important numbers for supporters back home! However, I do not need to cite biblical passages in order to demonstrate which of these two reflects God's usual way of doing things. Words like "growth," "fruit," "roots," "foundation," "perseverance," and the like convey the message clearly enough.

There is a wry saying among veteran China ministry workers: There are three things that come quickly with today's Chinese, and one that comes slowly. You can quickly get Chinese to come to church, admit that Christianity is an excellent religion, and even accept baptism; but true repentance and regeneration come more slowly. The same goes for building solid church leadership and healthy congregations. People don't become mature believers or capable pastors and teachers overnight. The process takes time, usually years, and requires solid relationships built upon mutual trust. Of course, we don't need to start from nothing, if we are connected in some way with those who have established those essential relationships. We can build on the foundation that others have laid, as long as we do not violate the trust and lose the respect they have won for us. Younger workers can inherit a great deal from those who have gone before, saving them much time, while they invest their efforts in earning the confidence of their Chinese friends by consistent Christ-like conduct.

Hard Questions

Now enters the foreigner who wants to make a contribution to the spread

---

18   Dana Robert, "Cross-cultural Friendship in the Creation of Twentieth-century Christianity," *International Bulletin of Missionary Research* 35, no. 2 (2011): 100–107.

of the gospel among the Chinese around the world. Several thousand are serving in China today in various capacities, and all want to help. How many of them, however, take the time and effort to learn the language and customs of their hosts? Are they aware that they are being watched and that their lives speak more loudly (even) than their lips? More importantly, are they willing to spend years building friendships that will provide soil for mutual understanding, sincere respect, and genuine cooperation in the Lord's work?

Dr. Robert asks penetrating questions: "In an age characterized by short-term service, what is the deeper meaning of friendship? ... Do today's young going into mission service commit themselves to specific persons from other cultures? Do they learn the languages or develop mutual reciprocity with the 'other'? ... Does anyone have time to make friends today, or is cross-cultural service a kind of global networking that looks good on a resume?"

RELIGIOUS DIALOGUE

E. Stanley Jones, the famous missionary to India, initiated a method of intentional conversation about matters of faith with his "religious dialogues." About ten people from different religious backgrounds would gather around in a circle, and then share their spiritual experiences. They did not argue, debate, or talk about ideas and concepts. They just related the story of their pilgrimage in knowing and serving "God."[19] Perhaps we can adapt this approach to our efforts to introduce our Chinese friends to Christ. Of course, we would first have to build a relationship of trust with them, and they would have to be willing to open up and tell us and perhaps a few others about their own quest for meaning in life. With younger people, especially students, that might be easier, since they have not known the trauma of the Cultural Revolution of the last century. Older scholars and their families would probably relax more if they were with friends. The leader of the discussion would gently guide the meeting, so that no one talked too much and there was no putting down of those with whom we disagree. Honest questions and gracious answers are totally in place, of course.

In some circles, "religious dialogue" has received a bad name because some of its proponents do not believe in the uniqueness of Christianity or the necessity of repentance and faith in him for eternal salvation. Of course, that is not what I am assuming here. Christians will be clear

---

19   See Richard W. Taylor, "E. Stanley Jones, 1884–1973: Following the Christ of the Indian Road," in Gerald H. Anderson and others, eds., *Mission Legacies*, 342–42.

about what they believe, but they will give others freedom to disagree and to state their own "take" on the journey of life. By restricting the conversation to personal experiences, moreover, much intellectual debate can be avoided. Jones observed that perhaps the greatest benefit of this type of meeting came from the self-reflection it engendered in the Christians themselves.

In the next chapter, we shall look at a few proven methods for proclamation of the truth of God, but I wanted first to emphasize the critical necessity of personal relationships and careful listening first.

CHAPTER FIVE
PROCLAMATION (1)

Jesus said that "This gospel of the Kingdom will be preached in all the world" (Matt 24:14), and issued commands that his disciples take the word of salvation to the ends of the earth. Proclamation of the gospel may take many forms and employ many different media and methods. You will find only a few of these briefly described below, though others are readily available.

INTERNET, RADIO, AND LITERATURE

Worldwide Web

We all know how the Internet has drastically transformed our world in the past two decades. Though sometimes it can be a source of immense frustration, this new medium has also added exciting dimensions to ministry. With a few strokes on the keyboard, we can send information to anyone who is "wired" to receive it. As the world sinks into recession, perhaps even depression, some types of Christian ministry become too expensive to continue. Not so the Internet! All over the world, and including China, people can access the Internet either free or almost so. Even with the "Great Chinese Firewall" in place, not all websites are blocked, and determined people can find ways to access almost any site.

Chinese users of the Internet now number more than the entire population of the United States. Though some websites are blocked in China, many are not. Christian content can be accessed without difficulty all over the vast expanse of the nation, at any time. That means that work done overseas can build up the church deep in the interior of China. People who don't know how to find a Christian church can receive solid biblical instruction just by turning on the computer.

Radio Broadcasts

For many years, when China was closed to the outside, Christian radio provided the only access to millions of Chinese who hungered for Bible truth. Now, with the doors wide open for study, tourism, business, education, and professional work, many have forgotten this powerful means of spreading the gospel in China. The truth is that most Chinese will never have a chance to hear about Christ from a foreigner, and hundreds of millions of them (ponder that number for a moment) have no contact with Chinese believers. Furthermore, millions of Chinese Christians lack the resources that we enjoy, and desperately need not only the basic facts of the gospel, but solid Biblical teaching.

Radio broadcasts are still probably the most effective means of reaching people in China. Please re-read that sentence. With all our emphasis on short-term trips to China by people who don't know the language and culture (and such trips do have some value), let us not neglect the awesome potential of radio, which beams soul-satisfying words in their mother tongue to countless thirsty listeners. Far East Broadcasting Company has served seekers and believers in China for decades. Their ministry continues to be extremely useful. CCNTV has joined FEBC in taking fine Christian programs of all sorts to China through the Internet as well. I urge you to inquire about how you may participate in what they do.

Christian Literature

For thousands of years, the Chinese have excelled in the written word. With a rich tradition of writings in philosophy, ethics, religion, essays, the novel, drama, and poetry, they have a literary heritage second to none. Recent decades have witnessed an explosion in the number of Chinese who are literate. Once the property of the educated elite, printed materials can now reach hundreds of millions of eager readers.

Christians have always prized the role of the written word. After all, we are "people of the Book," who believe that God has revealed his unchanging truth in the words of inspired men who have given us his inerrant Word in the Bible. Since the beginning of the Church, Christians have augmented the spoken ministry with writings aimed at both believers and pre-Christians. Seeking either to edify Christians or evangelize unbelievers, they have put their thoughts on paper, and influenced entire civilizations.

Books and other Christian literature have some advantages over preachers and evangelists. They can penetrate places people could never reach. They allow for quiet reflection, careful thought, and considered response. Available at any time, they can be read repeatedly, pondered, and passed on to others. They are also relatively cheap! Mailing a book costs much less than sending a speaker. Books don't have to be fed and lodged; they charge no transportation fees; they expect no honorarium.

Equally important in today's tense climate, they can be read in private, so they don't draw the attention of nosy authorities anxious lest a crowd gather to hear "dangerous" teachings. Printed—as distinct from electronic—materials can make a huge difference for both Chinese Christians and seekers all over the world. Thankfully, Chinese Christians know this, and have worked hard to produce wealth of resources in Chinese, a written language known by more people than any other except English. Publishers in Hong Kong, Taiwan, North America, and even now in China have issued a steady stream of excellent books, booklets, tracts, pamphlets, magazines and newspapers presenting the Biblical world-and-life view.

Many of these materials are translated from English, German, and other languages. Increasingly, however, Chinese authors are coming to the forefront. For example, one of my former students has written a massive commentary on the letters of John, which is part of a series of commentaries by Chinese scholars. Before long, Chinese may replace English as the leading language for theology! Meanwhile, non-Chinese can continue to share what we have learned with our Chinese brothers and sisters around the world, without ever leaving home.

STORIES OF CHINESE CHRISTIANS

In particular, stories of Chinese Christians and foreign missionaries to the Chinese find a ready audience in China. Starting with the Book of Acts, Christians have a heritage in the lives of disciples of Christ who have set before us examples of faithfulness and love. Think of Robert Morrison, who labored for decades to produce a Chinese Bible, dictionary, grammar, and dozens of other works covering all aspects of China's complex culture and society. Laboring under the most difficult conditions—even learning the language was illegal—he persevered, despite illness, the death of his wife, a full-time job, and the constant fear of discovery by authorities. Thousands of others followed in his footsteps, including J. Hudson Taylor, who adopted Chinese dress, and founded the China Inland Mission, whose members were known for and living among the people whom they came to serve.

In the twentieth century, John Song engaged in almost fabulous exploits as China's most famous evangelist. Who knows how many tens, perhaps hundreds, of thousands were converted through his powerful preaching, or how many thousands received miraculous healing from his prayers? Despite a debilitating disease that finally took his life, not to mention constant fatigue, bandits, Japanese bombing attacks, opposition from government officials or those whose businesses suffered when people repented of evil habits, he traversed China as well as much of South East Asia in epic journeys that are remembered to this day.

Lit-sen Chang (Zhang Lisheng) was a noted educator and proponent of Chinese religions, even a fierce enemy of Christianity, until he was converted at about the age of fifty. Afterwards, he poured all his strength and powerful intellect into communicating Christian theology in words and concepts that engaged traditional Chinese culture and religion as well as contemporary politics and theology.

Sometimes, the stone which the builders rejected turns into a major building block, as happened with Gladys Aylward, the "little woman" who became universally acclaimed for her stunning achievements in rural China, immortalized in Ingrid Bergmann's inaccurate but thrilling "Inn of the Sixth Happiness." David Adeney's health almost barred him from membership in the China Inland Mission, but he proved all the doctors wrong throughout decades of travels in China, South East Asia, North America, and the rest of the world. I met two men not long ago who had been greatly impacted by his ministry. Eric Liddell, hero of "Chariots of Fire," went on to missionary victories of Olympian stature. Others, like Wang Laiquan, served for decades in positions of relative obscurity while rendering invaluable service to the advance of the gospel. His own humility, sacrifice, and skill were indispensable to the early success of J. Hudson Taylor and the China Inland Mission.

For What Purpose?

What value does Chinese Christian history play in reaching Chinese worldwide? First, Chinese Christians receive encouragement by learning of their Christian heritage, which has hitherto been largely unknown to them. They see that they are not alone in their struggles against all sorts of obstacles. Second, these stories augment more didactic means of leadership development, furnishing models for evangelists, pastors, and others with responsibility in the church and in society. Third, stories supplement direct evangelistic tools. Sometimes stories can win people's hearts in a way that straight doctrine does not. In particular, these examples of courage and sacrifice appeal powerfully to Chinese, who admire those who suffer hardship for the good of others. Finally, historical accounts correct false impressions of missionaries as tools of foreign imperialism, and of Chinese believers as traitors to their country. Countering such prejudice forms a necessary component to any strategy to clear away obstacles to the growth of the church in China. Two of Global China Center's projects have proven to be effective tools for exposing Chinese readers to stories of faithful believers: *The Biographical Dictionary of Chinese*

Christianity and the three-volume *Salt and Light: Lives of Faith that Shaped Modern China,* in the *Studies in Chinese Christianity* series. Future volumes in that series will include biographies as well.

SMALL GROUP BIBLE STUDIES

All across the world, small group Bible studies have proven to bear consistent fruit. By "small group" I mean a gathering of no more than twenty people. "Bible studies" refers to meetings that focus on reading and discussing the Scriptures, with attention to application and time for sharing and prayer. The core content, however, is the Bible itself, not the life experiences or questions of the group members. For optimal effect, these groups will gather in homes, but meetings at school, work, or in a public place such as a hotel or restaurant can also be quite successful. The main ingredients are a small enough number of people to allow for questions and discussion; skilled leadership; and systematic study of the Scriptures.

Content

In my experience, it's best to start with Genesis, so that a foundation of biblical truth can be laid. If you begin with the Gospel of John, as many do, then you still have to go back to Genesis to find the source and meaning for terms like "in the beginning," "Word," God," "created, "life," and "light" (just to pick a few from the opening verses of John). Otherwise, our Chinese friends will have no idea of what the New Testament writer is saying. They may think that Jesus is just another "god" who can be placed into an existing pantheon.

Furthermore, without the Old Testament background, how can we explain the creation, fall, and process by which God began to redeem mankind? What about the importance of the Flood, or the call of Abraham, or the lives of the patriarchs and Moses, to which the New Testament so often refers? After the essential background has been laid, perhaps with study that goes from Genesis through Exodus 20 (the Ten Commandments), one can move on to the Gospels, starting with Mark or John, followed by Acts and then Romans. Yes, Romans! That challenging epistle gives a full exposition of Paul's Gospel in a way that leads one through fundamental truths to their practical application in personal and corporate life.

Systematic, consecutive study is important for several reasons: First, it teaches people how to read the Bible as a book, with attention to narrative flow and context. Topical Bible studies may introduce important ideas quickly, but they do so at great cost: Verses are taken out of context, and the general structure of the biblical story remains out of sight. Participants are introduced to a "cherry-picking" method of using the Scriptures as a mine for finding little truths at the whim of the leader or the writer of the study guide. They are not given an example of placing oneself under the authority of the Word of God as it is given to us by the divine Author.

Method

The point of a small group study is to evoke participation by each person in attendance. Lectures, even in small groups, do not allow interaction with the truth. One remembers very little from lectures anyway. How much better it is to study a passage of the Bible by asking carefully-prepared questions and giving everyone a chance to reflect and respond. Questions provide fertile ground for going deeper and wider. Errors of understanding will come out in the conversation and can be gently corrected by a closer attention to the text itself. In this way, people are shown how to study the Bible on their own, rather than always being dependent upon a teacher or "expert."

Published Bible study guides offer excellent help in formulating questions. The Serendipity Bible does, too. Campus Press in Taiwan has published a number of these in Chinese, as has InterVarsity Press and other organizations in the West. If you decide to write your own questions, it is best to start with observation (who, what, when, where, how?); then move to interpretation (Why is this said? How does it relate to the rest of the book and the rest of the Bible?), and finally application (What does this mean for our life today?). Outside reference works, such as study Bibles and commentaries, can be used by the leader in preparation, but these should be quoted only sparingly, and not used as a way of showing off one's knowledge or research.

Of course, there are pitfalls to this sort of Bible study. Domineering leaders can just talk all the time and stifle real discussions. Talkative members can go on and on, depriving others of a chance to speak. The group can run down rabbit trails rather than sticking to the text. A skilled leader will know how to ask questions rather than talk, gently remind everyone to allow others to talk, and bring the conversation back to the passage being studied. It's wise to set out ground rules at the very beginning and to remind folks of these when necessary.

The Bible itself will evoke all sorts of responses, including conviction of sin and guidance about how to trust and obey God. Let these be springboards for personal sharing and then prayer, but be sure also to give people freedom to raise problems at the end of the study so that people can support them in prayer. But remember to pray, rather than just heap all sorts of well-intentioned but probably unwelcome advice on the person who raised the issue! We have found that splitting into groups of men and women facilitates candid sharing and also gives each person more time to talk.

Meeting time should be limited by agreement. You can probably hold an excellent study within an hour, though it's not easy if the group is larger. Two hours should be plenty of time for almost any occasion. Ending with refreshments or even a meal adds a family atmosphere and gives people time to get to know each other better. Starting with a meal can work, but you have to be disciplined and begin the actual study on time!

In our experience, keeping both believers and seekers together has many advantages, though others choose to separate them into two groups. The Bible speaks to people at all levels of faith and all stages of their pilgrimage. As newcomers see believers share their insights and experiences, they grow in understanding. As believers share, they learn how to express the gospel in terms everyone can understand, and new leaders are developed. People disagree about this, of course, and a case can be made for introducing basic concepts to inquirers before inviting them into the main study, but that process should be brief. In my opinion, it is better to give them an extra opportunity to hear the basic outlines of the gospel, perhaps using the Apostle's Creed, just to orient them to fundamental concepts and terms.

However different may be the details of the content and method, small group Bible studies can serve as a powerful means of bringing people to Christ and fostering their growth into maturity.

EVANGELISTIC PREACHING

Every year, countless evangelistic addresses are delivered by Christian speakers to Chinese around the world. Perhaps Christmas provides the best opportunity for such messages, but so do Chinese New Year and other times when non-believers are willing to accept invitations from their Christian friends to attend an evangelistic event. As someone who has been asked to deliver evangelistic sermons on many occasions, I have had to think about what I should say, and how. Here are some preliminary conclusions:

Biblically Based

Evangelistic messages should be biblically based. Not only should they reflect biblical truth, but they should be based upon, and clearly expound, a passage from the Bible. I prefer to pick a whole paragraph, at least, as the text for an evangelistic message, so that several aspects and layers of God's truth can be shared in a natural way. Clear exposition of the Scripture is the best way to allow the Word of God to pierce to the hearts of unbelievers, evoking repentance and faith. The sermons of Peter, Stephen, and Paul recorded in the Acts of the Apostles offer us a variety of models, but all of them exemplify the power of the Word of the Lord to produce profound and lasting effects. In other words, we can trust the very words of the Bible, if clearly presented, to carry persuasive energy.

By building our sermon on a single passage, we aid the concentration of non-believers, who are probably not familiar with the Bible and find references to many parts of the Scriptures hard to follow. We show them the inner coherence of the Scripture; we let the intrinsic logic and poetic beauty of the Bible speak for itself. This sort of expository evangelistic preaching also lends credibility to our presentation as a message not from ourselves, but from our Master. Of course, we can refer to other parts of the Bible, as long as we make connections that are obvious once they are explained, and keep to the main thrust of the passage we are explaining.

God-directed

Our evangelistic sermons must focus on God: His greatness and his goodness; his majesty and his mercy; his power and his pity. Like the Bible itself, our preaching should aim to show just how holy are his judgments and how kind are his intentions to all who will humbly call upon him. He should be portrayed as Creator, Sustainer, Redeemer, Savior, and Judge, and not solely as Friend and Provider of good things to those who ask. Since Chinese culture lacks any tradition of a transcendent God, we need to draw out what the Bible teaches about his sovereignty over all the universe, his absolute distance from us, his immensity, and his freedom to act as he wills. Of course, we shall also speak of his love, grace, and forgiveness to all who truly repent and trust in Christ.

Honest about Sin

All too many sermons portray God as a vending machine that will spit out goodies if we just push the right buttons. Millions of Chinese have made a profession of faith in a God who will just give material benefits.

Christ-centered

Again, like the Scriptures, all of which point to Christ and the salvation that is found in him alone (Luke 24:44-47 ; 2 Tim 3:16) we need to portray Jesus as the unique, eternal, and fully divine Word and Son of God, as well as a human being just like us, except without sin. We can hold him up as an example, as long as we make clear that we cannot follow in his steps without the transforming power of the Holy Spirit. His miracles, too, reflect the majesty of his person and the ways in which he radiates the love of God the Father. Above all, like Paul, who knew nothing except "Jesus Christ and him crucified," we must declare the glory of his saving, atoning work upon the Cross, where our sins were borne in our place by the innocent Lamb of God. We must tell the wonderful story of his resurrection, ascension, and promise to come again.

Relevant

Throughout the message, we need to connect the gospel story with their own unique situation as Chinese. It helps to refer to concepts from their culture, such as success, family, and face. Praise for the good meal they may have just enjoyed is also in order! We can quote from Confucius' Analects selectively, or use Chinese proverbs, or acknowledge the pressures they face in a very competitive and lonely world. Above all, however, I find that frequent use of Scripture passages in Chinese conveys the most beauty and power.

To help them understand the nature and seriousness of sin, especially sinful motives, we can use examples from real life, as long as we do not reveal confidential information. I frequently adduce instances of my own failure, to show that I am human like them and to exhibit the liberating power of God's grace to enable us to be authentic before others. Maybe I do this too much, but they seem to relate to me as a result.

Spiritual

As I have traveled about to various Chinese churches, I am repeatedly told that though the "front door" to the church is wide open, with many flocking in, the "back door" is equally wide, with many going out, never to be seen again. Seeking to understand, I have asked about the message being preached, and have usually been told that Chinese are being offered mostly worldly, material benefits for faith in Christ. Too often, they are not being shown that their eternal condition hangs upon their relationship to a holy God who must deal with the sin that separates us from himself, and that only whole-hearted repentance, sincere trust in Christ, and a willingness to follow Jesus unto death will save them endless misery in hell.

Of course, Proverbs 16:20 is right when it states, "Whoever trusts in the LORD, happy is he!" Happy, indeed. We have peace with God; forgiveness of sins; light for our daily path; help in times of trouble; promises of provision and protection; inner transformation; intimacy with Christ—

and much more. But there are spiritual blessings, not material ones. They are the benefits that we should proffer to hungry souls, not success, or better health, or a happier marriage, though all these may well follow as the fruit of a life lived in full reliance upon God.

Chinese admit that they are very pragmatic and practical, even opportunistic. Well, we should explain the very real advantages of believing in Christ, but these benefits must be portrayed as primarily spiritual, not physical or temporal. Otherwise, when one prayer goes unanswered, or when difficulties come, the "back door" will be crowded with disappointed "converts" who probably never really trusted in Christ for their salvation.

Sowing, Not Reaping

Unlike most evangelists, however, I do not give an "altar call" of any sort. I do not find any place in the Bible where gospel preachers called for a show of hands or led people in a prayer to receive Christ. Such tactics seem highly manipulative and destined to produce shallow "conversions" that last only a short time. In the Scriptures, presentations of the gospel are climaxed by an exhortation to repent, believe in Jesus Christ, and be baptized. Baptism marks the entry into visible membership in the Body of Christ. Any other rite is simply a non-biblical accretion with dubious merit.

Of course, we should press the claims of Christ forcefully and with urgency and passion, lest they trifle with matters of life and death. We must point out that there are only two destinies, heaven and hell, and one way to eternal life. Though I urge new inquirers to take their time to learn as much about Christianity as possible, I also warn that any of us could be killed in an accident on the way home that very night, and caution them against needless procrastination, lest they perish in their sins. What I refuse to do, however, is to seek some sort of numerical validation for my efforts, or provide some sort of number for the hosts of the evening, to build our reputation. We should give God time to work!

We can seek to preserve the energy of the moment in various ways: Ask people who are interested in knowing more to sign up for a small group Bible study; invite them to church; or provide literature for sale or giving it away free of charge. I usually have my books available for people to purchase, since they may read something written by a person whom they have heard and met. I am always happy to sign my books, which gives them added value, it seems. (I make absolutely no money from these sales; all the funds go back into the Literature account of China Institute.)

Teamwork

As with most sorts of outreach, evangelistic meetings work best when they are organized by a local church or fellowship, to which people can be welcomed afterwards. When members invite their friends, a natural way of continuing the conversation exists. The visiting evangelist, or a local speaker preaching evangelistically, is only one member of a team of people who actually do most of the work of showing what faith in Christ looks like in daily life. Only by working together can we reap the most fruit.

"COLD-TURKEY" EVANGELISM

Although most Chinese become Christians through friends and after long exposure to the gospel, that does not mean that we should not take every opportunity to spread the Good News as widely as possible.

Probably more than a billion people in China have never heard the full story of God's salvation brought to us through Jesus Christ. How can we go to bed at night without doing all we can to give them at least one chance to encounter the only truth that will bring them to eternal life and save them from eternal death? How can we blithely go our way amidst the teeming crowds in any city in Greater China without praying for openings to tell someone about God's love for us in Christ? As J. Hudson Taylor famously said, if hearing the Good News once may not be sufficient to evoke true repentance and lasting faith, what about not ever hearing at all?

In my travels to East Asia, I make it a practice to share the gospel with as many people along the way as possible—on the airplane, in marketplace encounters, and especially when riding in taxis. Though going by bus or subway is cheaper, sometimes taking a taxi is the fastest and best way to reach one's destination. It is more expensive, but I see this modest outlay as an investment in God's kingdom, a "ticket" to a seat where I have an almost-"captive" audience of one person. I am sure others may have a better way to proceed, but here is how I do it.

A Basic Approach

I begin with questions about the driver's work, his family, his general outlook on life, expressing sincere interest and seeking to discern his mood and openness to conversation. After a while, I sometimes introduce the topic of Christianity by asking, "I hear that there are a number of Christians in [this city]. Do you have any friends or acquaintances who are Christians?"

If he answers, "Yes," I ask, "What are they like as people?" Usually the driver responds that Christians are good people.

I then inquire whether the Christians have told him what they believe. I am sad to say that most of the time they have not, so I then ask, "Well, do you mind if I take two minutes and tell you what Christians believe?"

Nine out of ten taxi drivers will say, with more or less enthusiasm, "Sure, go ahead." After all, they are lonely people whose passengers rarely engage them in conversation. And I am a paying guest.

Having obtained permission, I briefly tell the gospel story, beginning with the existence of one true and living God; his creation of the world, including mankind; his requirement that we worship and obey him alone; our fall into sin, the nature of indwelling sin, and the consequent personal and social frustration; and our inability to change ourselves (at this point they almost always express agreement!). The foundation having been laid, I tell how God's love for his creatures drove him to send his own Son, who is fully divine, into the world. Then I tell them about Jesus' the life, teaching, miracles, and finally death on the Cross.

"Much to their amazement, however, on the third day the disciples saw Jesus. They thought he was a ghost—after all, people don't rise from the dead, do they? But after more than a month with him, they realized that it was really Jesus, in a new and glorified body. He told them to take the news of repentance and forgiveness of sins to the whole world, then left them, promising to return at the end of the age, raise us all from death, and establish a new heavens and a new earth. Now all who truly repent of their sins and trust in Christ alone for salvation receive the Holy Spirit, who creates in us a new heart and enables us, slowly and gradually, to become better people, though we are always in need of God's daily forgiveness."

At this or some earlier point, I usually meet with pretty much the same response: "All religions are the same, for they all urge us to do good works." I agree that this is true, at least to some extent, and then go over what I have said very briefly, pointing out that the biblical God is unique, as is his Son Jesus; that our good works are never perfect (and they usually agree to this); that we need someone to die in our place and to give us power to change; and that salvation is by faith, not our moral effort.

"I have a question," they often say. "What is the difference between Roman Catholics and 'Christians'" (Jidutu, the Chinese word for Protestants)? At least in mainland China, Roman Catholicism and Protestantism are clearly separated as two of the five officially recognized religions (along with Buddhism, Daoism, and Islam, Confucianism being considered only a moral philosophy). First, I emphasize that both accept the same fundamental beliefs, as outlined in the Apostle's Creed and the

Nicene Creed. Then I point out the significant differences, including: A different Bible; a different source of ultimate authority; a different way to go to God the Father (through Jesus vs. through Mary); a different view of salvation (faith alone vs. faith plus works, plus…); a different view of the church and of the ministry; etc. This allows me, by the way, to express the essentials of the gospel once more.

Other Options

If the driver does not know any Christians, then I ask if he has heard what Christians believe. If he hasn't, then I ask permission to share the gospel, and proceed as I described above.

What if he says that he knows Christians and doesn't like them? Actually, that has happened only once, but it gave me an opening to ask why he didn't like his sister (in this case) and to agree with his objection to her, which was that "every sentence she says has a thorn in it." That allows me to talk more about the nature of sin; the imperfection of Christians; our need for forgiveness, and so forth.

Sometimes I try a different approach right from the beginning. In Taiwan, and increasingly in China proper, you will see something hanging from the rear-view mirror. Most of these objects appear to have some religious significance, so I point to it and ask, "What is this? What does it mean?" The response then usually prepares the way for further questions about his belief system and how well it's working for him. At some point in the conversation, I ask, "So how do you deal with failure to live up to your own moral standards?" If, as they usually do, they essentially say, "I try harder," I propose another way to handle guilt—faith in Jesus Christ.

Sowing, Not Reaping

I must emphasize that I see this sort of one-time evangelism as sowing only. I do not try to reap a harvest before the seed has had time to germinate. I merely want to introduce the person to the basic outline of the Christian message, trusting that God will use someone else or some other means to water the ground and eventually produce a crop of true repentance and lasting faith.

I never ask someone to pray a prayer to receive Christ. As I have pointed out before, and will discuss in more detail, I find no Scriptural warrant for such a practice. Only God can grant real repentance and heartfelt reliance upon Christ for salvation, and he usually does so after a long period of inquiring and learning about the Bible story and its meaning for us today. We should not rush the work of the Holy Spirit, who works when and as he wills, mostly on a timetable that does not match ours!

Follow up is essential, of course. That's difficult with taxi drivers, but some means could be used. Perhaps we can make up a card with the email address or URL of a Christian organization, or the call numbers of a Christian radio station. Most places in China, for example, and all of Taiwan, receive clear signals from the broadcast stations of Far East Broadcasting Company (FEBC). May churches in urban China have open websites, and we can always direct people to a local church, which in China would be a Three-Self Patriotic Movement/ China Christian Council congregation. These are legal and not hard to find. A number of tracts exist in Chinese that can be left with taxi drivers and shop keepers, or passengers we meet on public conveyances. These carry the message home with the person for him to ponder and perhaps pursue further. Most important of all, of course, is our reliance upon God through prayer. Unless the Spirit works, our words are in vain, but if he does, then miracles can result.

CHAPTER SIX
PROCLAMATION (2)

PROBLEMATIC PRACTICES

Over the past three decades, thousands of Christians, both Chinese and Western, have sought to introduce Chinese to the saving message of Christ. Though their efforts have paid off in a large number of genuine conversions, leading to the growth of the Chinese church in Asia and in the West, a few major mistakes have greatly reduced the effectiveness of this ministry. Scattered throughout this book are comments about these practices, which seem to me to be problematic. By that I mean that they lack biblical warrant or seem patently unwise. Here I shall briefly summarize those comments and add a few others. My purpose is not to denigrate the zeal, good will, or Christian character of those who employ these methods. I assume that everyone seeking to spread the gospel among the Chinese means well and intends to glorify God and bring good to our Chinese friends. "Zeal without knowledge," however, almost always reaps a harvest of frustration and failure.

Furthermore, just because something seems to "work" does not justify its use, nor does that apparent temporary effectiveness guarantee long-term and salutary results. A flash-in-the-pan blaze may be impressive and even exciting, but that doesn't indicate its fundamental value for baking an apple pie, much less roasting a turkey. We are seeking to bear fruit that will last, and that only happens when we abide in the Lord by allowing his words to abide in us (John 15:7, 16). Only as we "play the game" according to the rules will we win the prize of spiritual victory (2 Tim 2: 5). So, at the risk of offending many fine people, I offer the following comments on some commonly-employed tactics for helping Chinese come to know Christ and grow in his grace.

Inadequate Preparation

Although my wife and I went to Asia with virtually no knowledge of Chinese culture and history, as I described earlier in this book, we were given ten full weeks of intensive training in cross-cultural missionary work by veterans at the Overseas Missionary Fellowship international headquarters in Singapore. After that, we were required to spend two years in full-time study of the Chinese language, during which we were not permitted to engage in "ministry" to Chinese, though of course we were expected to make friends with them and to share our Christian faith with them as occasions arose.

During those two years, we were often given instruction in "how it is done" by senior workers. At the end of the two years, we were assigned to a Chinese church, in which we would have a minor ministry while we spent half the day in Chinese language study. All of this training was meant to keep us from making unnecessary mistakes through ignorance of the language and culture of the people we came to serve. As our language supervisor said, we were hoping to communicate complex concepts to a people with a difficult language and a rich culture, and it behooved us to learn as much as possible before we could expect to make much of an impact, and then we should be continually learning, in order to increase in our ability to understand and to communicate.

Nowadays, it seems that too many folks go to China without knowing much (as we did), but also with no intention of really putting in the time to acquire enough Mandarin to explain the gospel in terms that Chinese can understand and apply it to their own cultural context. For a variety of reasons, they skimp on language study, even when they are registered as language students, so that they can immediately start sharing the gospel. It would be much better for them to spend at least two years as listeners and learners, rather than presuming to be teachers and guides.

"Decisions for Christ" and "Praying to Receive Christ"

Another problem is the tendency, amounting almost to a compulsion, to get Chinese to make a premature profession of faith. Everywhere I go, I see the disastrous results of this misguided zeal. My experience over more than three decades has convinced me that most of these "decisions" do not produce lasting Christian discipleship. Quickie "conversions," usually expressed by a "prayer to receive Christ," and sometimes baptism soon thereafter, have filled Chinese churches with nominal "Christians" who know little of the faith, have not experienced new life, and bring confusion and even conflict into the Body of Christ.

Often, these conversions result in little more than a temporary lift for the one being evangelized and a "notch" in the spiritual "belt" of the evangelist, or worse, a number in his report to his donors and superiors. Reports of conversions may be required by superiors in the organization, but such numbers mean little unless they reflect true conversion, which is never in the Bible associated with a simple prayer or raising one's hand at an evangelistic meeting.

Nowhere in the Bible are we told to ask people to "pray to receive Christ," to "make a decision for Christ," or "receive Christ" simply by praying a prayer. Furthermore, there is no—as in not one—single biblical example of any evangelist or Christian bringing people to faith in this manner, or of an inquirer "coming to Christ" in this way. This indisputable fact should cause us to wonder whether we should follow the crowd in doing something the Lord and his Apostles did not either command or practice. Protestants have criticized Roman Catholics for adding "sacraments," considered to be "means of grace," that have no biblical basis, but is not this widely used practice not an example of just that?

It is true that there are promises that those who "receive him," that is, those who "believe on his name," will receive the right to become children of God (John 1:12–13). Statements such as this must be interpreted in the light of the larger context, however. The Gospel of John includes a definition of believing in Christ: a person will "continue in" his word (8:32); abide in him through prayer and meditation on the words of Christ (15:5, 7); and bear fruit (15:1–10). In the Acts of the Apostles, Peter and others exhort inquirers to "repent" and "be baptized" as signs that they have truly believed (Acts 2:38). Everywhere in the New Testament, baptism is rite of entry into the community of faith, and it commits one to a life of following Christ. Just praying a prayer or making a decision for Christ is never mentioned, much less as an indication that one has "become a Christian." Baptism, furthermore, is baptism into the Body of Christ, which normally means joining a congregation (however small) of believers in which the Lord's Supper is observed, there is regular worship and teaching, and some sort of discipline is practiced. Incorporation into such a "church" begins with baptism, and marks one as a Christian.

Such practices as asking people to make a "decision for Christ" also ignore studies that show that it takes, on average, three to five years, if not more, from the first contact with the gospel to a full and lasting dedication of one's life to Christ by people from a Chinese background. Another recent study has shown that Chinese young people are attracted to many aspects of the gospel, but stumble over the fundamental concept of the existence of God! Of all Chinese who "believed" in Jesus in the US, 85% fall away when they return to China.

REACHING CHINESE WORLDWIDE

Be patient! Please, please, do not be in a rush to get your Chinese friends to make "decisions for Christ" or assume that a sincere interest in the gospel—or even a desire to believe—indicates true repentance and faith. Let the Holy Spirit do his work, at his pace, and in his way. Assume that cultural differences, prejudices, and simple ignorance will require much exposure to Christian truth and life before your friend will know what it means to follow Christ.

Lack of Biblical Teaching

A twin problem is the lack of biblical teaching—from the pulpit, before baptism, and after baptism. Stories, testimonies, exhortations, and appeals to self-interest take the place of systematic presentations of the whole counsel of God. There is little focus on the Cross of Christ or the cruciform nature of Christian living, not to mention the implications of the gospel for family, work, money, and career ambitions. Many millions of professing Christians in China do not know the basic elements of the Christian faith, as summarized, for example, in the Apostles' Creed; nor can they recite the Lord's Prayer or the Ten Commandments.

"Clandestine" Ministry

No one knows how many people from the West, Korea, and Southeast Asia are living in China as underground "missionaries." Most of them go to a great deal of trouble to remain hidden from government detection and monitoring. Perhaps some of them succeed, but it is a fair assumption that the Chinese officials know about most of them and are watching them carefully, which is why I put "clandestine" in quotation marks above. Caucasians, in particular, are easy to spot and to follow. We can also assume that Chinese who associate with these foreigners are closely observed, as well, especially if they are present, or leading, at meetings with more than a few people. We can be pretty sure that such activities are well known to the authorities.

Thankfully, most government officials also realize that evangelical Christians pose no real threat to their power, for they are overwhelmingly non-political and only desire to worship and serve God. Perhaps that is why most foreigners are still allowed to conduct their evangelistic and teaching ministries without hindrance or molestation by local police. That tolerance does not indicate approval, however; nor does it guarantee that a sudden change of policy may not lead to quick action to terminate such activity.

We should also consider the impression that persistent violation of China's regulations against missionary work by foreigners makes upon officials. Are not Christians supposed to be law-abiding? What do they have to hide? Can they be trusted to keep their focus only on religious matters, or are they concealing another agenda, perhaps democracy and a change in regime? Why do they enter China on a visa that allows them to study, or teach, or work in a legitimate company, and then break the terms of that visa by spending most of their time doing something else? You can imagine the confusion this might engender in even the most sympathetic of government officials. You can also see why more than one foreigner has been expelled for just that reason.

True enough, the Apostles said that they must "obey God rather than men" when they were ordered not to preach the resurrection of Christ (Acts 5:29). Perhaps that serves as biblical authority for breaking the laws of China in order to obey the Great Commission, as early missionaries believed. We should remember, however, that Peter and the Apostles were citizens of the realm whose rulers they chose to disobey, and that they were prepared to suffer for their disobedience. Foreign Christians living in China risk only deportation. Furthermore, they come from countries such as the United States that have taken strong stands against various policies of the Chinese government, and thus represent, at least to some degree, "unfriendly" interests. They also follow in the train of those foreign missionaries whose entry into China in the nineteenth century was only made possible by the power of gunboats and forced upon the Chinese by "unequal treaties." We need to think and pray much about this.

Illegal Missionaries

Clandestine activity entails other costs as well. One has to be careful at all times. Communication by telephone and email must be in code or go through secure channels. Meetings could be disrupted by the police at any time. Everything takes place under a cloud of secrecy and tension, which can vary from mild to severe. Furthermore, everyone knows that the government is almost certainly aware of all this "secret" ministry. Officials often look the other way, but they harbor mixed feelings about foreigners who knowingly flout the laws of the land. Some express open contempt for what they consider to be hypocrisy, especially when student or work visas are used only as a pretext or "cover" for missionary work.

If foreign Christians think that God wants them to circumvent China's religious regulations, they must do so after careful consideration of the costs, especially the price that Chinese connected with them might have to pay. They should be invited by local believers who know the situation on the ground and can avoid unnecessary trouble. (There are, after all, some officials who really do not mind if foreigners work quietly in their midst to advocate doing good deeds.) And they must not jeopardize the safety of others by rash behavior, even if they sense God's leading to do so. I know of one Chinese university professor who invited an American theologian to lecture in his class on biblical studies, warning him clearly not to try to evangelize the students. The elderly American, saying that this was his last chance to preach Christ in China, stubbornly disregarded his host's warning and blatantly called for commitments to Christ at the end of his lecture. This was reported by a student, and the Chinese professor has been in trouble ever since. Now he can no longer ask any foreigner to give a lecture in any of his classes. All because of one overzealous and very misguided man!

Many foreign Christians believe that God has led them to engage in Christian ministry in China that technically violates the regulations in place at present. Some of them, who know China well, are fully cognizant of the risks involved for their Chinese Christian friends, and only seek to serve the local believers who invited them and who take full responsibility for the possible outcome. They do all they can not to provoke the government, and harbor no political intentions, so Chinese Christians trust them to behave discreetly and wisely. By no means do I want to disparage the purity of their motives or the value of their work. I am mostly concerned about those who almost dare the authorities to act by their flagrant transgressions of the law.

Political Advocacy

Christians should be wary of supporting organizations that advocate for political dissidents, even though they may be Christian. In fact, a great deal of confusion muddies the frequent claim of widespread persecution for being a Christian in China. Most of the examples given deal with Christians who were arrested for engaging in legal or political advocacy, rather than for simply attending church or preaching Christ. When Western Christians stridently take up their case in the media, they run the risk of giving the wrong impression both to Western believers and to the Chinese government. That is not to say that we are happy with the way that the Chinese suppresses dissent, or with the brutal tactics of many police. Of course, we wish that all Chinese citizens enjoyed the kinds of freedoms that we do in the West (at least at present). Nevertheless, political advocacy is different from evangelism, and though we cannot but admire Chinese who seek legal reform in their country, that does not mean that foreigners should join in that campaign.

I know many will disagree with me here, for there are calls for Christians in the West to speak out in support of our brothers and sisters in China who are in conflict with the authorities. Considering the historic, and now heightened, suspicion by the Chinese government that Chinese Christians are tools of American strategic policy, however, I think we should keep quiet for a while.

Financial Support for Chinese Christian Workers

From the very beginnings of Protestant missionary witness in China, debate has swirled around the question of whether to "hire" Chinese Christians to assist in evangelism and church growth. It seems that most early foreign missionaries and their organizations did provide monetary support for Chinese colporteurs, evangelists, "Bible women" who worked among their own sex, and those who assisted in literature and medical work. Karl Gutzlaff, a pioneer missionary in China, made a strong plea for relying almost entirely upon Chinese, who were paid and left largely unsupervised, to distribute gospel literature and preach the message far and wide. When at last some of his employees turned out to be deceivers and frauds, his strategy fell into disrepute, but the hiring of Chinese to work alongside foreign missionaries continued as a widespread practice well into the twentieth century.

Meanwhile, however, other voices spoke against this model of planting truly indigenous Chinese congregations. After all, foreign money almost always meant foreign control, along with identification with people whose governments were constantly encroaching upon Chinese territory and sovereignty. Agents paid by the Westerner could be expected to accept his religion, but why should anyone else turn away from traditional ways to identify with this foreign teaching? And how could dependence upon, and control by, missionaries be avoided? Supporting local ministers violates the three-self principles put forth in the nineteenth century by leading missions leaders: self-supporting, self-governing, self-propagating. These principles were taken by John Nevius from China to Korea, where they are credited with the tremendous growth of the Korean church, in contrast to the Chinese church in the early twentieth century. Most foreign mission organizations claimed to be aiming towards the establishment of an indigenous church. The China Inland Mission (CIM) was among the few that mostly succeeded.[20]

---

20   In Taiwan, careful studies have shown that there is an inverse relationship between Western financial support and growth. The indigenous groups have multiplied, while Western-supported groups lag far behind. The same pattern holds all over the world. See Allen Swanson, *Mending the Nets: Taiwan Church Growth and Loss in the 1980's.*

Above all, foreign money tainted the Chinese recipients, who were considered agents of foreign imperialists. Over the past two hundred years (more, if you count the experiences of Roman Catholics), persecution against Christians in China by the government has always arisen because of their connection with foreigners. Association with foreigners is suspicious enough, but financial support has all too often been the kiss of death.

Meanwhile, hundreds, and then thousands, of Chinese dedicated themselves to Christian ministry, founded self-supporting congregations, and began to learn how to direct their own affairs. As the call for "three self" principles became louder, Chinese were among the most vocal in advocating for "self-support, self-governance, and self-propagation." The great anti-Christian movement in 1926 heightened the tension and highlighted the risk of eating out of the white man's hand. When missionaries did finally try to put these "indigenous" principles into action, however, they often met with strong resistance from the Chinese whose livelihood still came from funds provided by overseas donors. They discovered that dependency is addictive. Chinese Christian workers who relied on overseas financial support resisted being "cut off." The large and costly institutions that had been established by missions organizations simply could not operate without infusions of foreign funds, for they were not sufficiently accepted by the leaders of Chinese society.

Weaning local Christians from outside support was moving slowly, until the war with Japan and then the Communist government made receipt of foreign donations impossible.

To the surprise of many, the Chinese church did not collapse when missionaries and their money withdrew. On the contrary, slowly, and then with stunning rapidity, the existing fully indigenous congregations multiplied, so that today they comprise the vast majority of Chinese churches. Official policy today forbids Chinese from accepting money from abroad, except for specific projects sponsored by the official Three-Self Patriotic Movement/China Christian Council. To give overseas money to local Chinese is therefore illegal. Receipt of such funds places the Chinese believers in danger of being accused of violating regulations concerning religion and of working for foreign interests. Usually, some roundabout way used to relay funds, and this involves further complications. For example, if the local Christian worker is "employed" by a "company" that pays him for services that he seldom, if ever, renders, he is breaking another law as well.

Even if an outside ministry thinks that paying Chinese Christians to spread the gospel will further the cause of Christ, we must remember that this not only constitutes violation of the law, but it further alienates the Chinese from his natural support base. It makes him independent of a local church, and can cause envy and resentment. It is possible that some ministries, such as student work, will in some places not take place soon without foreign funds, since local Chinese may not yet have a vision for them, but to step in prematurely with funds from overseas carries immense consequences. Given the history of foreign missions in China, and of the Chinese government's suspicion of overseas "cultural aggression," it seems highly imprudent to rush ahead. Perhaps more patient labor, training, and education within the Chinese church should be the higher priority, so that they can support needed personnel and projects themselves.

After all, by and large, China is not a third-world, impoverished nation. Its urban church and rural house church networks have financial resources adequate for most ministry, though they may perhaps in some cases lack the vision or expertise for certain specialized projects. Foreign funding is all too often a short-term expedient that produces short-term effects. These may make for good promotion at home, but may not be good for the healthy growth of the Chinese church, which is supposed to be what we long to see.

If a particular need exists that seems to demand temporary help from foreigners, one should turn to foundations and other organizations that have long experience and much expertise in this sort of stewardship of funds; they should be consulted and their services used whenever possible. I do not presume to know enough to object to all financial aid by foreigners to Christian work within China, but I am increasingly aware of the chorus of criticisms by Chinese church leaders themselves against this way of doing things, and so would urge extreme caution.

Theological Education in the West

Recognizing the pressing need for trained Christian leaders in China, many official and unregistered Chinese churches have been sending people with proven potential to the West for theological education in seminaries, and even for graduate degrees in theology, so that they can return to teach in local seminaries. At the same time, Western Christians, aware that they have a responsibility to share the rich heritage of theological, biblical, and pastoral theology resources they possess, have been eager to welcome, and even to offer financial support to, students from China. This procedure appears very attractive to the Chinese, since they can obtain both further training and prestigious degrees that will enhance their ministry back home. Western seminaries are also more than happy to extend their influence by educating a new generation of Chinese leaders.

On the other hand, very serious objections can be raised against this popular practice. For one thing, it is very expensive. A seminary or graduate education in the West costs much, much more than it would in China. It is also disruptive of the family. Either husband and wife are separated for several years, usually at a time when either the marriage or the children are young and need both parents at home, or the family comes along, further adding to the expense. During the long and arduous process, the student—usually the husband—spends most of his time in the library, trying desperately to keep up with the thousands of pages of technical reading in a field in which he usually lacks adequate background. He also does his best to earn the kind of high grades that he probably got in China, not quite realizing that to do so in a second language requires immense sacrifice of time and energy and imposes huge loads of stress upon an already pressured existence in a foreign land. Even more than for most Western seminarians, he is tempted to relax the devotional disciplines he had in China, and to dry up spiritually.

Depending upon the age of the children, by the time the degree is obtained they may have spent enough years in the Western schooling system to make it virtually impossible for them to re-enter the Chinese schools with any hope of competing with their classmates. Now the parents face another hard decision: Do they return to China and thrust their child(ren) into a situation fraught with anxiety, frustration, and possible failure, and thus deprive them of a university education, considered essential for success and therefore happiness by almost all Chinese parents? Or do they remain in the West for further studies to answer the call to serve in a Chinese church overseas? Love for their children often results in a choice that deprives the church in China of yet another valuable worker. Especially for those who go on to go a doctoral degree, it is said that fewer than two percent return to their homeland. Can we call this good stewardship?

But let us assume that the student graduates and returns to serve in a local church or teach in a local seminary. He has been "out of context" for several years—usually three or more. He has lost contact with his congregation and his culture. Having gained all his advanced education in English, he "thinks" in English. Having read volumes of books by Western theologians, he has absorbed Western ways of thinking and can talk about complex problems raised by liberal theologians. But does he know how to relate the Bible to Chinese philosophy, religion, and culture? Probably not. He can tell you about Moltmann, Pannenberg, N.T. Wright, and a host of other prolific writers like them, but can he expound the Scriptures in Chinese with sensitivity to Chinese questions? For reasons like these, at a conference recently, a distinguished panel of both Asian and American theological educators virtually begged the Chinese attendees to return home and teach in local seminaries. They argued passionately for the urgent need for theological education in Greater China to reverse the brain drain and to equip people who can serve effectively in a Chinese setting. We should take their pleas seriously. The other question, of course, is whether academic theological education per se is the best method of training church leaders, which we shall address later..

These are just a few of the practices that, though very common in ministry to Chinese today, seem questionable to me. May God himself grant wisdom and prudence to all of us who want to see his name and fame declared among the Chinese.

SPIRITUAL WARFARE

Any advance of the gospel among the Chinese will face implacable resistance from Satan and his demons. When Jesus was about to begin his ministry, he was tempted by the devil for forty days. Defeated, the enemy left Christ for a while, but returned often, especially in his last days on earth, when it was the devil who put it into Judas' heart to betray his Master. Everywhere Jesus went, he faced criticism from spiritual enemies like the Pharisees and Sadducees, and open conflict with demons who had taken possession of hapless people. He drove them out with a simple command, because he was the Strong Man who had come to despoil Satan (Luke 11:21–22), whom the Lord said he saw "fall like lightning from heaven" (Luke 10:18).

Followers of Christ can expect no less as they take the saving message of Christ to people who have never heard before, such as the Chinese today. The devil, whose main weapon is deceit, has held countless people in bondage to belief systems that contain just enough truth to appear plausible, and just enough error to keep people from God. Although many modern Western Christians look with suspicion on talk about demons, and particularly demon possession, both the Scriptures and ample experience of working among Chinese confirm the reality of the very personal activity of Satan in individuals. For example, those who worship in pagan temples sometimes become slaves of particular evil spirits, but most folks are held captive by false ideas and an unfounded sense of security as they worship beings who are not really gods. However gently we call people away from such folly, Satan will respond vigorously and sometimes violently.

Paul warned that non-believers are captured in a net woven by the world, their own flesh (including vain ideas), and the devil (Eph 2:1–3). He knew that Satan would disguise himself as an angel of light as he tried to seduce even believers from a simple trust in Jesus as Savior and Lord (2 Cor 11:3). We must not be unaware of his devices, which are as various as his malice is thorough. He can use illness, computer crashes, drugs, the occult, false teaching, doubt, envy, fear, pride, and even—though rarely—demon possession to keep people from knowing and enjoying God's love in Christ. Nowadays, he employs all the resources of the media to distract people. Sometimes he stirs up the civil authorities or even the masses to launch outright attacks on believers. More often, his tactics are subtle and less obvious, like the advertisements that promise happiness if we only buy a certain product, and the constant entertainment that keeps us from reading the Bible and doing good works, or nationalism and political passion, to divert our attention from the real issues of eternal life and death. I fully believe in the activity of Satan in this world as he strives with all his evil power to keep us from knowing and serving God. We must not neglect this aspect of biblical teaching and modern reality.

On the other hand, most of what goes under the name of "spiritual warfare" among Christians today seems to have little or no Scriptural support. The immensely popular novels by Frank E. Peretti, along with teaching by charismatic leaders, have spawned a worldview that is populated with demons who control everything and who must be cast out even from believers. Whether a true believer can be fully possessed by a demon has been debated, though we know that Satan and his minions can cause great damage to Christians. I am concerned not with that question, but with the larger concept of spiritual warfare as it is currently understood and waged in the church.

If we look at the only passage in the entire Bible that discusses spiritual warfare as such, Ephesians 6:10–20, we find that there is absolutely no mention of casting out demons or even of "binding" them. Instead, all the armor we are to don is meant to equip us with the truth to gain the victory over Satan's "wiles." In other words, since the devil's main weapon is deceit, our main defense is the truth, firmly believed and fully obeyed. Satan is a liar and the father of lies; he keeps us from loving God and loving each other by convincing us of falsehoods that deny God's Word, just as he did in the Garden of Eden.

More specifically, if we examine the entire letter to the Ephesians, we see that God plans to create a vast cosmic unity, bringing angels and saints together into harmony with himself through Jesus Christ (Eph 1:10). Through the preaching of the gospel and the work of the Spirit, people come to faith in Christ and are reconciled to God. That reconciliation brings them into a worldwide family, the Body of Christ, which knows no distinctions of race, ethnicity, class, or gender. So, we are duty-bound to preach this message of reconciliation and to live out its meaning in our lives with others (Eph 4:1–6:9).

Paul's language about spiritual warfare at the end of Ephesians, therefore, takes its meaning form what goes before, where we are urged to live together in humility and love; to avoid falsehood and greed; to renounce all lust and walk in love; to set aside pride and submit to each other; and to treat others as God, in Christ, has treated us. Satan will oppose every effort to bring people into a state of peace with God and with each other. In particular, he will spread all sorts of lies, in the hope that we will not believe God or imitate his love towards others. In this context, standing against Satan means to resist all his deceits and to hold, proclaim, and obey the truth as it is in Jesus, relying always on the power of the Lord through prayer in the Spirit.

Nowhere are Christians commanded to cast out demons as the principal means of waging spiritual warfare, though we may have to do so occasionally. We should also pray against the works of the enemy. But this cannot be the main emphasis of our campaign to advance the kingdom of God into territory held by the spiritual foe, Satan.

Much less biblical warrant can be found for the common practice of "binding" Satan or some evil spirit who is supposed to rule over a person or a place, or "commanding" an evil spirit to leave a person who has not otherwise evinced evidence of actual demon possession. According to Matthew 12:28–29, Satan is already "bound" by the "strong man," Jesus. We are never told that we should "bind" any evil spirit today. True enough, Satan prowls around like a roaring lion, seeking someone to devour (1 Pet 5:8), but we are told to "resist" him, not to "bind" him or any of his wicked subordinates (1 Pet 5:9; see also Eph 6:11). When facing someone clearly possessed by a demon (as indicated by speaking in a different voice, having supernatural physical strength, and recoiling at the mention of Jesus or of the Cross) we only need to command the spirit to leave. The current practice of "binding" does not need to be employed.

Nevertheless, we cannot ignore the Scriptural accounts of the ministry of Jesus and of the Apostles, the witness of the Early Church Fathers, including Athanasius, and the countless records of missionaries and others who have been confronted by persons who were demon possessed or otherwise harassed by evil spirits. I am no stranger to spiritual warfare, having been defeated by Satan many times. When we first arrived in Taiwan in 1976, I visited temples out of curiosity, not knowing that they were centers of evil spirits. Though my later difficulties as a young missionary did not all stem from direct spiritual attack—most resulted from inadequate faith—it became clear to me later that at least some of my illness and depression found their source in the activity of demons. I had been too presumptuous in casually exploring temples without first praying against the works of Satan. While trying to finish this book, I have been hit by one "bug" after another, in an unprecedented attack on my health. I do not believe that this is coincidental.

As strange as it may sound, on three occasions, I have had to cast out demons. Without any prior experience, but having received a bit of instruction in exorcism during training with OMF in Singapore, I found myself confronted by people who spoke with a voice totally different from their normal speech, and who exhaled a wickedness that was chilling to sense. I boldly commanded the unclean spirits to leave the afflicted person, insisting that they obey the authority that comes to all believers from the risen Lord himself. After a severe struggle, the demons departed, and the person "woke up" and said, "What has just happened to me?" Clearly, the name of Christ possesses a power greater than that of any evil spirit, and Christians may confidently confront obviously demon-possession with full reliance on the Son of God to gain the victory.

PATIENCE

As I have reflected on effective methods for reaching Chinese with the gospel, it seems that one theme keeps recurring: The need for patience. Without patience, coupled with perseverance, we are not likely to have a lasting impact on our Chinese friends or upon their society.

Patience in Preparation

A recent essay in a major China ministry newsletter stressed the need for long-term workers among the Chinese. The writer, who has extensive experience, was not trying to minimize the value of short-term visits to China for the purpose of gaining knowledge and vision for prayer and service. He was, however, calling for Christians to commit themselves to many years of life and ministry among the Chinese, starting with several years of preparation.

We must work hard and long to establish trust through listening, learning from, and loving our Chinese friends. Unless we invest in long-term friendships, we can expect only short-term results. Those who take the time to understand a few people well, to walk through life with them, and to demonstrate genuine love in a variety of ways, will be rewarded with a kind of loyalty seldom found in the West.

As a corollary, we should be patient in explaining the whole truth of God's Word, and not just select out a few verses in an effort to gain a speedy conversion, as I explained earlier when talking about effective Bible study. You probably have family members for whose salvation you have prayed for many years now. The same goes for our Chinese friends. Let us commit to pray for them daily, year after year, perhaps decade after decade, trusting in God to work his will in his way at his time.

CHAPTER SEVEN
POINTS OF CONTACT:
CHINESE CULTURE AND SOCIETY

For centuries Christian missionaries have sought ways to make contact with Chinese belief systems without compromising the biblical faith. In recent years, this effort has been included in the concept of "contextualization," which also speaks of ways in which Christianity can be lived out in truly Chinese forms, including worship, ethics, and society. From the beginning, fierce controversy has surrounded this topic, and various approaches have competed for supremacy. Without going into detail, let me say simply that I believe that the Christian view of general revelation teaches that people of all nations have been able to discern some elements of truth from their observation of the universe, including human nature and social interaction. Non-Christian religions, therefore, all contain teachings and even some rituals that reflect our creation in the image of God.

On the other hand, fallen men and women inevitably distort general revelation, with the result that cultures also feature a great many ideas, values, and practices that clash with the special revelation given to us in the Scriptures. There can be no real correspondence, therefore, between a non-Christian belief system and biblical Christianity. Since pagan religions begin from different starting points and develop along lines that essentially diverge from the biblical framework, it seems risky to speak of Christianity, or Christ, as "fulfilling" any non-Christian religion or practice, unless we mean only that what people long for and inadequately express in their religions and philosophies, Christ and Christianity offer in fullness. With Chinese theologian Lit-sen Chang[21] and many others, therefore, I prefer to speak of "points of contact" between Christianity and non-Christian belief systems and cultures, as well as the common experiences of people in society.

---

21 See especially his *Asia's Religions: Christianity's Momentous Encounter with Paganism*, as well as *Critique of Indigenous Theology*, found in G. Wright Doyle, ed. and trans., *Wise Man from the East: Lit-sen Chang*.

To be sure, if the gospel of Jesus Christ is to "take root downward and bear fruit upward" (2 Kings 19:30) among Chinese, it must be fully Chinese in character, not Western. Christians need to understand the hopes and fears, aspirations and anxieties, successes and failures, of non-Christian culture and society, and then apply the truth of God to their own context in word and deed.[22] That does not mean that we have to agree with all the worldly ambitions, both personal and political, that animate so much foolish behavior and engender so much conflict, but we should at least seek to understand and evince true empathy. Foreigners, especially, would do well to heed the words spoken to us by our OMF leaders in Taiwan, who urged us, in our relations with Chinese Christians, to "dream their dreams, and help them find ways to realize them," assuming, of course that these dreams were not in conflict with Scripture.

God has put powerful impulses and aching longings into each of us; even in our fallen condition, these reflect our creation in the divine image, and point towards our ultimate quest, which is for God himself, and for union with him. Christians can identify these and tap into them, and then bring all the resources of the Bible to bear upon them, by the power of the Holy Spirit and in living community with other believers. Gradually, both individuals and society will feel the effects of this kind of "salt and light" living, and ask about its Source. In any case, everyone around us will benefit from the truths that we speak and exemplify.

E. Stanley Jones, referred to earlier, sought to present a way of "following the Christ of the Indian road."[23] Without trying paint Jesus as a Chinese, as some have done, or assimilating both him and his message into Chinese religious and cultural ways, can we not attempt to portray our Lord in terms that make sense to our Chinese friends, and in a manner that commends him to them as the Word made flesh? As we ourselves sit with them, walk with them, and stand with them in their daily lives, let us also pray for wisdom and grace to communicate a Christ who has truly lived among us as one of us, and who, without for a moment compromising his utter holiness and transcendent truth, showed himself to be a man of his time, one with his people, and totally committed to their temporal and eternal welfare.

---

22   See Lit-sen Chang, *Strategy of Missions in the Orient: Christian Impact on the Pagan World*.

23   Richard W. Taylor, "E. Stanley Jones: Following the Christ of the Indian Road," in Gerald H. Anderson, et al., eds., *Mission Legacies*, 341.

HINTS AND SHADOWS

Let's explore ways in which Christians can speak to Chinese "points of contact"—existing conditions and concepts within their culture. First of all, let's look at some potential connections between traditional Chinese culture and biblical Christianity. We shall note both similarities and differences, and try to strike a balance between two extremes: Saying that there is nothing in Chinese culture that approximates, or reflects, the realities revealed in the Bible; and claiming that certain aspects of Chinese culture exactly correspond to Scripture. Below are a few examples of what we might call "hints and shadows" of special revelation that can be found, as aspects of general revelation, in traditional Chinese culture. Others reflect realities of life in modern China. These will be addressed in the following chapters.

The idea of God: The ancient Chinese worshiped a Supreme Being, called Shang Di, or Di, or Heaven (Tian) with many attributes similar to those ascribed to the God of the Bible. They also prayed and sacrificed to a host of spirits, lesser deities (shen), who remind us of the many "gods" of the biblical world.

Yin and Yang: Chinese have long believed that there are two fundamental principles that continuously interplay with each other to form all of reality. Does the Bible have any such idea?

Filial piety: At least from Confucius onward, Chinese have put respect for elders (especially parents), reverence for ancestors, and even some sort of "worship" for the spirits of the departed, at the center of their ethical system. How does this relate to "Honor your father and your mother"?

Confucian concepts: How do the ideas of benevolence (ren), righteousness (yi), and ceremony/courtesy (and proper observance of rites, li) compare with biblical concepts of love, justice, respect, and worship?

The idea of the Way (Dao or Tao): The Chinese Bible used dao to translate logos (word) in the opening verses of John's Gospel. Is this dao the same as the word (logos) of the Bible, or are there also significant differences?

Reward and punishment; heaven and hell: Chinese possess the idea that good and evil will be rewarded and punished. Through Buddhism, they received the concept of an afterlife where good and bad deeds receive their just recompense.

A legacy of the abuse of power, with the resulting resentment and occasional rebellion.

A strong sense of group identity: More than Westerners, Chinese have traditionally seen themselves as members of a larger group, whose interests they have identified with their own well-being.

An obsession with "face" and a corresponding fear of shame.

Science and the Bible: Has Darwin's evolutionary theory disproved Genesis?

The imperial system and the sacrifices at the Altar of Heaven in Beijing.

Intense pragmatism: Chinese focus on what works.

A keen sense of relative value: They seek the best bargain, and aim to make a profit.

Just a little thought will suggest ways in which the gospel addresses all of these concerns, and could fill these concepts with deeper meaning.

PRESSURE POINTS

First, let us glance at ways in which modern Chinese society prepares the way for the light, life, and love of God as expressed in the Good News. I shall call these "pressure points."

First and foremost, the breakdown of the family inflicts piercing and permanent pain upon untold millions. Divorce rates have skyrocketed, as adultery and busyness have stretched couples beyond their limited capacity to love. Older folks often feel abandoned by busy offspring. Children are neglected by two-job (and often divorced) parents, and pressured to perform academically in a system that produces lonely, tired, unhealthy, and frustrated youth. Pervasive pre-marital promiscuity has left young people with shattered dreams, jaded consciences, broken hearts, and STDs. Where can real love be found?

MARRIAGE

Chinese marriages are in trouble. Once, when I asked a Chinese pastor how the couples in his church were doing, he replied, "Worse even than American Christian marriages." He went on: "They are all too busy. Communication is lousy; they hardly ever really talk to each other. Conflict is dealt with by either 'cold war' (silence) or 'hot war' (screaming). It's a mess."

A Burdened Past

For millennia, Chinese women were mistreated by their men. From the binding of little girls' feet to the taking of concubines by their husbands, women faced daily denigration, drudgery, and disease. Death from preventable diseases was commonplace. At the same time, Chinese men were considered among the most hen-pecked in the world. Though husbands and wives were expected to treat each other courteously, and many did, the biblical standard of marital intimacy did not generally inform their view of marriage. In the twentieth century, conditions improved for women. The missionaries had initiated and supported campaigns for the end of foot-binding, education for girls, and equal regard for both sexes.

In the 1920s, this attitude then merged into another: The idea that a woman's worth depended entirely upon her contribution to society. Rejecting the traditional high regard for the roles of wife and mother (which had often been an excuse for subjugation), the "new woman" embraced an ideal of the equality of the sexes that amounted to identity in all respects except anatomy. The Communists enshrined this model of "liberation" for all women by requiring that they work outside the home, regardless of whether they wanted to. Meanwhile, their husbands, like men the world over, still expected their wives to do most of the housework and childrearing.

Marriage under Attack

Since the market reforms beginning in 1978—and long before that outside the Mainland—Chinese marriages have been buffeted by the gales of Western narcissism. The self rules. Today, pre-marital sex is rampant; extra-marital affairs are commonplace; domestic bickering and even violence are endemic; divorce rates soar annually. With both husband and wife pursuing success in their careers, there is no time to spend on nurturing their relationship. Rural couples find themselves separated by the need to find a job in the city, where temptations abound. Cheated wives back in the village commit suicide in droves. Like the rest of us, however, the Chinese have also embraced the romantic ideal, so they enter wedlock with high expectations for a fulfilling union. When the honeymoon ends, there are few communication skills to deal with conflict; hardly any good models to imitate; a lack of commitment to a lifelong bond; and the belief that you can change a mate as you do clothing.

Christ Brings Hope

The gospel speaks to this deplorable situation. Christ brings pardon of sins, and the power to forgive others. Jesus' example of self-sacrifice rebukes our selfishness and impels us to imitate him. Christian couples can pray with each other for their marriage, try to follow biblical teachings about relationships in general and marriage in particular, and rely on the Holy Spirit to change things. In the church, there are friends who can stand with us when we encounter the inevitable difficulties of living with a fellow sinner. Their friendship, example, and prayer can carry us through tough times.

OTHER PRESSURE POINTS

The mad rush to get rich—or just to survive—has created a life of long hours, constant pressure to succeed, intense competition, rapid turnover, sometimes awful living conditions, and—for millions of workers—withheld wages. What is the meaning of this rat-race? Where can security be found?

Massive migration to towns and cities has emptied some villages of all but the very old, the very young, and the women who must bear the burden of their nurture and upbringing. Newcomers to urban centers find themselves struggling to make a living in an unfamiliar environment. Lacking access to education, health care, or basic legal rights, they have to fend for themselves in a cutthroat world. Does anyone care? Is there no place to call home?

Fatigue, lack of nutrition, stress, and a highly degraded environment have produced a very unhealthy population, afflicted with cancer, respiratory illnesses, heart disease, and a host of other ailments. Lack of medical insurance and rising costs have bankrupted countless families, while a few well-to-do urbanites pay high prices for modern health facilities. Where can one find strength and healing?

Endemic, ubiquitous corruption at all levels, not to mention widespread exploitation by employers, has injected the poison of resentment and rage into the hearts of countless Chinese. Sometimes it explodes in violent demonstrations—more than one hundred thousand a year. How can one find the freedom to forgive?

Addictions—to sex, drugs, nicotine, entertainment, video games, Internet pornography have enslaved masses and robbed multitudes of the ability to live well, to love, and to work. Can these chains be broken?

Meanwhile, traditional religions have made a huge comeback, often fueled by funds from Taiwan, Hong Kong, and South East Asia. The old gods have new adherents in a land where atheism still claims official sanction, but where hungry hearts seek meaning and hope from the spirit world. These idols have never satisfied the soul, but they can blind one to the truth of God and ensnare worshipers in deadening darkness. Who will tell them of the one true and living God, who alone gives life, and light?

Running throughout Chinese society as an undercurrent that finds voice in story (like the Nobel prize-winning Soul Mountain), song, film, and desperate searches for reality, is a profound crisis of faith. Is there any real meaning to life? If so, where can it be found?

In all we do, we must seek to speak to the hearts and minds of those who are trapped in darkness and despair. Be an attentive listener, and try to weep with those who weep. Knowing the folly of attempting to answer a matter before hearing it fully, aim to understand the assumptions and aspirations of today's Chinese, and to hear their heartfelt cries. After we have gained their trust, we find that they ask us questions, and sometimes eagerly attend to our answers. Aspire to live lives of beauty and of love, marked by peace and joy. Those who are married should place a high premium upon family life, which often prompts the question, "Why is your home so different?" We must take every opportunity to share the Good News of Christ.

In our Christian congregations, we can model a healing community, as we care for each other and pray for each other; as we model lives that seek first God's kingdom and his righteousness, rather than material prosperity; and as we teach principles of wise and healthy living.[24]

SCIENCE AND THE BIBLE

Although not as anxiety-producing as the emotional and social tensions mentioned above, the question of the relationship between science and the Bible is another feature of modern Chinese life that causes intellectual conflict for many educated Chinese when they first encounter the story of the Bible and the idea of a creator God.

You might think it strange to see a discussion of "Science and the Bible" under the heading, "Points of Contact." Actually, however, the question of how Christianity relates to modern science has often proven to be one of the most fruitful entry points for opening the minds of educated Chinese to the gospel. Like most Westerners, they have been told that the findings of science, and especially of Darwinian evolutionism, have demonstrated that the Bible's account of beginnings is wrong, that miracles did not occur, and even that there is no God. When they discover that they have been misled and that evolutionism is a theory in crisis, they often quickly realize how many indications exist for intelligent design in the universe and even now remarkably reliable Genesis is for an understanding of origins.

We might ask our doubting Chinese friend, "Are you aware that more

---

24 My book, *The Lord's Healing Words*, which is also available in Chinese, was written to help both Christians and non-Christians enjoy better physical, mental, and spiritual health.

and more scientists are abandoning evolutionism because it lacks real scientific support?" At this point, I often refer them to literature, which you may find in the Resources section. Even without such resources, however, we can just ask a few questions.

Since science deals with recurring, observable events in the present, using experiments that can be verified, how can science speak to the origins of the universe, man, or life? No one was there to observe the beginning of the world, and no repeatable experiments or observations can be done on that unique event. Those sorts of things lie in the realm of history, which deals with one-time happenings in the past.

You say that science has disproven the existence of God. Where can I find the article that describes that experiment?

How could life have come from non-life; order from disorder; energy from nothing; personality from impersonality?

How could a scientific theory such as evolutionism be true while violating fundamental laws of science, such as the first and second laws of thermodynamics?

Where does information come from?

Have you heard that Darwin's theory of natural selection by random mutation has been shown to be mathematically impossible?

How could mutations produce a better, more "adapted" organism over time when 99% of mutations are harmful to the organism?

How could systems such as sight, breathing, circulation, digestion, reproduction have developed gradually over millions of years, when those systems require that all parts be present and working perfectly in order for it to function at all,?

Questions like these—and there are many others that could be asked—will at least give the evolutionist pause. Perhaps then he will be open to reading some of the materials suggested above. Then maybe you can introduce him to another theory, one that posits a personal, omnipotent, all-wise Creator who made the world out of nothing and who governs it to this day. I have found that many well-trained Chinese scientists very quickly see that this is a much better hypothesis to account for the world we see around us. In this way, their initial faith in Darwinism can be used as a contact point to put them into contact with God.

We turn now to a few elements of Chinese traditional culture and contemporary society that present points of contact with the gospel.

FILIAL PIETY

Many Chinese consider filial piety to be the crown jewel of their civilization. The core of Confucius' teaching, some aspects of filial piety reach back into the dawn of Chinese civilization, centuries before Confucius himself. Just what is "filial piety"? Traditionally, the concept has included at least three components: Obedience to one's parents; respect for all in authority; and some form of ancestor "worship."

Obedience to Parents

From the earliest days, Chinese have believed in, inculcated, and even enforced total obedience to parents, especially the father. Parents have had the right to tell their children what to eat, what to wear, what to study, where to work, and—until recently—whom to marry. They expect no questions, and may disregard their children's wishes, for they assume that they know best and their children don't know what is good for them. Of course, parents are obligated to provide for their children, and especially to secure for them the best possible education. But listening, understanding, admitting that they might perhaps not be totally correct—these are not generally considered to be parental duties.

Even after marriage, Chinese children have long fallen under the authority of their father and mother. The parent-child relationship takes priority over the husband-wife bond. Indeed, a wife is to obey her mother-in-law, even if she is verbally abusive, and your children "belong," in some sense, to your parents, not to you. If you are a man, your mother may be outraged if you pay more attention to your wife than to her. In the old days, families lived together in a large compound, but even now, when urbanization has to some extent given the nuclear family some private space, parents sometimes pressure children to visit much more than we would in the West. For millennia, Chinese children have been the only source support for aged parents. Even today, they often feel obligated to send their parents a major portion of their salary, even if they are not yet retired or don't need the money. You can imagine the sorts of marital conflicts that could arise if the young couples themselves don't have a lot of money.

Of course, modernization, including urbanization and globalization, has introduced massive changes into the traditional patterns. Children may now live not just across the city, but across the ocean, from their parents. Modern life rushes on at a pace that prevents long hours of leisurely time together, not to mention whole days with one's parents. Today's women don't necessarily want to obey their mothers-in-law, and their husbands can't enforce the kind of submission that used to prevail. It is even reported that the younger women will sometimes treat their mothers-in-law harshly, just as mothers-in-law had treated their daughters-in-law a generation ago.

Filial Piety and the Bible

Many—perhaps most—Chinese see no conflict between traditional Chinese filial piety and the Scriptures. After all, doesn't the Bible say, "Honor your father and your mother?" Certainly, Christian and Confucian ethics do agree that children should honor and (when small) fully obey their parents. Others (though not many) raise questions about the degree of overlap between Christianity and Confucianism at this point. Significantly, the Chinese translation of the Fifth Commandment does not use the word for "honor" [show respect], but employs two characters that incorporate almost the entire weight of traditional Chinese understanding.

Several questions need to be asked at this point.

What about the biblical teaching to parents: "Fathers, do not provoke your children to wrath" (Eph 6:4) and "Do not provoke your children, lest they become discouraged" (Col 3:21)?

What does the Bible's oft-repeated statement, "Therefore a man shall leave his father and mother and cling [cleave] to his wife" mean? Does it not strongly imply that marriage creates a major change in the parent-child relationship, which places a man's wife before his mother in importance?

If a wife is supposed to submit to her husband (Eph 5:22 ff; Col 3:28), does that not put a buffer between her and her mother-in-law? And if a husband should sacrifice himself for his wife, then should he not be willing to "die"—at least emotionally—in order to nurture and protect his wife?

If children should honor their parents, then who should have primary say in their lives, their father and mother, or grandparents?

Surely, aged and needy widows must be cared for financially by their children (1 Tim 5:3–16), but does a child have to send money home to parents who are both alive and able to earn income? If so, how much?

Just as with other points of contact, traditional Chinese notions of "filial piety" do not correspond totally to the biblical picture of the parent-child relationship. Instead, these concepts and terms reflect the creation of mankind in the image of God, and our universal fall into sin and darkness.

As God's image-bearers, we can discern some truth, but as fallen rebels, we twist and pervert that truth, so that we go astray in our minds and actions. How thankful we should be that God's special revelation in the Scriptures enables us to appreciate traditional values, and to be set free from "the aimless conduct [futile ways] received by tradition from [our] fathers" (1 Pet 1:18)!

SHAME

A Universal Experience

Students of anthropology are fond of drawing a distinction between "guilt" cultures and "shame" cultures. In the former, you feel bad when you have violated an objective moral standard, while in the latter you are ashamed when you fail to measure up to some norm of family or society. An oversimplified distinction would be that shame results from "failure" while guilt comes from "sin." Western society is—or used to be—an example of a "guilt" culture, and China is a prime exhibit for the "shame" cultures. Much has changed in recent years, of course. In both East and West, words and actions that used to be considered shameful are now flaunted openly and publicly, as if there was nothing wrong with them. But that is another subject.

Actually, even Westerners know about shame. Many of us have heard our parents say, "Shame on you!" or, "You should be ashamed of yourself!" when we spilled some milk, or our room was messier than usual, or we got bad grades in school. There is a great deal of shame arising from mistakes we have made in public, and even more from private addictions to pornography or alcohol. Still, most Chinese people really do fear shame more than Westerners, and have a correspondingly less acute sense of actual guilt for offenses against a righteous God.

You see this come out in various ways. Someone has promised to do something for you, but has encountered difficulty or even made another commitment, but doesn't tell you that he will be late or perhaps won't even be able to complete the job. He just says nothing, too ashamed to admit failure. Sometimes you don't find out until it's too late for you to find an alternative, leaving you angry and frustrated. "If only you had told me sooner!" you say, inflicting even more shame upon him. A sudden injury prevented one of China's main hopes for a gold-medal to drop out just before the race in the 2008 Olympic Games, provoking loud outcries around the nation, finger-pointing, and—it is reported—deep depression for the athlete himself. At least in the past, shame played an important role in the educational system. Teachers would employ harsh public rebuke to motivate poor students to do better. I have seen this even in Christian circles.

For traditional Chinese and other "Confucian" societies, there is little belief in a transcendent God, whose holiness and justice demand adherence to immutable moral laws; instead, the opinions of people are supreme. Family members, especially parents, teachers, friends, and society at large, are the ones whose opinion matters most. If they do not approve of me, I "die" inside from shame. Indeed, "death" happens not only subjectively, within me, but can take the very tangible form of public rebuke, failure in school, loss of a job, or even ostracism. We see the terrible potency of this bondage to others' approval in the number of suicides that took place during the Cultural Revolution, not just from unbearable physical torture, but from being mocked by huge crowds.

A sense of shame arises from two sources: We are finite, and we are fallen. Because of our limitations as creatures, we simply cannot fulfill all of the expectations that we or others have towards us. Most Chinese parents want their child to be "Number One" in the class, but only one student can earn that distinction. We are not as fast, or agile, or smart, or good-looking, or rich, or whatever, as some others are, and there is little we can do about it. We just can't "succeed" all the time! Too much shame arises from false ideas of "success." There is nothing shameful in coming in second—or fifth, or fifteenth—if you have trained as well as you could and run with all your strength. A child need not be ashamed of his alcoholic father, or uneducated mother, though that usually happens. Driving an old car, wearing out-of-date clothes, or living in a small house is not a matter for embarrassment, as long as you have worked hard and honestly, and done your best to be a good steward of limited resources.

Complicating matters, however, is that fact that we are fallen, infected with a moral malady that affects all we say or do. So, not only may I have a slender build by birth, but perhaps laziness has kept me from exercising as much as I could have. Or the reverse may be true: God gave me a solid, hefty frame, but I become overweight, even obese, from lack of self-discipline and from sloth. Then, I am ashamed of my appearance, not just because I don't resemble film stars or models in magazines, but because I haven't made of myself what I could have. Or maybe I know I am not as intelligent by birth as the next guy, but I am also aware that I could have worked harder to gain knowledge to make up for this deficit in innate aptitude.

Deeper still is the root cause of shame: My own pride. It's because I care so much about my image in the world, and believe that I should be, or could be, or am, better than either others think or than is really the case, that I am so shocked and shame-faced when I fail to measure up to their image of me, or mine of myself.

Surmounting Shame

The Bible speaks of shame in many places. The bottom line is: Those who trust in God do not need to fear the rejection of others, because on the judgment day they will not have to be ashamed (Ps 25:2, 3; 34:5; 119:6). On the contrary, people who forsake God for idols and unrepentant wickedness will be ultimately covered with shame (Ps 6:10; 25:3; 35:4, 26; 71:24). God's opinion matters infinitely more than the evaluations of those around us. No matter what they think, if we are relying on God and seeking to do his will, we do not have to be ashamed of "failure" (Rom 8:31, 34). Some say that the Christian message of forgiveness of sins should not be preached to people in a shame culture, since it makes no sense to them. That does not seem to be right. After all, as we have seen, real guilt often underlies our sense of shame. And even if others don't know, or care, about our offenses against the Lord's holy laws, God does, and he cannot overlook our transgressions.

No, we need to know the righteous requirements of God, by hearing and reading his commandments in the Bible, to be aware of our real reason for shame: Like Adam and Eve in the garden, we have disobeyed our Maker and are naked before his all-seeing eyes. We have done wrong, and nothing can hide that awful fact. What to do, then? Simply admit our moral failure and beg for his mercy. That mercy will surely come, because Jesus, the Son of God and the only man who had no cause for shame, allowed himself to be shamefully treated to an infinite degree, in our place. (Is 53:3 6).

OTHER POINTS OF CONTACT

You may have heard that some Chinese characters seem to reflect knowledge of the Genesis account of the Creation, Adam and Eve, the Flood, other early events, and even the sacrifice of Christ on the Cross. Though Chinese linguistic scholars reject the idea that their ancestors brought vestiges of primeval history into the ancient language, we can at least use these remarkable correspondences as an entry point to talk about the Good News.

The concept of the Emperor as Son of Heaven, especially when he offered sacrifices to a Supreme Being who had no image in the Temple of Heaven can also serve as a launching pad for a conversation about Christ. We can even try to show that the imperial system, with absolute authority vested in the Emperor, dimly reflects the sovereign monarchy of the one true and living God.

Then there is the legacy of the abuse of power, with the resulting resentment and occasional rebellion. As everyone knows, Chinese leaders have often abused power by lording it over those under them and seeking only personal advantage. Christians can point to the servant leadership of Jesus Christ, and can live out a counter-cultural leadership style in the home, the church, and in society. This cannot fail to spark curiosity.

A strong sense of group identity: More than Westerners, Chinese have traditionally seen themselves as members of a larger group, whose interests they have identified with their own well-being. For that reason, they often prove to be very dedicated members of a church where they find love, especially if the group is small. Much more so than individualistic Westerners, they tend to sacrifice for the interests of the community.

Intense pragmatism: Chinese focus on what works. Well, biblical religion is immensely practical! It "works" in all situations, at least in the long run. For example living according to the Scriptures will ordinary bring better health, happier family relationships, and success at work—though of course there are exceptions. We can legitimately point to these benefits of following Christ, even as we warn of inevitable hardship and emphasize the spiritual and eternal rewards for faithful disciples.

A keen sense of relative value: Chinese generally seek the best bargain, and aim to make a profit. Jesus told parables about this, like the treasure hidden in a field and the pearl of great price (Matt 13:44–46). Peter, who "left all" to follow Christ, spoke often of the preciousness of faith and its spiritual rewards, compared to gold and silver, which eventually perish (1 Pet 1:6–7, 18–19; 2 Pet 1:4), and Paul taught that "godliness with contentment is great gain" (1 Tim 6:6) and pointed out the folly of trusting in wealth (1 Tim 6:6–10). All in all, giving up everything else to gain eternal life is a good bargain!

THE ROLE OF CHRISTIANITY IN AMERICAN SOCIETY

Many Chinese have a love-hate relationship with America. On the one hand, they admire the wealth, power, and freedom that they see in the United States. At the same time, they do not respect our extreme individualism, rank hedonism, vulgar popular culture, gargantuan debt, political gridlock, and apparent intentions to rule the world as "hegemon." Since they also know that Christianity has played a prominent role in American history, they are curious about its positive contributions and perplexed at the contrast between "In God We Trust" and the degenerate, arrogant, and immature behavior of many American leaders and citizens.

My book, Christianity in America: Triumph and Tragedy, is meant to address this conundrum. To put it briefly, I try to show that when Christians have sought to be "salt and light," they have brought great benefits to all sectors of American society and culture. When they have presumed to be "savior and lord," however, they have caused immense damage. Furthermore, Christians have all too often succumbed to the worldly values and habits of their culture, and have lost influence and credibility as a consequence.

CHAPTER EIGHT
POINTS OF CONTACT:
CHINESE RELIGION (1)

NAMES FOR GOD

Traditional Chinese culture contains some remarkable "hints and shadows" of the gospel. These form points of contact for those who seek to share the truth and love of Christ with Chinese today. Perhaps the most obvious point of contact is the presence in Chinese of several names used to refer to "supernatural" beings whom they have worshiped. Two of these are Shang Di (sometimes written Shang Ti) and Shen, though the word for "Heaven" (Tian) is also sometimes used.

Shang Di

The name for the Supreme Being among the early Shang Dynasty was Shang Di. According to C.K. Thong in Faith of Our Fathers, he was believed to be unique; was never represented by an idol or image; was an "all-powerful and supreme Deity"; "sovereign of surrounding nations as well" as the Chinese themselves"; ruled the forces of nature; "governed the construction of cities, the outcome of wars, and the well-being and misfortune of human beings." Amazingly, he "received no cultic or manipulative worship".[25]

When the Zhou dynasty replaced the Shang, they believed that their supreme deity, called Tian (Heaven), was the same as Shang Di, and employed the two names interchangeably for a while. Later, Tian (Heaven) became the standard term. There is no evidence that either of these names referred to a being who had a beginning; Thong opines that he may have been considered eternal. Shang Di has become "a personal name for God, while Tian seems to be more of an abstraction" for the Deity. That is an important point.

---

25   Chen Kei Thong with Charlene Fu, *Faith of Our Fathers: God in Ancient China* (Shanghai: China Publishing Group, 2006) 79–81.

As you can see, Shang Di and Tian have some qualities similar to those of the God of the Bible. In addition, most Chinese know what these words mean, though they may have only a faint idea of their history. Thus, many Protestant Christians believe that Shang Di is the best—and indeed only proper—translation for the two major names for God in the Bible: Elohim (Hebrew) and Theos (Greek). Not only does it accurately render the meaning of the biblical terms, they say, but it also enables Chinese to connect immediately with the God of the Bible.

On the other hand, many other Chinese (and foreign) Protestants have resisted the use of Shang Di. Most importantly, Shang Di contains no element of plurality. It is the name of a particular, individual "deity." But beginning with the first verse of Genesis, the Old Testament contains many indications that there is some kind of plurality in God.

"In the beginning God (Elohim) created the heaven and the earth" (Genesis 1:1). The word Elohim is the plural for el, the generic term for "god." Later, we read, "Then God said, 'Let us make man in Our image'" (Genesis 1:26). The New Testament is much clearer, pointing to the existence of God the Father, God the Son, and God the Holy Spirit. In John 1:1–3, the word for "God" must allow for a "generic" reference to different entities ("persons," in theological language) of the same "sort" or "type."

Thus, where a passage in the Bible must refer to the entire Godhead and allow for plurality, or indicates distinctions within the Trinity, Shang Di simply will not do. In places like John 1:1–3 (to name only one of many), therefore, the use of Shang Di hopelessly muddles the concept of the Trinity, causing confusion as to the nature of the relationship between the Father and the Son. Since the Trinity is a fundamental concept in the Scriptures (though the word is not used), this seems to be a fatal objection to Shang Di as a translation of either Elohim or Theos.

There are other reasons for not using Shang Di as a direct translation for these biblical names for God. For example, it is the name of a particular deity, as we have seen. Theos, on the other hand, is the generic name for any sort of "divine" being in Greek. El—the singular of Elohim— serves the same purpose in Hebrew. Thus, there is a difference in kind between these biblical words and the Chinese name Shang Di. True, Shang Di means something like "Supreme Sovereign," and is thus more of a title than a personal name, as distinct from Yahweh, which is God's personal name in the Old Testament. Thus, one could argue that Shang Di approximates the meanings of Elohim and Theos as used in the Bible. On the other hand, a title is not the same thing as a generic term for "deity." Even though Shang Di does possess many of the attributes of the God of the Bible, should we take the name/title of a particular being worshiped by Chinese in former times and transfer that to the unique God of Israel and Father of Jesus? At best, we might use Shang Di as a rough translation for El Elyom—God Most High—one of the Old Testament names for God. But to identify a specific pagan god with the God of Scriptures seems unwise, no matter how close the resemblances may be. Is this not the very sort of thing that the Israelites were explicitly commanded not to do? (Exodus 23:13)

Shen

Is there any other Chinese word that could better convey the meaning of the Biblical words for God? The most commonly-used alternative is Shen.

Many have objected to Shen as a translation of either Elohim or Theos, because shen can also refer to lesser beings who are not transcendent. First of all, the Chinese have not traditionally believed in one truly transcendent "God." Shang Di and Tian (Heaven) have more similarities to the sovereign, transcendent God of the Bible. But, as we have seen, both these terms fall short as translations of Biblical words for God.

Shen, on the other hand, rarely expresses the idea of a single ruler of the universe. Most often, shen is used to describe exalted beings who rule the affairs of men, and who can benefit those who worship them properly. In this sense, these "gods" closely approximate the gods of Greece, Rome, and the Ancient Near East. As elsewhere, these gods are usually personified, and represent great men and women upon whom has been conferred divine status, sometimes by the Emperor himself. Sometimes, natural forces, such as wind and water, can be called "gods." Furthermore, the Chinese word shen, when used with guei (spirit, ghost) can refer to a less-than-divine being, especially an evil and malevolent one. Why would anyone want to use Shen, therefore, to denote the God of the Bible?

First, shen is a generic word, which refers to a class of beings whose special characteristic is superior power. They are also seen to be mostly spiritual and not of this world. Shen does not name a particular deity, as Shang Di does. In this way, it greatly resembles both the Hebrew el (singular of Elohim) and the Greek theos. It can thus be used to convey the idea of kind, or nature, or essential being, which Theos does in certain key passages of the New Testament (such as John 1:1).

Second, shen is almost always distinguished from guei (spirit, ghost, demon) by the addition of another word to show that "good" "gods" are not being referenced. Thus, by itself, shen does not carry the meaning of a lesser, evil, spirit being. Again, shen thus matches the use of theos in non-Biblical Greek literature, where the gods can either help you or hurt you, but are superior to the lower, malevolent spirit beings called "demons."

Third, since Chinese nouns do not carry endings to indicate singular or plural, shen can be either singular or plural—a necessary condition for accurate translation of either Elohim or of Theos when it refers to the entire Godhead in the Bible.

Fourth, in at least one key place in Chinese literature, shen is used, with another character, to refer to the Supreme Being. This fact demonstrates that the meaning of shen does not have to be limited to lesser beings.[26] That shen can also denote the false gods of the pagans is no objection, since the same is true of theos, as we have seen.

The Importance of This Question

Some have ridiculed those who in the past debated so fiercely this question of the proper term for God. They say either that Shang Di is the obvious choice, or that both terms may be used interchangeably, as we find modern Chinese Christians doing. From one standpoint, this is true. Chinese, being un-dogmatic and eclectic by nature, employ both terms for God without any sense of contradiction. On the other hand, if God is the foundational "term" in the Christian faith, and if the Bible is the Word of God and our only standard for faith and practice, then finding the best Chinese word to translate Elohim or Theos is essential for fidelity to God's revelation and even to the glory of his name among the Chinese.

The doctrine of the Trinity stands at the heart of the Christian faith as it is revealed in the Bible. Any translation that either obscures or distorts

---

26   See C.K. Thong, *Faith of Our Fathers*, 136, 144, and elsewhere. Though I appreciate the work done by Mr. Thong, and freely acknowledge the many similarities between some aspects of traditional Chinese beliefs and some aspects of the Old Testament faith, I believe he has overstated the case for these two faiths being identical in their conception of God. He and I have had a frank and amicable conversation on this knotty problem, and I greatly respect his superior knowledge of Chinese culture and classical literature. His book contains a great deal of solid information and fascinating reflections on parallels between traditional Chinese language and culture, moreover.

this complex truth about God must be rejected. As we have seen Shang Di hopelessly fails to communicate the plurality that somehow characterizes the very essence and being of God. First, it must refer to one single being, and cannot express the idea of plurality. Second, its reference is restricted to a particular deity, and thus cannot express the idea of deity, or that fundamental nature of the Triune God as found in the Bible, and especially in the New Testament.

This becomes crucial in passages like John 1:1, which says, "In the beginning was the Word, and the Word was with God, and the Word was God." In that last phrase, "the Word was God," "God" is a translation of Theos without the article, whereas, in the middle clause, "God" has the article in Greek. Simply put, this means that "The Word was with God" expresses the idea of two distinct "persons"—the Word and God. We know that the Word is the eternal Son of God, who became the God-man Jesus (John 1:14). "And the Word was God," on the other hand, means that the Word possessed from all eternity an essence, a fundamental nature, that was the same as that of God the Father. John is not saying here, who the Word was, but what he was. You may ask why this matters, but a simple survey of church history, down to the present time, will provide ample evidence that confusion about the true nature of Jesus and thus of the Trinity lies at the center of most heresies.

Looking Forward

The Chinese church has moved beyond the initial stages of pioneer evangelism in many parts of the world, including China itself. No longer does it need to accommodate unnecessarily to traditional Chinese culture (though we must always do our best to communicate in terms that people understand). Chinese Christianity now possesses a 200-year tradition of Protestant witness and theology; Chinese Christian scholars now rank with the world's best.

To meet the demands of competing world views and build a strong theological foundation for its future, Chinese Christianity must have at its disposable the finest possible vocabulary, and must adhere to the best possible translation and exegesis of the Scriptures. Thus, I propose the following compromise to the vexing Term Question: In ordinary conversation, and in some preaching, the word name Shang Di may be used some of the time, as long as it is adequately explained according to the full Biblical revelation. But, in most preaching and teaching, and in all translations of the Bible, Shen should be employed, as being the most accurate rendering of Elohim and of Theos.

YIN AND YANG

One of the most pervasive, and most profound, of all ancient Chinese concepts is that of yin and yang. You see its pictorial representation in the circle with two parts, one black and one white, arranged in an undulating fashion. Looking carefully, you can discern a black dot in the white section, and a white dot in the black section. Each part of this icon possesses meaning: Black and white represent polar opposites; their "two-peas-in-a pod" configuration shows that they are not absolutely opposed to each other, but merge and interact in a constant evolution of one into the other. The presence of the opposite color in each half indicates the lack of absolute contrast: There is some of each in the other.

"Unity of Opposites"

Yin stands for what is dark, moist, receptive, weak, feminine; yang for what is bright, dry, active, strong, masculine. As in the human world, so in nature as a whole, these two complement each other; they combine to produce a synthesis in an unending dialectic. They form a unity of opposites—which seems like a contradiction, but fits well with the Chinese view of change and motion, the constant transformation of things in this world.

Other complementary pairs include: Beauty and ugliness; difficult and easy; long and short; high and low; something and nothing; profit and loss; hard and soft; happiness and misfortune; wise and foolish; big and small; life and death; win and lose; offense and defense; advance and retreat; light and heavy; honor and disgrace; one and many; Heaven and earth. As one increases, the other decreases, until such a state of imbalance has been reached that the growing one declines and the other assumes prominence.

Biblical Pairs?

Does any of this accord with Biblical teaching? Can Christians find any truth in this fundamental Chinese construct? Of course! Aside from the obvious accuracy of the observations we have already mentioned, we see in the Scriptures some pairs, such as male and female; day and night; soul and body; flesh and spirit; pride and humility; strength and weakness. Clearly, the ancient Chinese were on to something when they discerned the presence of complementary, mutually-interacting pairs of contrasting qualities and forces. It would seem to me that one of the most important of these is the male-female relationship, in which each supplements the other and in which their union produces a beautiful synthesis. Even more obvious is the Incarnation of the Word of God, producing the God-man,

Jesus Christ. He is fully God, the Son of God equal in power and deity to the Father, and fully man, one of us in every respect, except sin. Here, it would seem, we have the perfect illustration of an infinitely beautiful synthesis of apparent opposites.

Fundamental Contrasts

On the other hand, many—perhaps most—of the paired ideas or realities found in the Bible represent basic opposition or at least essential difference—without the possibility of mixture. Thus, the Scriptures present light and darkness as opposing forces of good and evil—themselves irreconcilably different and distinct. Flesh and Spirit are everywhere contrasted (as creature and Creator). Light and dark; love and hate; righteousness and sin; truth and falsehood; faith and unbelief—these also, especially in the writings of John, stand for fundamental contrasts.

Even the union in mankind of body and soul (or spirit) is not a mingling, but a mysterious joining of two distinct "somethings." In Christ himself, the deity and the humanity remain distinct, as the ancient creeds insist. There is no co-mingling, but an eternal union of two separate natures, without division but without confusion. In other words, the Bible presents us with a certain essential dualism, not a fundamental unity of opposites. There is no white spot in the dark section! Furthermore, that dualism is not an equal one, as with yin and yang. Always, God rules: light overcomes darkness; spirit conquers flesh; life triumphs over death; love defeats hatred; righteousness rules over sin.

A Deeper Number

Finally, in the Bible, though the number two is important, there is another even more important number: Three! God himself is Father, Son, and Holy Spirit. According to at least one passage of the Bible, man is body, soul, and spirit (1 Thessalonians 5:23). The heavens contain the sun, moon, and stars. Faith, hope, and love are the cardinal virtues. Some scientists believe that even the universe displays a certain tri-unity: space, matter, and time. Space possesses three dimensions; time can be divided into past, present, and future. "The central entity in the universe is matter, which is essentially unseen energy, manifesting itself in motion and experienced in various phenomena."[27] At the very least, however, we can say that, in the Scriptures, three is more basic a concept than two.

Point of Contact

So, as with so much else in Chinese culture, we can readily admit some

---

27   Henry M. Morris, *Science and the Bible* (Chicago: Moody Press, 1986) 23.

similarities with some aspects of the Bible, but we must maintain the absolute priority of Biblical revelation, and the fundamental difference between any insights to be found in any human culture and the truths given to us by God in Scripture. Created in the image of God, men and women receive what the theologians call "general revelation." That is not enough, however, to enable us to know God or worship him aright. We need the special revelation that comes to us as we read the Scriptures and pray for the Holy Spirit to open our eyes to understand its truth. Thus, while we can happily affirm the good, true, and beautiful in any culture, including traditional Chinese culture, we must proceed from affirmation of the best in human civilization to proclamation of the saving gospel of Jesus Christ.

DAOISM

Beginning with the Syrian Church missionaries (often called Nestorians) who first tried to translate Christian vocabulary into Chinese, in the seventh century A.D., Christians have long noticed certain affinities between the Dao (Tao) of the Dao De Jing (Tao Te Ching) and the Logos (Word) of John's Gospel. Indeed, when the translators of the Chinese Bible had to select a term for the Greek Logos, they chose Dao, and with good reason. Just as logos carried a wealth of connotations in ancient Greek, some of them quite amenable to Christian usage, so dao (tao), both in the Dao De Jing and in some Confucian classics, expresses concepts that resonate with readers of the Bible.

For instance: The Dao is eternal, and omnipresent, permeating the entire cosmos. All things flow from it. It is "both one and many, transcendent and immanent."[28] Since dao also means, "way, path," it represents the fundamental principle of human action as well. One thinks of Jesus' statement that he is the "Way" (John 14:6). Followers of the Dao, which is the Way, will imitate it by ceasing from striving, self-seeking, confrontation, and anxiety. They will give way and not fight, and will happily avoid recognition and public power.

At the same time, however, and providing difficulty for those who would see a direct correspondence between the Dao of Laozi and the Logos of the Bible, the Dao is also "impersonal, . . . being and nonbeing, action and nonaction. . . All opposites and contrasts are harmonized in the

---

28   John D.L. Hsu, "Taoist, Taosim," in A. Scott Moreau, ed., *Evangelical Dictionary of World Missions*, 930. See also the chapters on Laozi and Daoism in G. Wright Doyle and Peter Xiaoming Yu, *China: Ancient Culture, Modern Society*, 139–46.

Tao."[29] The Dao is the "One who is the primordial being or, the Chaos.
. . The Tao functions spontaneously, without any will or purpose . . . Tao
functions totally through natural processes and emerges from natural
processes, hence it is not like a creator who creates the world through will
and purpose."[30] For Christians, the impersonal nature of the Dao makes
identification of it with Christ impossible.

Recently, however, a prominent Chinese Christian evangelist has challenged the traditional interpretation of the Dao De Jing and has produced
not only a new translation but a long and detailed exposition of what he
considers to be the essential identity of the Dao of Laozi and the Logos
of the Bible. He adamantly opposes the idea that the Dao is impersonal
or nameless, and re-translates many passages of the Dao De Jing to try to
demonstrate the fundamental correspondence of the Dao and the Logos,
or Christ.[31]

In the opinion of many Chinese scholars, both Christian and non-Christian, there are two problems with this view: First, most scholars cannot
accept such a radical re-translation of the *Dao De Jing*, as if all previous
translators were completely wrong. Second, though very striking similarities definitely do exist between the Dao of the *Dao De Jing* and the Logos
of the Bible, there seem to be too many contrasts.[32] I greatly respect the
learning of those who emphasize the amazing, sometimes very beautiful,
echoes of the Bible's description of the Logos in the *Dao De Jing*, but
must also respect the scholarship of those who believe that irreconcilable
differences make any direct correlation impossible. For now, I follow the
traditional interpretation of Laozi's classic—a book that I love, by the
way.

In other words, I think we should take these undeniable similarities as
contact points and conversation-starters. That enables us to appreciate
what Laozi received through general revelation, without compromising
the unique status of the Bible as special revelation. As for religious
Daoism, though it does possess very interesting emphases, such as

---

29   Hsu, "Taoist," 930.
30   Choong Chee Pang, "Taoism," in Scott W. Sunquist, ed., *A Dictionary of Asian
Christianity*," 820–21.
31   *Tao Te Ching*, Yuan Zhiming and Yuan Zhiming, trans., *Lao Tzu and the Bible*,
Chen Shangyu, trans., (Bloomington, IN: AuthorHouse, 2010). C.K. Thong adopts a
similar approach in *Faith of Our Fathers*, 298–310.
32   I have laid out these comparisons and contrasts briefly in *The TAO of Lao Tzu
and The LOGOS of the Bible: Comparison and Contrast* for your consideration.
Available at chinainst.org.

non-action and the search for immortality, and though these can also be considered useful openings to the gospel, most Christians have thought it too similar to Chinese popular religion to be considered as much of a bridge to non-believers.

CHAPTER NINE
POINTS OF CONTACT:
CHINESE RELIGION (2)

CONFUCIANISM

With the influence of Confucius and Confucianism once again rising in China, Christians must find effective avenues of approach to deal with this pervasive cultural force. As with other elements of any culture, Christians can take several possible stances: They can utterly ignore Confucianism; totally reject it; assimilate it into Christianity with little critique; or affirm certain aspects of it while challenging, correcting, and even replacing others with biblical truth.

To ignore this major component of Chinese culture, and to proceed with evangelism and teaching of believers without reference to Confucianism, would seem to be the height of folly. Likewise, utterly to reject a great cultural hero and a predominant feature of Chinese life and thought for more than two millennia would amount to total contempt for generations of very intelligent people. On the other hand, simply to endorse traditional Confucian concepts without subjecting them to a careful biblical examination would be to engage in syncretism. The best course, therefore, would seem to be to strive for a balance between affirmation of those planks in the Confucian platform that accord with the Scriptures and respectful rejection of those that contradict Scripture, while filling in gaps with God's truth.

Careful Consideration

First of all, Confucius himself, and Confucianism generally, deserve our careful study. If we are to understand either traditional Chinese civilization or the recent resurgence of Confucian ideals in public life, we must take the time to listen, to read, and to ponder this essential core of China's identity. I suggest beginning with a general survey of Chinese culture and society, to put Confucianism into context. China: Ancient Culture, Modern Society, which I co-authored with Dr. Peter Yu, provides such an

overview. Next should come an attentive reading of the Analects of Confucius, the main text of Confucianism. Perhaps the best edition is The
Analects of Confucius: A Literal Translation with an Introduction and
Notes, by Chichung Huang, published by Oxford University Press. For
a very brief introduction, see the recent article on Confucius in China
Today, reviewed at globalchinacenter.org. After that, you can familiarize
yourself with the other three of the "Four Books": Mencius, The Golden
Mean, and The Great Learning. From there, the vista widens to include
studies such as those contained in the resource section of this book.

Profound Respect

The more you study Confucius, the more you will respect him. Christians can, without reservation, agree that Confucius was a great scholar,
a great teacher, and a great man. Otherwise, how could he have exerted
such a powerful influence on such a great people for such a long time?
Even if some of the popular claims made about him may not be completely verifiable, there is enough that is substantial to elicit our esteem.
More than a dozen readings of the Analects have only deepened my
admiration for him.

Appreciative Comparison

We do not have to agree with all that Confucius and his followers have
said and done, but we can easily admit Confucianism's many significant
agreements with biblical concepts. For example, both Confucius and the
Bible teach that children should obey their parents; the young should
respect their elders; wives should submit to their husbands; "slaves"
should obey their "masters"; and citizens should submit to those in
authority over them (Eph 5:22–33, 6:1–3, 6:5–8; 1 Pet 2:13–25, 5:5; Rom
13:1–7). The Confucian concept of "benevolence" (ren, or jen) enjoys
some overlap with biblical "love." Confucius' "negative Golden Rule"—
do not do to others what you don't want them to do to you—finds its
"positive" counterpart in Jesus' command to treat others as we would
have them treat us.

In particular, the breakdown of the family in modern society, including
the huge generation gap, cries out for a return to a regard for our parents,
forebears, and siblings. The Scriptures provide no warrant for the rank
individualism, unbridled hedonism, narcissistic self-pre-occupation,
indiscriminate self-expression, and vulgar behavior that characterize
much of current Western, even Christian, culture today.

What is wrong with a proper and balanced regard for politeness and
etiquette—what Confucius would call li? We don't have to return to

the elaborate rituals of traditional Chinese society in order to enjoy the benefits of gestures of respect and ceremonies that help to control our baser impulses and express reverence and honor for people and occasions. I think of graduation exercises, presidential inaugurations, silence and applause at concerts, and of course Christian worship.

Likewise, the Confucian "harmonious society" recently trumpeted by the Chinese government resonates with passages in the Bible that urge Christians to strive for peace (Eph 4:1–3; Col 3:15; Titus 3:1–3; Heb 12:12; 1 Pet 3:8–12). Strident, angry confrontation and disputing are everywhere denounced in the Scriptures, and there is no biblical warrant for violent revolution.

Ever since Confucius, Chinese have extolled the value of hard work, and especially of diligent study. Can anyone say that these virtues are foreign to the Bible or useless to us today? Confucius' emphasis upon a reverent contemplation of the best that has been handed down to us from the past does not conflict either with the Fifth Commandment or the Bible's repeated calls to study the Scriptures and the examples and teachings of those who have preceded us.

Respectful Disagreement

On the other hand, we cannot ignore major points of contrast between the Bible and Confucianism. I will here name only a few.

Filial piety must be balanced by parental responsibility to treat their children with respect; to listen to them carefully; to allow them freedom to grow into responsible servants of God; and not to "exasperate" them or cause them to lose heart (Eph 6:4; Col 3:21). If parents displayed more patience and humility towards their children, and less self-righteous pride and know-it-all instruction, perhaps their offspring would respond with less rebellion or inattention (Eph 4:1–3; 5:21; Col 2:1–4; 1 Pet 5:5). For example, the Bible teaches that a young woman may marry the man she chooses (Gen 24:57–60; Num 36:6).

Again, while young children are commanded to obey their parents, adults who marry must "leave father and mother" and cleave to their spouse; as they establish their own household, the locus of authority shifts from parents to husband (Eph 5:22–33). We should note here that Confucius' own marriage ended in failure, and that the Analects contain virtually no teaching about this fundamental relationship.

In the church and in society, all those in positions of leadership must follow the example of Christ, who humbly served others, rather than the imperial pattern that has dominated China up to the present (Matt

20:25–28; Eph 6:9; 1 Pet 5:1–4). Husbands must "submit" to their wives by setting a Christ- like pattern of servant leadership and self-sacrifice (Eph 5:25–31). If we take the Scriptures as our guide, there is no excuse for the abuse of authority that seems endemic in Chinese society.

In particular, females of all ages—including young girls, adults, and aged women—must be treated with the utmost respect, care, and tenderness, for they are equally made in the image of God (Gen 1:26–27; 1 Pet 3:7). Anything else is an affront to our Maker and to Christ, who died and rose for both women and men. Though leadership and authority in the home and in the church is reserved by Scripture for men, that does not mean that women should be deprived of honor or the opportunity to exercise their abilities and gifts in appropriate spheres.[33]

Other major areas of disagreement include the Christian teachings on epistemology (how we know the truth) and salvation. The Bible claims to be the revealed Word of God; Jesus himself said that he spoke only words that had been given to him from God the Father (John 12:44–50). Confucius was humbly unassertive, even somewhat agnostic, about the spiritual realm, whereas Christians believe that God has revealed absolute truth about this world and the one to come, and that this knowledge finds its focus in the person and work of Jesus Christ. Unlike Confucianists, Christians do not rely solely on human observation, reason, or tradition for authoritative information about life and death; they have grounds for believing that the Scriptures are inspired by God and furnish a sufficient guide to eternal verities (2 Tim 3:16).

As for salvation, Confucius and his followers concentrate upon how to live well, and prosperously, on this earth and in this age. The Bible does not neglect such matters (see, for example, the Book of Proverbs), but affirms that our relationship with God trumps all other concerns. In contrast to Confucianism, Christians believe that human beings are both good, since they are created in the image of God, and also evil, since they are all fallen (Gen 1:16, 31; Rom 3:9–18, 23).

Furthermore, where Confucius placed his hopes on the power of humans to improve themselves through study, effort, and conformity to ritual, the Bible teaches that we are dead in sin, slaves to sin, and under condemnation by a righteous God who must punish evil (John 8:34; Eph 2:1–3). The only way for us to be reconciled to God is through sincere repentance and faith in Christ (Rom 3:21–26). Improvement of our character

---

33   For more on this controversial subject, see, for example, Wayne Grudem, *Systematic Theology*, 937–44, and *Evangelical Feminism and Biblical Truth*; and Wayne Grudem and John Piper, *Recovering Biblical Manhood and Womanhood*.

only comes by the power of the Holy Spirit, who is given to all who rely solely on Christ for salvation (Rom 7:6; 8:12–13).

Extending this core belief outward to society, Christians do not look for a perfectly "harmonious society" on this earth. While they are under obligation to do all that they can to show love for their neighbors and to improve conditions in the world, they place their hopes for a perfect society upon the return of Christ, when he will usher in a "new heaven and a new earth, in which righteousness dwells" (2 Pet 3:13). Their expectations both of individuals and of governments are limited, therefore. When humans fail to practice justice, Christians are saddened, even outraged, but they are not surprised, nor do they harbor hatred against those who have disappointed them. Instead, they pray for their leaders and practice such good works as God enables them to perform, serving as "salt and light" in a dark world (1 Tim 2:1–2; Titus 3:8; Matt 5:13–16).[34]

We see, therefore, that while Christians can affirm much that Confucianism teaches, they believe that God has provided them with an even more valid, complete, and useful body of knowledge in the Scriptures. And not just information: They rejoice in the grace of God, who has given them new life, brought them into fellowship with himself and with other believers, made them children in a new family with God as Father, empowered them to experience substantial moral change in their lives, and sent them into the world with a mandate to reflect the glory of God by word and deed. Whenever they can, they will join hands with followers of Confucius to promote all that is good and right; when it is necessary, they will gently and respectfully point Confucianists away from the great Chinese Sage to Jesus, the Only Savior.

BUDDHISM

Buddhism is growing. In Taiwan, this ancient religion has experienced a powerful resurgence in the past twenty or thirty years, with new temples, monasteries, seminaries, a large charity organization, and increasing public presence in the government and the media. After the anti-religious fervor of the Cultural Revolution, Chinese on the mainland began to revert to their traditional Buddhist beliefs and practices, helped greatly by visiting tourists from Taiwan, Hong Kong, Singapore, and other parts of Southeast Asia, who expressed interest in seeing temples and then donated large amounts to have them rebuilt and refurbished.

For our purposes, "Buddhism" is not the same as Chinese popular religion,

---

34   For more points of both comparison and contrast, see the end of this volume for my books *Confucius and Christ* (in Chinese) or *Jesus: The Complete Man* (in English).

though most Chinese probably don't know the difference. Roughly speaking, there are two main types of Chinese Buddhism (itself one of two major kinds of worldwide Buddhism): "Traditional"—Chinese, Zen, Tibetan, etc., and "Modern"—found in Taiwan, North America, and elsewhere.

Similarities with Christianity

Despite fundamental differences, there are actually quite a few surface similarities between Buddhism and Christianity. Perhaps we can call these "conversation starters," since they provide points of superficial contact that can lead to deeper discussion.

Buddhists see clearly the transitory nature of this life, and advocate achieving distance from its passions and desires by meditating upon just how fleeting is our short stay on this earth. In that sense, they agree with Christians, who are urged by the Bible not to set their hopes on earthly things (Col 3:1; 1 Pet 1:13). To Buddhists, the cause of our inner discontent lies in our attachment to this world, with which Christians would agree, at least to some extent. Jesus, after all, pointed to the reward that would come in the next life, and Paul advocated walking by faith, not by sight, while John commanded that we should not love this world, or the things in it, or be captivated by lusts arising from excessive entanglement with the world.

The problem of suffering occupies a central place in Buddhist teaching. The Buddha himself was overcome by the suffering he saw one day, and sought to find the way out of what seemed to be an endless cycle of misery. His solution was to meditate, as we have seen, on the ephemeral quality of this earthly existence, and thus to tame the desires that are attached to it and thus evoke pain. The Bible also speaks often about suffering. Jesus did a great deal to alleviate pain and sickness while on earth, and from one standpoint, you could say that he came to this world in order to bring an end to suffering for his people.

The importance of enlightenment is another similarity between Buddhism and Christianity. Actually, "Buddha" means "the Enlightened One," for he believed that our basic problem stemmed from ignorance, from which he wanted to free his followers. Jesus, too, came to bring light. In fact, he claimed that he himself was the light of the world (John 8:12). Paul prayed that God would enlighten the hearts of his readers and urged them to walk as children of light. Both Jesus and Paul assumed that ignorance of God and his truth kept people in darkness, and they claimed to bring liberating light.

Inner transformation through meditation also plays a key role in both Buddhism and Christianity, for the real battle takes place in the mind. If we are to respond well to the vicissitudes of life, we need to transform our minds, so that they hold to right thoughts based on true reality. That requires constant pondering of the eternal verities, to keep us from being led astray by what we see around us.

Both Buddhism and Christianity possess a collection of sacred writings, which are taught and studied by faithful disciples.

As distinct from Confucianism, Buddhism advocates "broad love" (not confined to family or nation). Christianity, likewise, tells us to consider everyone we meet along the way to be a "neighbor" whom we are to love as we love ourselves. Buddhism, like Christianity, enjoins upon its followers the necessity of doing good deeds, especially works of charity. Modern Buddhism in Taiwan has seen the formation of huge charitable organizations that are matched by those that have been funded by Christians worldwide for centuries.

Another similarity lies in the belief in moral standards. Both religions have concepts of virtue and vice, and their ethical precepts often overlap. Likewise, both believe in merit and demerit, in the sense that our good works and our bad works have significance for our future destiny (Roman Catholics would agree even more closely with Buddhists than Protestants, because they think that Christians can acquire merit before God by doing virtuous deeds.) As a consequence, both popular Chinese Buddhism and Christianity teach that there will be rewards and punishments in the next life, when the righteous will be happy and the unrighteous will suffer torments.

In the Pure Land tradition, Buddhist believers are promised a blissful existence in a Western paradise. Some simplify the requirements for this sort of salvation to the point of offering it to those who chant the name Amitabha (Amituofo) with faith in the Buddha. Virtuous actions were also encouraged, of course.

When Christians speak of Christ, who came from heaven to save mortal humans, Buddhists refer to both the Buddha and to many bodhisattvas, people with special merit who defer their own entrance into Nirvana in order to assist mortals still on earth gain buddhahood.

Some features of Chinese Buddhism find at least superficial counterparts in certain practices of Roman Catholicism, such as praying to the saints, offering incense, emphasis upon merit, priests, monks, and temples. The bodhisattva Guanyin (Goddess of Mercy) bears a close resemblance to

Mary in Roman Catholic devotion; some, indeed, observe that the transformation of Guanyin from a male to a female deity took place at about the time the Christianity became known in China.

Modern Buddhism devotes less attention to rituals, and concentrates instead upon internal transformation through meditation and strict mental control, thus somewhat resembling evangelical Protestantism more than Roman Catholicism or "high-church" Protestant worship.

Differences

Though conversations between Christians and Buddhists may start with the similarities noted above, at some stage the fundamental differences between the two faiths need to be pointed out.

They hold different scriptures to be authoritative. Christianity has a smaller, well-defined canon, which is closed. Furthermore, the Christian Scriptures are basically historical in nature, utterly devoid of myths and complex philosophical speculation. The New Testament was composed by Jesus' immediate disciples or their associates, unlike the accounts of Buddha, which were only written down hundreds of years after his death. Whereas the vast body of Buddhist sacred writings contains books that are both filled with myths and mutually contradictory, the Bible is self-consistent as well as historically accurate.

Christians believe, of course, in a single Creator God, utterly unlike the atheism of original Buddhism or the polytheism of popular Chinese religion. He is the fundamental Source, Goal, and Life of the universe. Our purpose is to know, love, serve, and worship him.

Far from being illusory, creation—including each individual soul—is considered both real and good in the Bible. Our moral problem and mental suffering results from "total depravity." The root of our troubles is not ignorance, but a willful turning away from God and his will that affects every department of the human personality.

For that reason, Christians believe that we all need a divine-human Savior, one who can reconcile God and men because he fully partakes of both natures. Because of our moral degradation, we stand under God's wrath; no amount of self-cultivation can make us good enough to deserve entrance into God's presence. Thus, we need a propitiating sacrifice.

For Christians, Jesus Christ is not just a great teacher, or even a godlike bodhisattva, but the unique divine Son of God and son of Mary, who entered into history, lived, died, rose again, and ascended into heaven. Faith in him will bring a righteous standing before God, which qualifies us to draw near to God as beloved children of a heavenly Father. We do not claim any merit, but wholly rely on the merit of Christ on our behalf. Salvation is by faith, not works.

This faith results in regeneration, not repeated reincarnation. It is a once-for-all experience in this life, which gives us a new heart that can begin to obey God by the power of the indwelling Holy Spirit. Again—Christians do not rely on self-effort to overcome sin.

Good works are, of course, required of all believers, but they are the fruit of the Holy Spirit, who works in us as we call in faith upon God to change us. Christianity, unlike traditional Buddhism, is a "worldly," or "world-transforming," faith. Especially in its Protestant form, Christianity urges all believers to be "salt and light" in this world, and not to flee from it into a monastery.

All those who trust in Christ become members of the church, which is the Body of Christ; this is their new and true family, and is an international fellowship.

Rather than hoping either for rebirth into a vague Western Paradise, or the melting of the soul into the World Soul in Nirvana, Christians hold to the promise of the return of Christ, which will end history and usher in a new heaven and new earth.

For these and other reasons, Christians try to avoid unnecessary mental and even physical pain, and respond to suffering when it does come, not by denial of desire but by the cultivation of proper desires and renunciation of sinful ones. They do not seek to kill all longings, but to direct them towards God.

The many apparent similarities between Buddhism and Christianity offer useful points of departure for conversations that reflect genuine respect but also move towards greater clarity. Though they do not have to make unnecessary concessions to Buddhism in the process, Christians may move from these points of contact to a presentation of their faith that answers the longings, and even some of the God-given insights, of their Buddhist friends.

POPULAR RELIGION

In recent decades, Chinese popular religion—sometimes called folk religion—has staged a massive comeback, especially in the countryside. In a land where religions of all sorts were banned and apparently banished forever during the Great Cultural Revolution (1966–1976), things have returned to "normal," with the added presence of Christianity. Tens of thousands of temples have been rebuilt or newly constructed, many of them elaborately decorated and furnished. "Ghost palaces" and "hell houses" have been built to attract tourists. In the 1990s, overseas Chinese visitors financed much of this construction, but now the funding comes from local sources, as people return to the ancient rhythms of their ancestors.

The world of Chinese folk religion is populated with ghosts, buddhas, demons, gods, and a variety of invisible beings who are believed to have influence over the affairs of this life and the next. In particular, ancestor worship has resumed its central place in Chinese piety and religious practice, with offerings and prayers to departed relatives who, if happy, can bestow blessing, but if unhappy—or hungry!—can blast people with baneful curses, including disease, infertility, and financial loss.

These gods exist for the benefit of their worshipers, and are expected to deliver very tangible goods and services to those who pray to them—healing, children, deliverance from demons, good harvests, a job, a mate, etc. When they do not, one simply goes to another god residing in another temple or shrine, in a true "free market" of religion. In essence, Chinese folk religion is dominated by pragmatism and utilitarianism, not a personal relationship with the Lord of the universe.

Enter Christianity

During the 1960s, when all of these beliefs and practices were labeled "superstitious" by the government, temples were shut down or converted to secular uses, as were Christian churches. This eradication of folk religion left a vacuum of faith, which demanded to be filled. That is when Christians began to penetrate the rural areas of China with a new message, one of hope, joy, and peace. Jesus was a new god, more powerful than the old ones, who could deliver you from demons, disease, danger, and destitution. Believing firmly in the power of God, fervent evangelists traveled all over the interior of China, proclaiming this new "god" and urging people to put their trust in him. Usually young and lacking a sound knowledge of the Bible, these zealous preachers often portrayed Christ as a replacement for the old deities, and in the same terms: He could do more for you than they did!

Of course, many Christian evangelists preached a pure gospel of salvation by grace alone through faith in Christ alone; that is the real source of the incredible growth of the Chinese church in the countryside. Even they, however, either could not shake off the pragmatism, utilitarianism, and this-worldly focus that pervaded Chinese culture. Though they may have believed the gospel of redemption through the cross and resurrection of Christ, they may also have so couched their preaching, and directed their prayers, as to give the impression that Jesus and God were very similar to the deities of folk belief.

Some of this derived from the clear teaching of the Bible. God can work miracles; prayer to him in Jesus' name does result in deliverance from demon oppression, inner peace and joy, and—often—physical healing. When we follow biblical principles, we shall, generally, enjoy better health, happier homes, and a measure of material prosperity. On the other hand, these biblical truths and realities appeal so strongly to Chinese pragmatism that in some places more than 60% of "conversions" take place after someone has been healed through prayer to God in Jesus' name. Even mature Christians often give testimonies that focus on material and temporal blessings rather than spiritual benefits that accrue to those who trust in Christ.

This sort of pragmatism and utilitarianism affects not only the rural churches, but those in the cities, too. And not just poor and uneducated people, but highly-intelligent, well-educated churchgoers as well. Even in the West, where Chinese churches are filled with PhDs, the testimonies you hear have mostly to do with answers to prayer for healing, a job, a visa, a child, or academic success—precisely the same message being conveyed in the simplest country congregation in rural China.

Baneful Consequences

The results are not good for true Christianity. Rather than preaching that we should seek God for spiritual blessings; thank him for forgiveness of sins, reconciliation, and access to him in prayer through Christ, and stress the hope that we have of eternal life with him, both clergy and laity tend to fix their eyes on this world. The Cross loses its centrality; God becomes a means to an end; faith the instrument of accessing worldly goods and services. Of course, when your prayers aren't answered, you can easily lose hope. One knowledgeable observer said, "Millions of Chinese Christians are one unanswered prayer away from leaving the church." That is why the "back door" of many churches is just as wide as the "front door."

Before we criticize such pragmatic and utilitarian features of Chinese Christianity, however, it might be good for Western believers to examine our own prayer lives. Perhaps we, too, have our hopes set on this world, rather than on God and the grace to be brought to us when Christ returns. Are we going around angry with God for not giving us something we really want? What about our "prosperity message" preachers? Are they not saying the same thing, with their "name it and claim it" religion? As former TIME Magazine religious editor Richard Ostling once told me, this "health and wealth" preaching is real journalistic "news": never before in church history have Christians preached, or believed, such crude heresy. From the "therapeutic," feel-good sermons of many preachers, such as Joel Osteen, to the baser appeals to desires for health, beauty, prosperity, and earthly happiness of too many others, our own "folk religion" looks just as worldly as does that of millions of Chinese churchgoers.

What to Do?

For those who want to see God's kingdom advance among Chinese, the question is urgent: What can we do about this revival of Chinese folk religion and—even more important—about the pervasive influence of pragmatism and utilitarianism among Chinese Christians?

First, we should remember Jesus' words, "Let him who is without sin cast the first stone." Let us first take the beam of worldliness out of our own eye; only then will we see clearly enough to help our Chinese brothers and sisters. After all, Western "health and wealth" preachers are widely heard in villages deep within the Majority World. I once heard a Benny Hinn sermon in the foothills of the Himalayas! One Chinese church leader has said, "Your prosperity message is ruining our church!"

Even within orthodox, evangelical circles, we need a deep revival of true devotion to God and Jesus Christ, worked within our worldly hearts by the Holy Spirit. Is it not possible that we should re-examine our comfortable lifestyles to see where they reflect a fixation on earthly comforts? Maybe we need to set an example of self-denial and radical discipleship. On the other hand, maybe some staid and sensible Christians in the West need to recover faith in a God who truly does work miracles, including healing and deliverance from demons, and who provides our daily necessities if we ask for them in faith.

Then, we should pray that Chinese preachers would proclaim Christ and him crucified, as John Song and other twentieth-century revivalists did with such power. The Bible clearly teaches that Jesus healed people from various illnesses, drove out demons, and even occasionally fed those who had followed him into the wilderness to hear his teaching. He sent the chosen disciples out to conduct a similar ministry of preaching, healing, and deliverance during his life on earth, and the Spirit-filled apostles likewise both preached and engaged in healing and exorcism. Furthermore, the Christians in Antioch and elsewhere were encouraged to contribute food to the famine-struck believers in Judea. We may, therefore, freely pray for people to receive healing, release from demonic oppression, and satisfaction of their real physical and material needs. In doing so, we are imitating Christ himself, whose good works displayed the generous compassion of the Father.

On the other hand, as I said above, we must be very careful not to present a gospel that closely resembles popular Chinese religion. In other words, we have an obligation to place repentance, faith, conversion, and forsaking all to follow Christ at the center of both our proclamation and our own practical living. Addressing the legitimate earthly concerns of our hearers and neighbors, we should also point them to their greater, and even desperate, need for reconciliation to a holy God, entrance into his heavenly kingdom, and deliverance from an excessive preoccupation with this world.

CHPATER TEN
"PERFECTION" OF BELIEVERS

Christians will never, in this life, become morally perfect. However, in this chapter I want to talk about a few ways in which we can help Chinese who have expressed an interest in Christ, or who have professed faith in him, to become mature and productive members of the Body of Christ and effective witnesses of Christ.[35] First, we should state our goal: The establishment of healthy, growing, biblically-based congregations. All the methods we might employ to help people believe in Jesus for salvation must, one way or another, and as much as possible, flow from, and issue in, the local church.

BAPTISM AND THE LORD'S SUPPER

When a person has been given repentance, genuine faith, and a changed life by God's Spirit through faith in Christ, he should be baptized. In the early church, inquirers (called "catechumens") were enrolled in a three-year course of instruction and probation, after which they would be received for baptism. Missionaries to China in the nineteenth century varied in their policy toward converts who sought baptism, some allowing it immediately after a credible profession of faith, with most requiring months or even longer, during which the seeker would be instructed in the basic tenets of the faith and its implications for daily life. Always, a visibly transformed life was seen as a prerequisite for baptism. The methods of John Nevius deserve our careful attention for many reasons, including his insistence that those who said they had believed in Christ be given six months of intensive teaching, during which they were observed, before being interviewed for possible baptism.[36] Hasty administration of this rite of initiation into Christ and his church has probably caused more damage both to individuals and to the name of Christ than anything else, since it has filled the churches with nominal "Christians" whose testimony sullies the reputation of the Lord and whose fleshly conduct stirs up conflict within the Body of Christ.

Those desiring baptism should be taught the general outline of Christian doctrine, as contained, for example, in the Apostles' Creed and the Nicene Creed. In addition, they need to know the overall structure of

35   See Eph 4:13–16; Col 1:28.
36   See Samuel Chao, "Conversion Methods: Theory and Practices," in R.G. Tiedemann, ed., *Handbook of Christianity in China*, Vol. 2: 1800–present, 425–25.

the Bible and the narrative of creation, fall, and redemption in Christ. Coming from a background lacking any sense of a transcendent God, they must be taught about a Sovereign Lord who created the world, governs, it, sovereignly saves those who trust in him, guides and provides for his people, and will one day renew the world. Not only his love, but his holiness and justice must be presented, so that a proper reverence for him will lead to obedience flowing from faith.

Baptism joins the true believer with Christ, and signifies his total forgiveness by God as well as his commitment to follow Christ, even unto death. I always ask people, "Are you willing to follow Jesus even if it leads to loss of a job, a lifetime of singleness, and even death?" If the answer is "No," I tell them to go home and think about it further.

As Paul explains in Romans 6:1–23, baptism involves dying with Christ to the old life of sin and rising with him to a new life of holiness and full consecration to God as his willing servants. He repeats this later in the same letter, reminding us that because of the mercies of God in Christ, we are to present ourselves to God as a living sacrifice (Rom 12:1–2). Sacrifice involves death, death to self, to sin, to the world. But the Christian believer accepts this sort of "death" in order to enjoy life with God in Christ, now and forever.

Baptism also joins us to the local expression of the Body of Christ. The leaders of the church usually administer baptism, and afterwards the newly-baptized persons are welcomed to participate in the Lord's Supper, which was previously not available to them. In some churches in China, inquirers and visitors are required to leave the service before the Lord's Supper is celebrated; in others they are simply told not to receive the bread and the cup. The Lord's Supper is a family meal, for those who have publicly declared their faith in Christ through baptism. It is celebrated as part of the ongoing life of the church, as a remembrance of the death of Jesus for our sins, his presence with us now, and his promise to return. In some way that we cannot understand, as we partake of the elements by faith, in true repentance and forgiving all those who have offended us, we receive grace from God, both in a renewed sense of his love for us, and in a fresh infusion of energy to live for him.

HOUSE CHURCHES

A Heavy Burden

Not long ago, I visited a large American church that was about to cut staff because of insufficient funds. One major reason: Their huge mortgage. A Chinese congregation where I preached was about to decide whether to acquire property being sold by a defunct American church. Some members opposed the move, fearing that the purchase would exceed their resources. Indeed, conflict over buying, building, and budgeting for buildings may have split more churches than any other issue. In China, some large networks of unregistered churches have erected huge, costly, and elaborate structures, only to see them torn down by the government.

A "Simple" Solution?

Both the Bible and church history point towards another way of "doing" church. Wherever the gospel has spread the fastest and taken deepest root, believers have met primarily in homes. There is no record of Christians meeting in buildings specifically designed for worship for the first few hundred years of early church history. The initial group of believers in Jerusalem met from house to house (Acts 2:46),[37] and Paul refers frequently to home-based churches (Rom. 16:5, 19; Col. 4:15; Phil. 2). In China, the number of Christians has exploded in recent decades, with most of that increase coming from home-based meetings.

Advantages of Home-based Churches

Home-based churches enjoy a number of advantages over those tied to a "church" building.

Cost: Meeting in the home of a believer avoids the immense cost of buying (or building) and then maintaining a large building. The money saved could go into salaries for pastors, evangelists, missionaries, and other church workers, as well as widows, orphans, and others in need.

Flexibility: As the church grows, or as members move away, venues for meetings can be altered easily. If persecution arises, smaller units are harder to attack than concentrated ones.

Size: Home-based meetings are necessarily "small." Even a very large house cannot accommodate more than about 100 people, which is still a small enough number for relationships of love we see in the New Testament. Smaller congregations can engage more easily in the "one another" activities that are so prominent in the New Testament. (Rom. 12:10–15; 1 Cor. 11:33; 12:25; Gal. 6:2; Heb. 10:24; James 5:16; 1 Peter 4:9–11). Imagine a Lord's Day gathering that actually followed Paul's instructions in 1 Corinthians 11:27–22; 14:26–33, and see whether it could take place in a large room filled with hundreds of people.

---

37   They also gathered in the Temple, but not for their specifically Christian meetings, and not after Jerusalem was destroyed by the Romans in A.D. 70. For two centuries, Christians did not seek to build a "temple" for worship.

Pastoral Care: It's hard to get "lost" in a home-based group. People know each other well enough to notice an uncustomary absence or sad expression. They also feel more comfortable to share their burdens with each other.

Evangelism: Many non-believers who won't enter a religious building feel quite comfortable in a home. Family members who wouldn't attend a typical church can hardly avoid hearing what goes on in their own home, or see the love between Christians.

Leader Development: It takes both time and money to prepare a man to preach to, and lead, a large congregation. The head of a household, or an elder chosen from among the group, can be trained more quickly to teach a Bible lesson to people whom he knows.

Body Life: Each believer can exercise his or her spiritual gift much more easily in a home-based group than in a larger congregation based in a special building. Almost naturally, people's needs are known and met by members of the congregation.

Love: As members grow in knowledge of each other, they will naturally be stimulated by the Holy Spirit to reflect the love of God the Father and of Jesus to each other. Big congregations, with hundreds of attendees at each meeting, do not generally make really close fellowship possible. Smaller groups have time and "space" to enable individuals to share their lives with other believers and sacrifice for one another. This sort of love is not only a powerful healing instrument in God's hands, but an essential requirement for effective witness to the outside world, as Jesus made crystal clear on his last night with his disciples (John 13:31–33).

Problems

Of course, traditional church buildings provide some benefits, and house churches are not without problems, as both the New Testament and recent Chinese church developments attest. They can become narrow and focused only on themselves. One strong man or family can dominate a group. Heresies and sects can develop unless there is input from outside. Nevertheless, it behooves us to encourage Chinese believers to return to the biblical pattern of meeting in homes and develop the sort of stron fellowship that can only occur in smaller groups.[38]

---

38 For some suggestions on how to overcome common pitfalls of house churches, see G. Wright Doyle, "A Theology of House Churches," http://www.chinainst.org/en/articles/christianity/a-theology-for-house-churches.php.

EQUIPPING OTHERS TO SERVE

The Mandate

Jesus has commanded his church to "Go into all the world and preach the gospel to every creature" (Mark 16:15). That command, like similar ones in Matthew, Luke, John, and Acts, has never been rescinded. Furthermore, despite heroic faithfulness over many generations, the world has far more unevangelized people than ever before, most of whom will never hear unless someone crosses cultural boundaries. In mainland China and Taiwan, though Christians are numerous, more than one billion people have likely never heard a clear presentation of the gospel. "The harvest truly is plentiful, but the laborers are few. Therefore pray the Lord of the harvest to send out laborers into His harvest" (Matt 9:37–38). Like Jesus' disciples, we must ask God to raise up more willing workers. Almost everyone agrees that the most urgent priority in the Chinese church today is leadership development. With many millions of people attending meetings, capable shepherds are in drastically short supply.

The Means

How can Christians participate in mobilizing a contingent of well-equipped laborers for this field? First, we should pray daily for the Lord of the harvest to thrust people out of their comfort zones into the heat of the battle for the souls of millions of Chinese. Other than our personal life with God and with our family, what can be more important than this? We can intercede for those who have gone, and we can ask God to prosper their work. We can pray also for those who send others. Dozens, perhaps hundreds, of organizations are dedicated to putting Christian witnesses among the Chinese around the world. What if you "adopted" one or more of these, received their information, and remembered them in your prayers?

Second, we can set a good example by plunging into the effort with our time and money.

Third, we can support those whom God has moved to offer themselves for service to the Chinese, either in the West or in Asia.

No one person, church, or organization can hope to evangelize China's vast population, or edify the growing number of Christians, or equip church leaders. This task is so huge that the entire church around the world must be mobilized to fulfill the Great Commission as it refers to the Chinese. Reaching out to Chinese living overseas must be a team effort, involving both Chinese churches and local believers. Therefore, we should not only seek to minister to Chinese ourselves, but to mobilize others for service among the Chinese.

Both Chinese and Westerners

Missionaries recognized long ago that China would be evangelized by its own people, who are in almost every way better equipped than foreigners. Thus, our primary focus should be on helping Chinese seekers to know Christ, and then on training them to disciple others in their own language. But that is not enough. Both because of the Great Commission's mandate for all nations to be engaged in the spread of the gospel, and because there are not enough Chinese believers to do the job alone, Westerners have a role to play. The difficulty is that those of us who are not Chinese face numerous obstacles to effective ministry. It's not easy communicate Christ cross-culturally. People from other backgrounds have worldviews, values, histories, pressures and prejudices that strongly affect their ability to hear, believe, and live out the Christian faith. If Westerners are going to serve them effectively, they need information, training, advice, and a support structure.

Earnest Efforts

Thousands of trainers within China are joined by many others from outside, mostly Chinese, to teach new leaders. Usually meeting in secret for intensive classes lasting a few weeks, but sometimes in "underground" seminaries with full three-year programs, unregistered ("house") churches are working hard to educate teachers and pastors for their vast flocks. Meanwhile, the official church has more than a dozen seminaries, and many more training centers, around the nation, most of which are evangelical in theological orientation, despite the official "liberal" theology of the overall organization. Chinese Christians outside the mainland— in Hong Kong, Taiwan, North America, Singapore, and elsewhere—do their part to equip workers for this vast harvest. Many, perhaps most, of their graduates spend at least some time each year within China.

A number of Christian organizations devote some or all of their attention to mobilization of Chinese ministry workers. Without attempting to be comprehensive, and without seeking to compare, some of these are listed in the Resources section at the end of this volume.

Discipling Others

Immediately after issuing his summons to prayer, Jesus himself called twelve men to himself and instructed them (Matthew 10:1–42). In the same way, we should each be seeking to train others to share God's truth and love among the Chinese. Notice that Jesus spent most of his time with a few people, and that he almost always spent time with them in what we would now call a small group, even as he also taught the multitudes. We need to focus on a few individuals, and the most effective way to do that might be in gatherings of two or three. If we have opportunities to teach larger groups, these few should be with us to watch. "The things which you have heard from me in the presence of many witnesses, these entrust to faithful men, who will be able to teach others also" (2 Timothy 2:2).

REACHING MEN

What you are about to read may sound politically incorrect, but I think the reason for it will become clear as we progress. For several reasons, it seems to me that those who want to reach Chinese worldwide with the gospel of Christ in a lasting fashion must consider the strategic importance of concentrating at least some of our energies upon reaching men.

Why Reach Men?

In all societies, including China, most leadership positions are occupied by men, even now. Traditional cultures, in particular, continue to emphasize the role of men as fathers, husbands, elders in society, and leaders in the church. Simply from a sociological standpoint, if we are going to influence a family, a village, or even a nation, it would seem that capturing the allegiance of men would be wise.

Think of some of the most common problems that women face: Distant or abusive fathers; absent, irresponsible, violent, or even unfaithful husbands; domineering bosses; corrupt political and business leaders—most of whom are men. Experienced counselors all know that many problems presented by women stem from the faults and failings of the men in their lives. There is more: In China today, Christian women outnumber men by a large margin. This disparity means that it's very difficult to find believers for them to marry, much less suitable candidates for the position of elder, deacon, and pastor. The loneliness of women without Christian husbands and fathers, not to mention the misery of those who succumb to various pressures and marry unbelievers, compel us to work hard to redress this imbalance.

Though he taught women and included them among his band of followers, Jesus devoted most of his time to the training of the Twelve (and perhaps also of the Seventy), who were, of course, all men. We may say that contemporary social customs necessitated such a move, except that Jesus broke so many conventions, and demonstrated such tender care for women, that he cannot be accused of simply bowing to prevailing mores. Likewise, Paul, who highly esteemed a number of women for their contribution to the Lord's work, chose men to be his most intimate companions.

Paul's instructions for church leaders (surely for elders, and probably also for deacons) assume male leadership in the churches that he founded. That concept has been vigorously challenged in recent years, and is highly disputed today, but perhaps we should inquire further into possible reasons for such a focus. Setting aside the theological and exegetical questions, there are practical matters to consider as well.

So, it would seem that both biblical precedent and pragmatic considerations point toward investing a significant amount of time and energy in bringing the gospel to men and then training them to be mature Christian leaders in the home, church, and society.

How?

Reaching Chinese men effectively demands a comprehensive review of not only the methods we use, but the very content of our message. "Masculine" elements of the biblical gospel can be highlighted: God as King and Judge; Jesus as a man's man, and an example to all men; valiant men in narrative portions; specific teachings to men; etc. In particular, we need to show how the Word of God speaks to men's concerns, including family and work and their special temptations (such as pride, ambition, autocratic leadership, and lust).

Furthermore, we must be intentional about this, making sure that we make time to evangelize men and then disciple them. This can be done using methods such as men's Bible studies; books translated into Chinese, and mentoring individuals. See the resources section for more information.

LEADERSHIP TRAINING

Virtually everyone agrees that the greatest need among Chinese Christians is for qualified leaders, especially men. The number of professing believers has grown so fast that leadership training has not caught up. As a result, millions of Chinese Christians lack adequate spiritual oversight and care. Heresies and sects have proliferated, while the average churchgoer remains largely uninstructed in the Scriptures and often even ignorant of the basic articles of the faith, much less the general teaching of the Bible about doctrine and life.

Addressing the Problem

Fully cognizant of this dire situation, countless leadership training schools and programs have been developed. As I have said, the Three-Self Patriotic Movement operates over a dozen seminaries and many more Bible institutes and educational programs for lay leaders, while unregistered churches have organized a variety of ways to train pastors and evangelists. Often the participants willingly suffer deprivation of food, comfort, and even sleep in order to gain more knowledge of the Bible.

In recent years, more foreigners have entered the scene, sometimes by invitation, often on their own, with a wide panoply of offerings, such as short-term seminars with foreign lecturers using interpreters; translated materials; radio and Internet courses; and literature of all types. A number of overseas seminaries have either dispatched faculty to China for short-term sessions or welcomed Chinese Christians to study in their schools in Hong Kong, Singapore, the Philippines, and the West. There are also online courses, in English and in Chinese, that can be listened to, or even taken for credit, by anyone with Internet access.

Advantages of formal education programs include maintenance of standards; a well-rounded curriculum; community life; several qualified instructors; and, of course, recognition by churches where graduates want to serve.

Limitations

All of these efforts spring from a sincere desire to equip leaders for the Chinese church. Some are more effective than others, of course. More and more, sophisticated urban house churches want their pastors to have an earned theological degree from a foreign-based theological seminary (the TSPM schools not being an option for them). Of course, the academic quality of these degrees is generally quite high, and the holder of an M.Div. returns to his church with greatly increased status.

On the other hand, academic theological education, especially residential schooling, suffers from well-known limitations: As we saw earlier, it takes one away from his church and often from family as well, for several years. The returning scholar has often lost contact with the people whom he once knew well, both because of his absence and by reason of the nature of his education, which is highly academic and Western. Chinese-language seminaries try to overcome the cultural gap, but they, too, focus on academics, despite attempts to inculcate spiritual life and provide practical training. The hard fact is that schools are academic institutions, and they must maintain standards that emphasize knowledge that can be measured by tests and papers, rather than spiritual maturity, Christian character, or an ability to "deliver" the truth effectively. Such programs are also quite expensive.

A New Leadership Training Course

As an example of a different way to train leaders, allow me to briefly outline a pilot program recently begun at China Institute. Without claiming to have produced something novel or better, but hoping to make a small contribution, we have launched a Leadership Training Course that tries to avoid some of the problems noted above. Starting in 2012 with a few students and intended to last three years, the course is based on a careful reading of the Scriptures, using the New International Version Study Bible in Chinese. Students read the Bible according to a plan that alternates between the Old and New Testaments; look up cross references; study the notes at the bottom of the page; and memorize a few verses each week.

Their homework consists of selecting two verses each day, one teaching a basic doctrine, the other relating to the Christian life, and copying them into a growing file that becomes their own theology-and-life sourcebook. They are supposed to share what they have learned with at least one person each week, converse regularly with a spiritual partner and with a mentor, and participate in small group discussions. Always, the emphasis is upon union with Christ, character, community, and growing competence in leading small groups and home meetings, and discipling individuals. They will also read books on church history and study one or more of the classic summaries of the Christian faith (such as the Westminster Confession). Since the greatest need is for mature men, we have decided to limit the course to brothers in Christ.

We have begun to see both the promise and the problems of such an approach. It seems that the hardest thing is for these busy men to develop the habit of daily Bible reading, study, and recording of their thoughts. Sharing what they have learned with others each week has also not come easily for some of them. We are still experimenting with this, but I hope that the mere mention of an alternative approach—and there are many more available—will stimulate your thinking.[39]

MENTORING AND COACHING

Not long ago, I sat next to a Chinese brother who has crisscrossed China for many years, talking with hundreds of house church leaders. When I asked, "What should foreign Christians pray for concerning the Chinese church?" he replied, "Our greatest need is for mentors for leaders."

"Why is that?" I queried.

---

39 A much more comprehensive treatment of alternative ways to train leaders by Dr. Malcolm Webber can be found at www.leadersource.org.

"Because they can't learn from each other. They are too proud, too afraid of losing face, to open up to each other. More than once, I have attended training sessions with them, and have noticed that they don't talk to each other; they rely on the foreign instructor."

Two Americans who have visited China dozens of times nodded in agreement. It seems that there is little precedent for a Chinese leader of any sort to admit any need or to ask for advice from his peers, much less his subordinates.

Mentoring, Coaching, and Counseling

We all know what teaching—or lecturing—looks like: An "expert" stands up front and talks to a group of students. For decades now, Chinese church leaders have availed themselves of such instruction. The result? "They come out proud of their knowledge, but unable to apply it to daily life—their marriage, family, or church. It's especially bad when they receive advanced theological education; it only seems to make them more arrogant," said the man I quoted earlier. Others have confirmed this assessment also.

What, then, is mentoring? It differs from counseling, which assumes that you have a problem and another person has the wisdom and skill to help you solve it. Nor is it the same as coaching, which involves occasional discussions, perhaps over the telephone, with a skilled advisor, who guides you through the decision-making process and assists you in setting goals and devising realistic means of achieving them. Mentoring requires multiple face-to-face meetings with a person who is older, more experienced, or skilled in the areas in which you want to grow. At its core, mentoring is a life-on-life relationship that reproduces what the mentor has acquired over the years in the life of a younger, or less experienced, "disciple."

Mentoring takes place in normal family settings, perhaps in a master-apprentice arrangement, and in a variety of contexts. Sadly, it is often lacking in churches and Christian organizations. We are good at presenting information to people, sometimes even at helping them solve problems, but we often fail to share our lives with them in a way that effects lasting change. Jesus, of course, was the supreme Mentor, whose example we should all strive to emulate. Books like The Master Plan of Evangelism by Robert Coleman have shown how he made disciples over time.

Varieties of Mentoring

Of course, there is no one-size-fits-all pattern of mentoring. We are all influenced by a variety of people and media, and can benefit from the experience and wisdom of others in many ways. The best way to mentor others is to spend time with them in a number of different contexts over a period of months or years. There is just no substitute for personal contact, both one-on-one and in small groups. Once a relationship has been established, however, mentoring can be carried out by less frequent, even long-distance communication, as long as the older person shares his heart transparently with the younger one. Such a process can develop into coaching, in which you are led to manage your life and work more effectively, and it will often include counseling, when you need a listening ear, a sympathetic heart, and godly advice.

We can even be mentored by books! How many of us have imbibed precious lessons and constructed models to follow from reading the stories of people whom we admire? I know I have. Many of my mentors are people who lived long ago and far away. In other words, mentoring takes place in multiple ways; the key thing is for us to be intentional about helping others to reach their potential.

COUNSELING

With Chinese families falling apart, hundreds of millions of people migrating to cities and others left behind to carry the burden in the countryside, endemic official corruption and cutthroat competition, and other distressing social changes overtaking them at dizzying speed, millions of Chinese are anxious, angry, depressed, and confused. They desperately need someone to listen to them, show love to them, and point them towards God, who alone can infuse love, joy, and peace into their troubled hearts.

Within the church also exist millions of unhappy believers whose lives are marked by tension, worry, broken relationships, and insufficient aware-ness of God's power and his gracious presence. Everybody is so busy that few have time really to understand. Pastors and other leaders struggle to keep up with the rapid influx of new adherents, much less to slow down and care for those who are hurting. Inadequate teaching on communica-tion, conflict resolution, and Christian community life leaves Christians estranged from each other and from God, with nowhere to turn for help. Lack of skilled counselors means that most must suffer silently and alone.

This situation does not have to go unchecked, however. God has placed within the Body of Christ sufficient resources to minister to the needs of each member. His Spirit indwells every believer. If we look to him, we can daily experience his unconditional love for us. His promises to forgive, to guide, and to provide can lift our eyes away from ourselves and our surroundings to his throne of grace and the inexhaustible rivers of his mercy and might, available to those who put their trust daily in Christ. Regular and systematic exposure to the Scriptures—both through private reading and through public reading and exposition—can re-direct our eyes to our heavenly Father, the God of all comfort, who comforts us in all our affliction (2 Cor 1:4).

Individual believers can help each other as they walk the narrow path of faith in a dark and dangerous world. Though we ourselves are beset with manifold weaknesses and sins, we can remind our friends that there is a God who rules the universe with justice and with love, and who is near to the brokenhearted when they cry out to him (Ps 34:18; 145:18). Strengthened by his promises, we can speak words of faith and hope to those who are plagued by doubt and even despair. Each Christian can be used by God to "comfort the fainthearted [and] uphold the weak" (1 Thess 5:14). As we humbly and patiently "bear one another's burdens," we can restore those who have gone astray (Gal 6:1–2). If our own minds have been enlightened by the Bible, we shall have heavenly wisdom to guide others who are perplexed (Jas 3:17; 2 Tim 3:16).

Effective Counselors

In this sense, each Christian is "competent to counsel"[40] other believers, as we rely on the Holy Spirit to guide us in applying relevant portions of the Word of God to those in need of encouragement and enlightenment. I shall call this "informal" counseling.

Requirements for effective informal counseling include a sound knowledge of the Bible, a close walk with the Lord, humility, personal integrity, wisdom from God, faith that God can change people, persistent prayer, and great patience.[41] Effective counselors will be aware of their own sins, at peace with others, and convinced of God's love towards them. They will listen long and hard before they speak words of advice, much less words of rebuke.[42] Realizing that we are all members of the Body of Christ and need each other, they will do their best to incorporate those whom they counsel into fellowship with other believers; they will not try to "save" them or be their only source of emotional support. In fact, they

---

40   The title of an influential and controversial book by Jay Adams.
41   See Jas 3:17–18.
42   See Jas 1:19.

will resolutely resist the temptation to be "Christ" to anyone; like John the Baptist, they will do their best to point people to the only one who can save us and satisfy the longing of our hearts.

God has also placed into the church some people who are especially gifted at counseling. Perhaps Paul refers to them when he speaks of those who "encourage" ("exhort" in the NKJV) in Romans 12:8. While some can expound the Scriptures in a general way to a group of people (and everything I said about expository evangelistic preaching applies to the regular feeding of God's flock with the explanation of the Scriptures), gifted counselors know how to apply the Bible to particular people and their unique problems. They communicate love and acceptance, without condoning sin or feeding self-pity. Speaking the truth in love, they enable fellow Christians to grow up into maturity in Christ.[43] God seems to give them unusual insight into the hearts and minds of those who are trapped in sorrow or sin, and to guide them in saying just the right word to bring light and liberty.

These individuals need to be trained, equipped, and empowered to exercise their gift in the church and in the world. Though pastoral counseling has not yet developed in mainland China, the Chinese churches in Taiwan, Hong, Kong, Singapore, and the West have gained a great deal from the various Christian counseling movements that have sprung up, especially in North America, in the past fifty years. Some good books have been translated; others have been penned in their own language by Chinese authors. Opportunities for receiving training include full-time academic programs in seminaries, part-time distance-learning courses, and specific conferences and workshops. I personally have benefitted from all sorts of these, in addition to reading.

For believers, it seems to me that non-Christian psychology-based programs, while opening doors to secular employment, hold the risk of your receiving training that is very much at odds with the Bible and is therefore of little real use in helping people. If one does choose to get a secular counseling degree, it should be augmented with a great deal of exposure to biblical counseling principles through reading, courses, and seminars.

A Few Key Points

In my experience, there are a few central principles and practices that have proven to be extremely effective. I offer them only as examples of the many ways in which God's Word equips believers to help others with their problems.

---

43   See Eph 4:15.

The Speck and the Beam (Matt 7:1–5)

When I am angry with someone, I ask God to show me the beam in my eye (Matt 7:1–3). That is, I assume that my very strong reaction of outrage may arise from a similar sin in my own life that I am not seeing at the time. When I pray this prayer, I request that God would show me how I am violating his will in a way that is like what the person with whom I am angry is doing. Sometimes this may not be obvious. Perhaps I don't lose my temper and say hateful things when I am angry, as he (or she) does. But I probably find that, like him, I am failing to "speak the truth in love" and to speak in order to edify others (Eph 4:28). In that way I am equally guilty.

Then I pray for God's perspective on my sin. That is, I seek to feel the "beam-ness" of what I may have thought was a "speck" in my eye, to feel the seriousness of it, so that I do not deceive myself into thinking that, even though I may be guilty of a similar offence, his is much worse than mine. In fact, I need to realize that my fault is equally great, and that Jesus had to die for me so that I would not be plunged into hell.

As John and Paula Sandford point out in The Transformation of the Inner man, the promise that things will go well with us if we honor our parents is matched by the corollary that if we have encountered a serious problem, it may be connected with our not honoring our parents in some way (Eph 6:1–3). Even the best parents are imperfect, and will fail to love their children as they ought. All children, therefore, are, to some degree at least, angry, perhaps even outraged, by their parents' failures. This initial reaction comes from our being made in the image of God, but it all too soon degenerates into resentment, self-pity, pride, and other sins.

When we grow up, God often puts people and situations into our lives that evoke intense negative feelings. When that happens, we should ask, "Does this person remind me of my mother, my father, or both?" I find that it is almost always one of these three possibilities! Then we can search our hearts to see whether we have forgiven our parents (or other significant people in our past). We probably have not. After that come repentance for our resentment, and a heartfelt cry for forgiveness. We are also likely, to some degree, not respecting our parents for what they have done, so that needs to be confessed, too. Then there is the fact that we probably resemble them, so maybe we are to some degree guilty of a fault similar to theirs; that, too, needs repentance. Or perhaps I cherish an idol in my heart, which the person to whom I am reacting so strongly (in fear, anger, or envy) is challenging my possession of that idol. I need to confess and renounce my idolatry before I will be able to relate calmly and kindly to the other. When I have gone through these steps, I find that my anger dissipates and that God has begun to liberate me from ancient, deep-seated fears, resentment, and self-enslaving inner vows ("I'll never trust anyone again!").

We could use the Bible to help people in many other situations, such as worry (Phil 4:6–7), fear (Ps 27:1), guilt (Rom 8:1; 1 John 1:9–2:2), doubt (James 1:5–8; Rom. 4:19–22), envy (James 3:14–16; 4:1–5), and lust (Matt 5:28) The core of what I am saying is that the Scriptures really are adequate to enable us to bring light, liberty, and life to people who really want to be delivered from their sins.

CHAPTER ELEVEN
PARTICIPATION IN THE
BODY OF CHRIST

PARTNERING WITH CHINESE CHRISTIANS

I shall never forget a conversation I had with the late David Adeney, one of the most widely-respected and loved missionaries among the Chinese. He was about 75 at the time, but still full of zeal and energy.

"What is your burden these days" I asked.

"To mobilize the Chinese church," he replied immediately. "They are the ones who will evangelize China."

Indeed, he had spent much of his life doing that very thing. He trained Chinese student leaders in Asia; founded Discipleship Training Centre in Singapore to equip Asian Christians; and taught at a Chinese seminary in Hong Kong. After "retiring" to the United States, this intrepid Englishman traveled incessantly, speaking at Chinese churches and conferences and counseling young Chinese believers who sensed God's leading to serve their people. His impact was immense, and lasting.

A Potent Force

There are thousands of Chinese churches outside of Mainland China—in Hong Kong, Taiwan, Singapore, South East Asia, Australasia, Europe, North and South America, even Africa and the Middle East. Within China itself, hundreds of thousands of congregations, some tiny, some huge, burn with a desire to see their countrymen come to know God. Often at great personal cost, they are bearing witness to Christ in countless ways, and their labors are effective, as phenomenal church growth testifies.

Do They Need Us?

"Well, then," some are saying, "Let's just leave the task of sharing God's Word among the Chinese to the Chinese church itself. They don't need us." Wrong! For a variety of reasons, Chinese believers welcome our participation in their mission to glorify God among their own people and even among the nations.

For one thing, though numerous, Chinese believers are relatively rare. Though in some places, like Wenzhou, as much as one-tenth the population may profess faith in Christ, in other areas they are a tiny minority. You can visit countless villages in China without a gospel witness; walk for blocks in any of China's mega-cities without encountering a believer; enter dozens of towns in Taiwan of over 40,000 without a single church. Though the gospel came to Taiwan more than one hundred years ago, and about 2,000 churches dot the island, active Christians account for no more than 1% of the total population of more than 23 million.

In Chinese churches generally, cultural and historical factors have created a gap between ideal and practice, theory and conduct, the Word and life in the world. Certain characteristic traits among Chinese, such as the desire for "face," make it hard for them to resolve conflicts or build genuine fellowship based on honest admission of weakness and need. We could go on, but the fact is that the whole church around the world, being the Body of Christ, needs every member. We need them (a major topic in itself!), and they need us.

Equipping Chinese Christians: An Urgent Crisis

Everyone agrees that the greatest need among Chinese churches around the world is for capable leaders. Whether in Taiwan, North America, Europe, or China itself, there is a dearth of pastors, elders, and teachers who can feed God's flock with the Word of God. In China itself, Christians lack solid Bible teaching, and are thus vulnerable to sects, heresies, and cults. Trained leaders are woefully few.

I remember vividly meeting a young man at a conference in Macau in 2006. He was the Youth Pastor for his church in northern China.

"How many kids in your youth group?" I inquired.

"Six thousand," he replied.

As a result of lack of teaching and shepherding, many Chinese believers have little grounding in the Scriptures with which to guide their life at home, at work, and in society. They are prey to cults, sects, and heresies, and may not have the knowledge to resist worldly values and Satan's wiles. I personally know of several Chinese churches in the United States who are looking for qualified pastors, and there are many others.

Responding to the Crisis

Over the past few decades, dozens—perhaps hundreds—of different ministries have sought to remedy this lack with solid biblical education for Chinese believers, and especially present or potential leaders. Some of these efforts have paid rich dividends. Others have been less effective, either because they were too theoretical or because they did not apply the Scriptures to the Chinese situation.

How Can We Help?

When my wife and I were new missionaries in Taiwan, one of the experienced workers said, "The most important thing you can do is to make friends with your pastor and his wife." There is probably a Chinese church in your town, perhaps even your neighborhood. Call the pastor and invite him and his wife out to lunch, or home to dinner. Just say that you would like to know how they and their church are doing, so that you might pray for them. Listening attentively to these dedicated, hard-working, and probably lonely servants of God will not only bless you, but encourage those who are on the front lines. That will lead to prayer and perhaps action that they suggest.

Ask them, and our Chinese brothers and sisters will themselves tell you what you can do to strengthen their hands. Perhaps they need training, or recommendations of good books, or a place to take a much-needed vacation, or English teachers for a summer outreach project. Let them tell you, but ask!

TAIWAN'S STRATEGIC ROLE

Now is the time to re-direct the attention of Christians to the importance of Taiwan and its people. Not only does this island have a desperate need for the gospel, but it also plays a strategic, even vital, role in the building of God's church in China.

The Need

Sadly, most Western Christians, and even many Chinese, have neglected Taiwan in recent years. Since the opening of China and the realization that God has been doing a remarkable work there, most foreign Christians have focused on that land. Some mission agencies in Taiwan have closed down operations and switched their personnel to the Mainland. Even overseas Chinese believers have given up on Taiwan and have concentrated upon evangelism and house church leadership training in China.

Some missions strategists consider Taiwan to be sufficiently "reached," or even adequately evangelized, compared with the hundreds of millions of those in China who have not yet heard the gospel. They point to the existence of almost 2,000 churches, 200,000 adherents, seminaries, publishing houses, bookstores, television broadcasting, and other signs of vital Christianity on the island. But they seem not to notice that though "reached," Taiwan is not yet evangelized. More than 23 million people live on Taiwan. As I said, less than 2% of them are active Christians. In fact, most of those living in Taiwan have never, ever, heard even a simple presentation of the gospel. That's a population greater than Alabama, Arizona, Georgia, and Iowa combined! They do not know Christ; they have little way of hearing about him.

Political Crisis

The Chinese word for "crisis" combines two characters, one meaning "danger" and the other "opportunity."

With more than 1,200 missiles targeted on Taiwan, and many other military and economic weapons at hand, China could easily subdue the island. Despite political freedom—indeed, partly because of it—Taiwan faces almost unprecedented challenges today. The Communist and Nationalist Parties fought a bitter civil war after Japan surrendered at the end of World War II. After their defeat, the Nationalists retreated to Taiwan, where they ruled until Chen Shui-bian's DPP won the presidency in 2000. Since then, the opposing parties have been locked in an increasingly vicious struggle for power. The spiral of mutual mistrust and hatred deepened after his re-election by a razor-thin margin in 2004. Chen's administration was marked by economic slowdown, intensive ethnic strife (much of it fomented by Chen and his supporters), legislative gridlock, volatile relations with China, estrangement with the U.S., and ever-increasing scandal. Chen and his wife and several members of his family and ranking staff were convicted of corruption. After the Nationalist (KMT) party returned to power in 2008, relations with the People's Republic of China warmed, but the threat still remains, and the fundamental problem of Taiwan's de facto independence is intolerable to China's rulers.

Social Crisis

Taiwan's people are unhappy. You will not be surprised to learn that Taiwan's millions, crowded into burgeoning cities, suffer all the ills of a life without God. Though materially well off, they are spiritually dead; emotionally starved; mentally confused; harried by the cares of life; broken-hearted by broken marriages. Their frenetic search for wealth has largely succeeded, but at the cost of the family, the soul, and personal peace. The crime rate, divorce rate, and use of drugs alarm everyone. Homosexual practice spreads; sexual immorality is commonplace, as are abortions. Society seems to be coming unraveled. Everywhere is a sense of insecurity and fear, even as people trample the temple courts in a desperate search for "life."

Religious Crisis

Most of Taiwan's people are enslaved to worthless idols. Buddhism, Taoism, and popular Chinese religion are flourishing, using methods borrowed from the Christians (seminaries, small groups, literature, music, evangelism, charitable work), enjoying strong government support, commanding respect and allegiance in all sectors of society, and building on their ancient roots in the soil of Chinese culture. Surveys have shown that more than 90% of this highly-educated populace believe in the gods of their ancestors.

On special days, you can see them burning paper money to the spirits of the dead and offering food on altars to various "gods" at home, on the street, and in richly-ornamented temples. Children are fed a steady diet of myths from these religions each day in school; television news reports feature national leaders paying homage; and the large Buddhist relief organization makes headlines each time disaster strikes. For a graphic description of the powerful hold of traditional religions on the population of Taiwan, read Jennifer Su's Dead Women Walking.

The Christian church constitutes a tiny minority. With some exceptions, Christian churches struggle to survive, much less to grow, while millions of souls remain outside their doors in darkness. Some say that Christians are too busy making money. Others point to a "gospel" that lacks life-changing power: "Believe in Jesus, and it will go well with you—in this life!" is the common theme. Evangelical publishing houses print translations of books from the West containing liberal theology. Prominent seminary teachers and preachers avoid saying that the Bible is inerrant, and are silent about the Cross of Christ or the radical demands of discipleship. The market is not good, so publishers think that they have to print what appeals to the popular taste, rather than solid biblical teaching.

Surely, this under-evangelized island deserves our prayers.

Taiwan is Open

On the other hand, even if your goal is to reach China's millions, Taiwan is an ideal place to start. Unlike mainland China, Taiwan enjoys complete freedom of religion. Though there may be problems with Christianity in Taiwan, there are many who are doing much good. Thousands of excellent books are available in Taiwan for their growth in Christian understanding. Some seminaries provide excellent training for future pastors and current church leaders. Dozens of mature churches offer fellowship, teaching, and constant reminders of the imperative of evangelism.

Evangelism and Training

Perhaps most valuable of all is the witness and teaching of mature believers from Taiwan who travel to China to train church leaders, carry on evangelism, or serve as salt and light in various professions and business. Since Taiwan's relations with China improved markedly after the election of 2008, contacts between Taiwan and the Mainland are already expanding rapidly. More than a million Taiwanese already live in China; now traffic will flow in both directions. Hundreds of thousands of tourists from the mainland now crowd Taiwan's most popular locations. With these increasingly close ties to mainland China, Taiwan can serve as a base for helping believers who already speak Mandarin to reach out to their kinsmen across the narrow straits.

Taiwan's Christians have grappled for fifty years with the complex challenges posed by modernization, urbanization and prosperity—just the issues perplexing many believers in China today. They come mostly from the middle and upper-middle classes. Highly educated, sophisticated, and mobile, they travel the globe for business, education, and fun. They are internationally-minded, savvy, and poised to make a difference. Christian scholars in Taiwan have done solid work in theology and the relationship of the gospel to Chinese culture.

A recent survey discovered—surprise!—that trainers from Taiwan are usually more attuned to the real needs of China's believers than the Westerners who seek to build leaders there. They know the language, understand the culture, and build long-range relationships. From years of observation and friendship, they have discovered what works best in China. In other words, they don't go in with a "one-size-fits-all" curriculum taught in a foreign language by strangers from an alien background.

The church in Taiwan cares greatly about their brothers and sisters and unsaved countrymen in China. They conduct a wide range of activities in order to share with them the love and truth of God in Christ. Radio and television broadcasts are taped in Taipei. Literature for both believers and non-believers pours off the presses in Taiwan. Far East Broadcasting Company has an office in Taipei, where eight hours of programs are produced daily, half of them evangelistic. Hundreds of letters come back monthly asking for counsel or answers to questions about the faith. These broadcasts reach all of China, including Tibet, in Mandarin and several dialects or minority languages.

Thousands of Taiwanese Christians live in China and consciously seek to set a Christian example and share the truth of the gospel each day. Others visit or even live in China for tourism, business, and education. Depending upon the quality of their life and witness, they can make a significant impact. Many churches have been planted in major Chinese cities by Christians from Taiwan.

Knowing that the greatest need in China's church is for biblical literacy and accurate understanding of the Christian faith, Taiwan's church engages in innumerable efforts to train leaders. Pastors and elders are sent out by many—perhaps most—churches to house churches in China to train their counterparts in week-long intensive classes. Some of them have been instrumental in bringing relational healing and reconciliation to estranged church leaders and their wives. Seminary professors teach advanced courses, some of them for degrees. Far East Broadcasting Company produces mid-level biblical instruction, leading to a certificate, to thousands of Christians with pastoral responsibility in China's house churches. House church leaders are asking seminaries in Taiwan to offer short courses for them to attend in Taiwan.

Exchange

The new development is actual formal exchange. A meeting was recently held at which representatives from the leading official church seminaries in China met with their Taiwan counterparts for a three-day conference on cross-strait cooperation in theological education. Since many from the Chinese side are evangelicals, there is tremendous potential for further cooperation. This is a truly astounding advance, with amazing potential. Taiwan also recently hosted a conference of involving Chinese biblical scholars from all over the world, including China.

The Challenge: Help Wanted

Well, then, should we in the West just let our brothers from Taiwan carry the ball? Of course not! There's a lot we can do to help. First of all, we should pray regularly for Christians in Taiwan and for the missionaries who seek to encourage them. They are a tiny minority in a sea of pagans. Often what they need most is a listening ear and sincere prayers, for they face tremendous challenges not only in fast-paced and idolatrous Taiwan, but also on the mainland.

Second, we can support those organizations that serve Christ in Taiwan, such as OMF International, TEAM, SEND, the Conservative Baptists, the Southern Baptists, the Navigators, YWAM, Awana, China Ministries International, China Evangelical Seminary, Campus Evangelical Fellowship, and many more.

Third, opportunities for serving in Taiwan abound. Without fear of government surveillance or harming local believers, foreigners may live openly as followers of Christ and participate in church life with local Christians. Taiwan is also a great place to learn Chinese. Several language schools offer excellent instruction, even in Christian terminology, unavailable in China. English teaching, business and other open doors beckon those with faith and love. Anything we do here to strengthen the hands of believers in Taiwan, or to add to their number by personal evangelism, will have an effect on the growth of the church in China, sometimes almost immediately.

Taiwan's time may be limited. Who knows how long this situation will last? China's leaders, perched atop a very fragile and shifting mountain of power, could use any of several pretexts to "re-unite" Taiwan with the motherland. We don't know what will become of religious freedom then.

ENGLISH-SPEAKING CHURCHES

For a number of reasons, many Chinese attend English-speaking churches. These may be English-language congregations connected to a Chinese church, or churches of native English speakers led by Westerners. For some ethnic Chinese who are brought up in English-speaking countries, English is their native tongue. Others, however, prefer to worship with non-Chinese even though they may not be fully at home in English. Many students and scholars who have come to the West to study want to take advantage of every opportunity to hear and practice English. Others, having left home for a new culture, want to identify as much as possible with that culture. Still others simply do not want to associate with fellow Chinese very much while they are overseas.

Chinese churches are generally very friendly and welcoming, but newcomers often feel pressure either to believe in Jesus quickly or, if baptized, to spend a lot of time in ministry within the church. The message usually focuses on what we must do for God, rather than what he has done for us, whereas it seems that in Western churches, the emphasis more often falls upon God's grace, and newcomers do not sense much pressure to accept the gospel or to serve the church. Also, the perception that Christianity is a "Western" religion still persists, leading to the idea that one should learn about this faith in English, not Chinese.

When ethnic Chinese return from the West, they often find adjustment to a Chinese-language congregation difficult. Perhaps they only know how to "do" Christianity in English. Often, they appreciate the strengths of English-speaking churches that I mentioned above. Or maybe they want to avoid the legalism and pressure to perform typical of Chinese-speaking congregations. Whatever their reasons, English-language churches in Asia, such as the one that two of our colleagues serve in Taipei, fill an important need.

Making the Most of this Situation

Though we may not fully approve of the various motives that bring ethnic Chinese to Western-led churches, we can thank God for this opportunity to reach people who might not otherwise hear the gospel.

For example, three Chinese undergraduates were recently baptized in our American church. They are all members of the Chinese Christian Fellowship (CCF) at the University of Virginia (which my wife and I advise) and had attended the church over the past couple of years. They appreciated the rich music and liturgy and solid biblical teaching of our church. Several of our elders and pastors have spoken frequently at their fellowship's meetings and annual retreats. My wife and I had regular contact with the students, and they have taken courses at the university taught by members of our congregation. They have invited their non-Christian friends to church also, and gather together in the foyer after the service—it is like an extra meeting for them. Most CCFers return to Asia for the summer; they take their faith with them and share it with family and friends.

As I said earlier, another group of Chinese, mostly graduate students and married people, gathers for a Sunday school class in Mandarin between services. Your church's ministry to ethnic Chinese will look different from ours, but I have no doubt that each congregation can make a huge impact, as long as we rely on the Holy Spirit to reveal God the Father to those we serve through Jesus Christ. All churches, including ours, have many faults and failings. As we ask God to work in and through us despite our sins and limitations, and as we employ a variety of approaches, he can demonstrate his truth, beauty, and goodness to people who desperately need the blessings that only God can bestow.

CHAPTER TWELVE
PERFORMANCE OF GOOD WORKS

LISTENING
A Nagging Question

When I first went to Asia, I longed to share with Chinese "the unsearchable riches of Christ." I still do. That's why I have preached, taught, and written so much! Indeed, I spent the first fifteen years or so of my ministry trying to communicate the gospel as clearly as possible, and that is still my aim. For the past twenty years or so, however, a slow realization has been dawning upon me, and has come to the forefront in my approach to missions. What if I haven't really understood the people to whom I have been speaking? What if I am answering questions they are not asking? Am I speaking to their hearts? To their deepest beliefs and convictions? Do I know their fears, their hopes, their dreams? When I speak and write, do I couch my words in terms they can really understand? Have I adapted the form (not the content!) of my message to their unique culture, in such a way as to bring real conviction of sin, profound faith in God, and clear awareness of the Lord's will?

Another Way? The Importance of Listening

Slowly, I am beginning to see another way to reach Chinese, both Christian and pre-Christians, with God's love and truth: Listening. James tells us to be "Swift to hear, slow to speak" (James 1:19). In Proverbs we read, "He who answers a matter before he hears it, it is folly and shame to him" (18:13), and describes a fool as one who "has no delight in understanding, but in expressing his own heart" (18:2). Job's would-be counselors first sat with him in the dust for a whole week, wordless—and even then their pre-conceived ideas prevented them from effective ministry! Jesus spent thirty years leaning Jewish culture from the inside, and only then began to preach. And he was the sinless Son of God.

About thirty-five years ago, at the beginning of my ministry, I read a little book called The Awesome Power of the Listening Ear. It made a profound impact on me at the time, and its title still rings in my ears. The author basically said that people want to be heard, and understood. Only then will they listen to us. And only then will we know what to say, and how. Recently, a very good Chinese friend finally got up the courage to say to me: "You Americans come to us saying, 'Let us help you solve your problems.' But you don't even know what our problems are! You don't take time to understand us."

Listening to the Chinese

For those of us wanting to reach Chinese, listening must come first. Listening begins with diligent language study. Even then, linguists tell us that our priorities are learning to (1) listen; (2) speak; (3) read; and (4) write. All too often, we are eager only to acquire the ability to speak. As we continue language acquisition, we must also dig deeply into the culture. For the Chinese, this means absorbing their long history. Chinese culture abounds in complexity, depth, and scope, and there are a variety of ways to become slightly familiar with some aspects of it: watching Chinese movies; reading Chinese literature; listening to Chinese music; visiting Greater China; viewing Chinese art; scouring the Web; attending a Chinese church. Above all, we can get to know a few Chinese well, simply by asking questions and listening to their responses. We need first and foremost to listen to God each day. Only as we "receive with meekness the implanted word" shall we be able to become "doers of the word" and bridle our tongues enough really to listen to others (Jas 1:21–22, 26).

TEACHING ENGLISH

Over the past several decades, teaching English has proven to be one of the best ways to reach Chinese with the gospel, not only in China and Taiwan, but in the West. English is the international language, with no replacement in sight for the foreseeable future. Businesspeople, airline pilots, scientists, tourists, scholars—all use English in international settings. Within China, the number of people who are studying English or who are already able to read or speak it to some degree almost equals the population of the United States! Ability in English opens doors to further education, better jobs, travel abroad, and essential knowledge. Perhaps most of all, English is a required subject for the college entrance exam. That is why hundreds of millions of Chinese people do all they can to acquire this difficult language.

Difficulties

On the other hand, a recent blog states that "Behind the eye-catching number that 300m people either are learning or have learned English in China is a depressing reality. Classes are extremely poor, the teachers themselves not fluent in English. Rote memorization is the norm."[44] The same is true in Taiwan, I believe. Let's face it: English grammar is complicated; English pronunciation and spelling are a huge mess; the wide use of idioms and slang makes ordinary conversation far different from what they learn in textbooks. And, above all, contact with native English speakers is hard to come by. These are some of the reasons why teaching English, in Asia or elsewhere, presents such a marvelous opportunity to demonstrate God's love and live out his truth.

Opportunities

Besides the massive demand, other features of teaching English make it very useful. The teacher builds a relationship with students that lasts at least a few months, and sometimes longer. Students see the teacher in a variety of settings, allowing them to observe him closely. Class discussions and homework, including journals, provide chances to explore questions of meaning, such as "What do you think success is?" "What is the main thing in life?" Cultural holidays, such as Thanksgiving, Christmas, and Easter, require some explanation. Outside of class, teachers are available for individual relationships, which often become open and candid, granting even more platforms for the explanation of Christian truth. English teachers also have a recognized and respected role in society, one that is entirely legal, so they don't have to try to hide anything. They are performing a needed service that is highly appreciated. Above all, their loving conduct wins credibility and friends.

Avenues to English Teaching in China and Taiwan

Christian organizations offer many openings for teachers of English and other subjects in China. They provide some training, orientation, and field support. Frequently, teachers are placed in a team, so they can encourage each other. These organizations generally have very good relations with the school and the government. One disadvantage of being placed by a Christian organization is that you must raise your own support. In a crumbling economy, that could be a huge obstacle. Another possible danger within China is that teachers are scrutinized very carefully for any breach of contract regarding sharing their faith. ELIC is one of the more well-recognized agencies, but there are many others that can be found online.

---

44   R.L.G., "English in China: How many English learners in China?," *The Economist*, September 1, 2011, http://www.economist.com/blogs/ johnson/2011/09/english-china.

Secular companies also find jobs for teachers. Some of them also provide orientation, training, and on-field support. The advantage of going with them is that you don't have to raise your own support; you can be financially independent even in a recession. Individuals can find their own position online or through contacts as well. This is a bit risky, since there is no network of experienced and connected people to protect these individuals from possible misunderstandings or failure by the school to keep their part of the bargain. Unless, that is, the contacts are completely reliable.

Preparing to Teach

However you go, you need to prepare. Read about Chinese history, culture and society. I suggest China: Ancient Culture, Modern Society to begin with, which I wrote as an introduction to China for all who are interested, but specifically for those who desire to serve among the Chinese. Gather a group of prayer supporters who will uphold you in what will be a very challenging, though rewarding, endeavor. Develop habits of drawing close to God in the Word and prayer daily. Get into very good physical condition. Take a course on teaching English as a second language. Begin tutoring someone now. Acquiring ability in Mandarin, either here or there, will be a great asset. Ask God to guide you, provide for you, and prosper your efforts to share his love with people in very great need. Begin to thank him for what he will do in and through you!

Aware of the Great Commission and of the 1.2 billion+ Chinese who don't know Christ, I am asking God to raise up 1,000 Christian men to go to China and 100 to Taiwan as English teachers. Will you join me in that prayer? "Pray the Lord of the harvest to send out laborers into his harvest" (Matt 9:38).

"BUSINESS BY THE BOOK"

For several decades, Christians have realized that doing business in China, or with Chinese, can open doors for the spread of the saving message of God's love in Christ. Sometimes this is called "business as mission," but this term would seem to raise some questions. Just why are you engaging in commercial activity? Just to make converts? Surely there must be some other way of thinking about and defining why Christians would want to do business in China or with Chinese people.

Larry Burkett wrote Business by the Book to help Christian business people to do their work in a way that glorifies God and benefits everyone, including shareholders, employees, and customers. The "Book," of course, is the Bible, which contains a great deal of material about how we can conduct ourselves in the marketplace in such a way that biblical principles are honored, and in the conviction that God's Word would not lead us astray or into bankruptcy. Without at all trying to be comprehensive, let us look quickly at just a few of these general guidelines.

First and foremost, of course, Christians should adhere to strict standards of honesty and integrity in all dealings with others. That means keeping contracts and even verbal commitments; factual, true, and accurate advertising; paying all taxes; taking and giving no bribes; offering the products and services that we promise, at the price and time we stated; and not substituting inferior materials or sloppy performance that deviate from the original agreement.

Since Christians are commanded to love others as we love ourselves, all our policies and procedures must be governed by love. Employees are not machines to be used, or slaves to be exploited, but they are people created in the image of God who deserve our respect and care. Even if the owner or boss is a workaholic who doesn't mind ruining his health and family, he should not impose the same standards on those who work for him. At least one full day should be set aside for rest, and the overall workweek should not exceed fifty or, at the most, sixty hours. That includes overtime and "occasional" or "unexpected" calls for extra work. A wise manager will factor these into his overall business plan, so that his workers will not be worn out or fuming with resentment when they are called upon to perform well. Working late at night and on weekends puts enormous strain on marriages and keeps parents from giving their children the attention they deserve and need. Healthy, rested, and happy employees come to work motivated to do their best and are less distracted by other concerns than those who have been required to spend too much time at the office or factory.

Working conditions need to be as pleasant as possible, though of course within reasonable limits. Adequate lighting, fresh air, and proper heating and cooling will enable people to work with more efficiency. Factory owners should give their employees living quarters that they themselves wouldn't mind dwelling in, and provide times of rest and vacation that prevent burnout. Wages must be paid on time and in full, at the owner's expense if necessary.

Perhaps most of all, genuine concern shown by the boss will evoke loyalty and dedication from employees. Taking time to ask how your assistant is doing, and even to pray with them, will add a boost to their moral and make coming to work something to which they look forward rather than something they dread. Occasional informal gatherings where bosses and their subordinates than get to know each other will only strengthen the bond between them. There is no need to obliterate the natural and necessary distinction of rank and responsibility, but neither is there any justification for lording it over those who work for you.

As always, setting a good example will encourage employees to do their best. In contrast to worldly men, Christian bosses will not expose their workers to temptation by taking them to night clubs for drinks and flirting with girls whose bodies are for hire; nor will they make improper advances on associates or employees of the other sex. In addition, if owners and bosses deliberately take a lower salary in order to live more simply and pay better wages, they will not only gain affection and loyalty but also point people to the pattern of Christ himself who, "though He was rich, yet for your sakes . . . became poor, so that you through Him might become [spiritually] rich" (2 Cor 8:9). The lavish lifestyle that all too many Christian entrepreneurs display speaks only of power, privilege, and unbridled pleasure, not the self-sacrificial love of Christ.

In other words, if Christians in business behaved according to their beliefs as they are expressed in the Bible, they would be so strikingly different that others would naturally ask, "Why are you behaving like this? What motivates you? Can anyone make a profit doing business this way?" Unless God is foolish, which is patently impossible, obedience to his written revelation cannot bring anything but real and lasting prosperity and the kind of success that really matters—godliness, contentment, and our "daily bread." (Ps 1:3; Josh 1:8). Those who seek to be rich, on the other hand, will run into all sorts of trouble and into "many and foolish and harmful lusts which drown men in destruction and perdition. For the love of money is a root of all kinds of evil, for which some have strayed from the faith in their greediness, and have pierced themselves through with many sorrows" (1 Tim 6:9–10). On the other hand, "godliness with contentment is great gain" (1 Tim 6:6). Jesus flatly promised that if we seek first the kingdom of God and his righteousness, all necessary material needs would be given to us (Matt 6:33).

Those who sense God's leading to serve him in the marketplace can gain access to sectors of Chinese society closed to others who engage in teaching, for example. They can contribute to the general welfare by providing jobs and needed goods and services at a fair price, and by their radically dedicated lives they can demonstrate the love of God in Christ in the midst of a very dark and dishonest society.

MEETING PRACTICAL NEEDS

When Jesus told his disciples that they were the salt and light of the world, he commanded them to let their light shine in such a way that "men will see your good works and glorify your Father in heaven" (Matt 5:15). His disciple, Peter, who heard these instructions, repeated them later in his First Epistle, in which he exhorted his readers to do good works that would testify to God's goodness and greatness (1Pet 2:15; 3:6, 13, 17; 4:19). Paul gave the same teaching (Gal 6:110; Tit 3:1, 8).

The Second Commandment cited by Jesus is, "Love your neighbor as yourself." Christians naturally seek to obey this mandate, for they know God's unconditional love for them in Christ, which is not because of what they have done. When they love others around them, therefore, they are not responding to the other's loveliness, and they expect nothing in return. Simply because they are created in God's image, like everyone else, they seek to honor the inherent worth of each individual and to reflect God's character in their own lives. When they see people in any kind of need, they naturally want to help, just as God constantly provides for all that they need, and as Jesus demonstrated the generosity of the Father by healing, casting out demons, and providing food.

The Lord and his apostles made it clear that we must first meet the needs of fellow believers, such as widows and orphans in the family and in our congregations (1 Tim 5:3–8, 16). Jesus set the example by feeding not everyone, but those who had followed him into the wilderness to hear his teaching (Matt 14:13–21; 15:32–38). In the famous passage about helping others as a way of ministering to him, he distinctly said that we must do good to "these My brothers"—meaning those who belong to the family of faith. We are not to feel burdened to minister to the wants of everyone indiscriminately. On the other hand, Jesus healed all who came or were brought to him, as did Peter and Paul. Furthermore, the parable of the Good Samaritan implies that my "neighbor" is anyone in my presence with a desperate need.

Though China has developed amazingly in the past three decades, enormous problems still plague the nation, and hundreds of millions of ordinary people still do not enjoy the prosperity that many in the cities now consider normal. Medical care comes at a very high price; education costs too much for poor people and may not even be available to urban migrants; children with physical handicaps or parents who cannot afford to care for them are abandoned or placed in orphanages with those whose parents have died or been separated by divorce and cannot provide for them. The elderly lack the safety net once promised to all, and millions of unemployed search in vain for jobs. The blind and the deaf languish in loneliness and hopelessness, while women caught up in the sex trade endure daily degradation and abuse, with no chance of gaining their freedom. Victims of natural disasters struggle to survive long after the catastrophic events destroy their homes and deprive them of a livelihood.

Both Chinese and foreign Christians long to bring tangible evidence of God's love to these people. Their hearts broken by such overwhelming needs, they are trying to find ways to step into these gaps with a helping hand. The efforts of nonprofit organizations are often resisted by the government, partly to keep from losing face. They labor under restrictions in China, which has little tradition of civil society and nonprofit service work. The government is always suspicious that these non-governmental organizations NGOs will somehow try to subvert their power and authority. Despite this official resistance, as well as their severely limited resources, much encouraging work has been done by a variety of groups and individuals. A few examples will show what is possible.

Foreign and local Christians supply funds and personnel for orphanages, or volunteer to assist the overworked staffs of institutions run by the government. They bring life and love and hope to both adults and children, who sometimes then ask why they have come. Though infants need people to hold them and talk to them, perhaps the greatest benefit comes when the staff are encouraged through teaching, training, or just a listening ear. Short-term visits from teams of believers with musical ability have lifted spirits and awakened talents in the children, also.

Children of migrant workers in the cities may not be allowed to attend the local public schools, so programs for their education have been offered by concerned Christians. Even when they are welcomed into the local schools, their needs for tutoring and other assistance are great.

Medical care costs a great deal more than it used to, and may still not be available to people living in the countryside or in poorer areas of large cities and towns. Christians have stepped in to work with existing hospitals and clinics to provide extra help or specialized medical care at no or very low cost. Some foreign medical people have chosen to live in China on a long-term basis; many others make shorter visits to offer their expertise for free.

Some urban churches have organized relief and ongoing ministry to earthquake survivors; others have been blocked by government officials. Going in under the name of a church or Christian organization is not necessary, however; you can still find ways to join, or come alongside, government agencies. The purpose is not to gain some sort of reputation for doing good, but to give to those in desperate need. God will get the glory somehow, even if Christians are not allowed to claim credit for their good deeds.

A number of Christian organizations based in Hong Kong provide both medical help and further training for Chinese medical personnel, especially in less developed areas. Since 1994, MSI Professional Services (msips.org) has dispatched teams of physicians and other medical personnel to Yunnan and Chongqing Municipality for short-term education and treatment, as well as placing permanent workers in communities. They have offered education and treatment in a variety of specialties, including dental, eye, and emergency medicine. For more than twenty years, Jian Hua Foundation (https://www.jhf-china.org) has sent teams of medical people on short-term missions to provide care and training in China's less-developed areas. More recently, they have found opportunities for long-term workers in medical care, orphan care, and community development. Foreign believers can donate to legitimate charities in China through recognized vetting firms, or send their contributions to registered foundations that have been allowed to work in China.

Christians are not the only ones with a heart to serve the poor, uneducated, and sick people in China. Several Buddhist, or Buddhist-led foundations, have been active also. One of these is the Li Ka Shing Foundation, also based in Hong Kong. The founder, Mr. Li, has donated several billion dollars to selected causes in China, where he was born, as well as overseas. Shantou University now boasts a world-class library and a growing reputation as a leader in education reform because of Mr. Li's largess, but it is only one of almost two dozen institutions in China, Hong Kong, and Singapore that have received major financial support. Partly because of Mr. Li's own experience, as well as his commitment to help those who are weak and marginalized, the foundation has established rural health clinics; treatment centers for the poor; cleft-palate treatment programs; hospice care centers; and facilities to care for the mentally retarded. The Shantou University medical school participates in a number of these, and has instituted innovative training methods as well. Other similar institutions in Asia, North America, and Europe, have been able to launch new initiatives with the Foundation's support. Though the Li Ka Shing Foundation may be the largest of its kind, it is not the only one.

Imagine what dedicated Christians working in such charitable organizations could do. Not only could they participate in such a way that people see their good works and glorify their Father in heaven, but they would demonstrate the love of Christ and may even be able to have an influence upon policy in a gentle way. Meeting physical needs has always been part of God's strategy for demonstrating his goodness and greatness among the Chinese. Many early missionaries, like Peter Parker and Hudson Taylor, were physicians. Missionaries, including Taylor and his wife, and also Timothy Richard, sacrificed a great deal to alleviate the horrible suffering inflicted by the great famine of 1876–1877. The examples are too numerous to record, and they remain powerful reminders today of the multiple ways in which Christians can serve as salt and light in society, to the glory of God the Father.

OBEYING THE LAW

When ordered by the authorities not to preach the resurrection of Jesus from the dead, Peter declared, "Whether it is right in the sight of God to listen to you more than to God, you judge. For we cannot but speak the things which we have seen and heard" (Acts 5:19–20). Inspired by those words, as well as by the oft-repeated Great Commission issued by the risen Christ, missionaries and evangelists have often ignored prohibitions against preaching the gospel, preferring suffering to guilty silence.

To Obey or Not to Obey?

After a period of toleration, Roman Catholic missionary activity in China was prohibited in the mid-eighteenth century, and had to be carried on clandestinely and at great risk. The first Protestant missionaries faced the same legal restrictions in the early 1800s. Some obeyed, and worked either outside of China or, later, in areas where treaties allowed them to preach the gospel. Others chose to disobey the law, and plunged into the interior of China to test the limits of official opposition that, they discovered, varied from place to place. The warm reception they were often given by the general populace, and occasionally by the local gentry, encouraged them.

The same contrast can be found today, both among Chinese Christians and foreigners who want to share the gospel among the Chinese. Many choose to work with the officially sanctioned Three-Self Patriotic Movement/China Christian Council, where regulated Christian activity is approved. Most Chinese Christians, and many—perhaps most—foreigners, prefer to operate outside the restrictions of the TSPM/CCC. They do not believe that the government should dictate to the church or that the church should serve political ends. In particular, they want the freedom to engage in teaching and evangelism without being restricted by designated places, times, and personnel. The law does not allow foreign Christians to teach in unregistered congregations; to make disciples; to evangelize publicly; or to contribute money to local Christians. Those who violate these rules can be expelled, and their Chinese friends will face increased suspicion, surveillance, and perhaps even punishment. We have mentioned other difficulties with "clandestine" work earlier.

Obeying the Law

Many foreign Christians have chosen to honor the regulations concerning religious activity by non-Chinese, citing the examples of Joseph, Daniel, and Nehemiah, who worked within the "system." A variety of avenues for communicating God's love to Chinese remain open: the Internet; radio; distribution of Scriptures and Christian literature; legitimate relationships formed through business, education, the arts, and travel; medical and mercy work; equipping Chinese Christians living outside of the mainland; genuine hospitality to Chinese now in the West; partnership with experienced organizations that know how to serve the Christians in China in a way that does not disturb the peace; low-key contacts by wise, discreet visitors to China who refrain from open evangelism or training. As always, Taiwan, Hong Kong, Singapore, Macao, and other such places are still fully available to those who would seek to reach Chinese worldwide with the gospel. In these fully lawful roles, they not only make a contribution to the building of a healthy Chinese society, but earn trust, respect, and open doors, as a recent issue of the MSI Professional Services Bulletin explains and illustrates (msips.org).

Both of our organizations follow this path also. Almost all of our "religious" activity takes place outside of mainland China, not only because we think this is the most strategic way of reaching Chinese worldwide, but because we want to avoid unnecessary trouble, both for ourselves and for Chinese who deal with us. Thus, we openly share the gospel in North America, Taiwan, and England; prepare literature in Chinese; publish web sites that are available to Chinese around the world; and equip others to serve among the Chinese. Likewise, our academic and scholarly work is done within the bounds of the religious regulations, through legal publications, conferences, lectures in Chinese universities, and conversations with Chinese scholars both inside and outside of China.

We have found that we don't have to break any rules to have full scope to evangelize non-Christians, edify believers, and equip present and future leaders for the Chinese church and society. In fact, we have our hands full! We have neither the right nor the desire to criticize others who seek to obey the Great Commission differently. Each of us must answer to conscience and, finally, to God, and there is no room for judging the servant of Another, though there is plenty of space for respectful disagreement and discussion.

PRAYER

Believing the many promises in the Bible about God's willingness to answer the prayers of his people, I am convinced that the most "practical" "good deed" we can perform is to pray for our Chinese friends and for their nation's leaders. Whenever we encounter illness, poverty, unemployment, temptation to compromise, conflict, broken relationships, anger, sadness, and confusion, we can come humbly before the Throne of Grace and ask our Father to show mercy to those who are in need. In my experience, the Lord sometimes heeds the requests of even those who have not yet placed full trust in Christ, to demonstrate his power and his pity. As I said earlier, Chinese are very practical, pragmatic folks. When they see our genuine love and know that we are praying for them, they greatly appreciate it. If God actually "comes through" for them and brings healing, reconciliation, guidance, a job, or any other benefit, they are usually quite open and sincere about their gratitude, and this sometimes leads to their conversion. In our years among the Chinese, we have witnessed countless instances when God graciously responded to petitions. Our resources are severely limited, but his are infinite. Let us draw upon his wealth and power with boldness!

CHAPTER THIRTEEN
PARTNERING WITH GOD

IT TAKES TIME

At a recent meeting of American China ministry leaders, several speakers called for new workers who would commit themselves to long-term service among the Chinese. That concept was also highlighted in a recent Bulletin of MSI Professional Services, every article in which dealt with "The Long-Term Approach." With most young Americans shrinking from commitments of any sort, including marriage, this plea for a willingness to invest many years in China ministry could not be more timely, or more challenging.

The fact is that effective cross-cultural work takes years to develop.

It takes time to learn a language as rich, complicated, and difficult as Chinese.

It takes time to gain even a little knowledge about the history, culture, religion, art, literature, politics, social values, psychology, and inner soul of people from this ancient civilization.

It takes time to adjust to life in a new place, with food, customs, and environment so different from ours.

It takes time to build friendships, especially since Chinese people value what we do more than what we say, and don't commit themselves to strangers quickly.

It takes time to establish trust, to earn a reputation for honesty, sincerity, and good will.

It takes time to acquire the right to speak about matters of eternal significance.

It takes time to overcome well-founded prejudices against Americans and their nation's depraved popular culture and "hegemonic" foreign policy.

It takes time for Chinese, who have virtually no concept of either a transcendent God or of original sin in their background, to gain a sense of the holiness of God and our need for Christ.

It takes time for them to become familiar with the basic story line of the Bible and to see its relevance to their life.

It takes time for God's Spirit to work in their hearts, creating a hunger for him, a repentant heart, and genuine faith.

Though we are often impatient, God is not. He knows his own plan, and follows it without haste. Our job is to wait upon him and to work with him as his humble servants, not seeking to rush him or conform him to our timetable. We are partners with God, to be sure (1 Cor 3:9), but we are very junior and subordinate servants, not his masters.

HARD WORK AND SUFFERING

When my wife Dori and I had been in Taiwan as new workers with Overseas Missionary Fellowship for only a few months, a conference was held for people at our stage of missionary service. One of the speakers had served for thirty years in Malaysia and then in Taiwan. I have never forgotten what he said: Missionary success will not come without "hard work and suffering." In his case, he and his wife had been sorely tested by severe health difficulties and the loss of a child, not to mention numerous setbacks, in their efforts to serve God among the Chinese. But they kept on, persevering in the strength of God and the hope of his promises.

If the examples of Jesus, Paul, the Apostles, and countless missionaries over the centuries is any guide, we cannot expect to see fruit from our labors to reach Chinese with the gospel unless we, too, are committed to "hard work and suffering." Indeed, it seems that "no pain, no gain," is a fundamental principle of effective cross-cultural ministry. This principle applies to those in the West who want to befriend Chinese students and scholars just as much as it does to those who "forsake all, and follow Jesus" to Asia. There is no short cut to spiritual "success." "The hard-working farmer must be first to partake of the crops" (2 Tim 2:6). So, "endure hardship" is a command that comes to us with the same force as it did to Timothy (2 Tim 2:3).

Such hardship may consist simply of making a telephone call instead of watching your favorite drama or football team on TV. Or it may involve inviting a Chinese person to share in a special family occasion, rather than keeping the warmth, love, and joy all to yourselves, as Americans are wont to do. Or God may call you to pack up, sell your house, and move to Asia, so that you can live out your life in the midst of a watching and very needy people.

To make any lasting spiritual impact on the Chinese, we shall have to commit ourselves to prayer, diligent study of the Bible, and disciplined study of their language and culture.

In our case, since leaving Chapel Hill in 1975, we have encountered quite a number of challenges. Dori found living in hot, humid, noisy, congested, and sometimes disorderly cities very trying, especially since she had spent all her life in small, semi-rural towns. For me, learning Chinese has been a decades-long struggle with my incredibly poor memory. It is immensely difficult for me to retain bits of specific information, like vocabulary, in my mind ever since college days, and Chinese is nothing if not a collection of tens of thousands of discrete data!

During our first two years in Taiwan, my health broke down and I became depressed. I have never quite regained the stamina and vitality I had when we boarded the plane in 1975. As I said at the beginning of this book, I struggled with chronic pain, mild depression, and fatigue until 2004, when I was miraculously healed of the pain, but the fatigue persists, despite regular exercise and frequent naps. Injuries to my back and knees in Taiwan and China continue to slow me down, limit my activities, and impose a daily regimen of remedial exercises (joined now by exercises for injured hands). I am glad to say that the depression lifted when I began to deal with unhealthy thought patterns.

Living in another culture put strains on our marriage; additionally, we were not able to have a child until we had been married fifteen years. Two times I have been "fired" by Chinese bosses who were angry with me; once I have had to separate from an organization because of policy differences, though relationships remained intact. I have failed twice at establishing a viable fellowship for Chinese in Virginia.

I could go on. This short list is not intended to evoke either respect or pity, but simply to show that I am aware that gospel advance among the Chinese will not go unopposed by the world, our own flesh, and the devil. Only if we persevere, relying on God's grace and power to forgive and to change, will we be able to continue long enough to see significant results from our feeble and sin-tainted labors. But we will see such fruit! God's Word will not return to him empty, but will accomplish the purpose for which he sent it (Isa 55:11).

A BEAUTIFUL LIFE

While in Taiwan on a visit a few years ago, I spoke with a woman who serves as a missionary in the Middle East. As she explained to me her understanding of her basic mission, I knew immediately that I wanted to make it my own as well. Her goal is "to live among them a life of beauty; a life of health; a life of love, so that they will want to ask, 'What is your secret?'"

Did not our Lord Jesus say, "You are the salt of the earth... You are the light of the world... Let your light so shine before men, that they may see your good works and glorify your Father in heaven" (Matt 5:13, 14, 16)? His disciple John wrote, "The Word became flesh and dwelt among us, and we beheld his glory, the glory as of the only begotten of the Father, full of grace and truth" (John 1:14).

The once-impetuous and voluble Peter had obviously changed his approach by the time he penned these words: "But sanctify the Lord God in your hearts, and always be ready to give a defense to everyone who asks you a reason for the hope that is in you, with meekness and fear; having a good conscience, that when they defame you as evildoers, those who revile your good conduct in Christ may be ashamed." (1 Pet 3:15–16)

Even the Apostle Paul, a preacher and a teacher who believed in the power of verbal proclamation, exhorted the Christians at Philippi to "Do all things without complaining and disputing, that you may become blameless and harmless [innocent], children of God without fault in the midst of a crooked and perverse generation, among whom you shine as lights in the world, holding fast the word of life..." (Phil 2:14–16)

Long ago, missionary to India A.G. Hogg wrote, "Christian preaching is interpretation; and in order to be effectual, the missionary's preaching has to be the interpretation of a life which he is living with the people and for the people. . . And this life must be of a distinctive quality which will make men wish to discover its spiritual secret."[45]

What if those who seek to influence Chinese sought first to live a beautiful life—one filled with love, joy, and peace? What if we made it our goal to be "quick to listen, slow to speak" (Jas 1:19)? Non-Chinese, especially, might do well to aim to understand before we presume to share our opinions. Chinese rightly consider themselves practical people, who value actions more than words. Perhaps we should re-orient our priorities, putting "show" in front of "tell."

---

45 Alfred G. Hogg, quoted in Eric J. Sharpe, "A.G. Hogg," in Gerald H. Anderson, et al., eds., *Mission Legacies: Biographical Studies of Leaders of the Modern Missionary Movement*, 336.

PARTNERSHIP WITH GOD

After all, we are not engaged in our mission, but God's. He was the One who decided to save fallen men and women from their sins, and to initiate a grand design that stretches from eternity past to eternity future. The entire Bible speaks of his sovereign grace and holy judgment; it displays his awesome power and his condescending pity; it broadcasts his wisdom, which we cannot hope to fathom. His ways are not our ways! His timing is not our timing. Sometimes he works much more quickly than we would consider possible; more, he seems to effect his purposes at a snail's pace, while we fret impatiently. Always, however, he accomplishes his will (Eph 1:11). Nothing hinders him from carrying out his plan to save his people.

So, as I said at the outset, prayerful waiting upon him each day and all day must be our highest purpose. The "chief end of man" is to "glorify God and enjoy him forever," the Westminster Shorter Catechism famously declares. Let us begin by honoring him in our hearts and minds, by dwelling on his beauty, majesty, kindness, compassion, holiness, righteousness, wisdom, power, and grace, as revealed supremely in the life of our Lord Jesus Christ, and by the gentle illumination of the Holy Spirit as we lovingly meditate upon the very words of God.

Martha was a good woman, and she meant well. She will surely be in heaven with her sister. Mary, however, knew something even more vital: That sitting at the feet of Jesus to hear his word, and then to pour out her heart in utter adoration and worship, regardless of the cost, was what our Lord really desired. This entire book has been written to earnest people who want to "do" things to honor God by someone who has "done" a lot, much of it in haste and without seeking the Lord's face or his strength. Certainly, God has good works which he has prepared for us to walk in (Eph 2:10), and he wants us to be active, zealous, effective "doers of the word."

Jesus said, "I am the vine, you are the branches. He who abides in Me, and I in him, bears much fruit; for without Me you can do nothing" (John 15:7). All our words and deeds must spring from an intimate relationship with our Lord and Savior, in whom alone do we find life in its fullness. The Director of OMF in Taiwan told us when we arrived that "the greatest contribution you can make to the Chinese is your experience of the grace of God." Those words still ring in my ears, reminding me that only by feeding on God's majestic mercy each day will I have anything to offer my Chinese friends. It has often been said that "being precedes doing." "Being" involves resting and rejoicing in the love of God for us in Christ.

The Bible says that the Father is seeking worshipers, people who will fix their minds and hearts on the Truth as it is in Jesus, and offer their love and their lives to him by the power of the Holy Spirit (John 4:24).

This brings to a close my very brief introduction to different ways of reaching Chinese worldwide. The doors are open; millions of Chinese are hungry for hope and truth; and resources for presenting Christ to them abound. I pray that these pages have stimulated both your heart and your mind to be worshipers of God, and to do all you can to take part in this strategic ministry, and all to the glory of our great God, to whom be praise and honor forever, through Jesus Christ our Lord and Savior. Amen.

THE AUTHOR

G. Wright Doyle received a B.A. with Honors in Latin from the University of North Carolina at Chapel Hill in 1966; a B.D. (M.Div.) with Honors from the Virginia Theological Seminary in 1969; and a PhD. in Classics from the University of North Carolina in 1975, with a dissertation on St. Augustine. He studied Mandarin Chinese at the Taipei Language Institute in Taiwan (1976–1978, 1980–1981). From 1980 to 1988, he taught Greek and New Testament at China Evangelical Seminary, Taipei.

Since 1989, the Doyles have lived in Charlottesville, Virginia, where they reach out to Chinese connected with the University of Virginia through Bible studies, friendship, and advising Chinese Christians. Wright has preached in Chinese churches and taught intensive courses on the New Testament and Systematic Theology for Chinese language seminaries in North America and Taiwan. He has presented papers at academic meetings and lectured at universities in mainland China, England, Taiwan, and the United States.

Wright is the co-author of *China: Ancient Culture, Modern Society*; English editor of the *Biographical Dictionary of Chinese Christianity* (bdcconline.net); editor and translator of *Wise Man from the East*: Lit-sen Chang; co-editor (with Dr. Carol Lee Hamrin) of the Wipf & Stock series, *Studies in Chinese Christianity*; and principal contributor to globalchinacenter.org and chinainst.org. He supervised the translation of Gingrich and Danker's Greek-English Lexicon into Chinese, and prepared an abridgment of the Chinese edition of Carl Henry's *God, Revelation, and Authority.*

He has also written *Christianity in America: Triumph and Tragedy*; *Jesus: The Complete Man*; and *The Lord's Healing Words.* Seven of his books have been translated and published in Chinese.

The Doyles have one married daughter.

Resources

The literature on Missions, China, and Christianity in China is vast and growing. I have only read a tiny portion of what is available. The following list contains some of the sources that have helped to inform my limited understanding. Since these are all easily available by searching the Internet, only author and title are listed for books. A few are briefly described. Reviews of many of the books listed below can be found at chinainst.org or globalchinacenter.org.

Pastoral Theology

Edwards, Jonathan, Religious Affections. The definitive analysis of true and false religious experiences.

Lovelace, Richard F., Dynamics of Spiritual Life: An Evangelical Theology of Renewal.

————, Renewal as a Way of Life: A Guidebook for Spiritual Growth. An adaptation and abridgment of Dynamics of Spiritual Life.

Missiology

General

Miller, Darrow L., Discipling Nations: The Power of Truth to Transform Cultures.

Moreau, A. Scott, Gary R. Corwin, and Gary B. McGee, Introducing World Missions: A Biblical, Historical, and Practical Survey. An excellent introduction for students and prospective cross-cultural witnesses to Christ, though adjustments will need to be made for those living in China.

Ott, Craig, and Stephen J. Strauss, with Timothy Tennent, Encountering Theology of Mission: Biblical Foundations, Historical Developments, and Contemporary Issues. A clear, comprehensive, concise, and convincing overview.

Taylor, William D., ed., Global Missiology for the 21st Century: The Iguassu Dialogue. A veritable encyclopedia of missions theory by evangelicals from all over the world.

Winter, Ralph, and Steven C. Hawthorne, eds., Perspectives on the World Christian Movement: A Reader. This comprehensive volume is essential reading for anyone who wants to be involved in cross-cultural ministry. It introduces all aspects of the world Christian movement under four headings: The Biblical Perspective, Historical Perspective, Cultural Perspective, and Strategic Perspective. The entire volume deserves repeated, thoughtful, and prayerful reading.

Reference Works

Anderson, Gerald H., Biographical Dictionary of Christian Missions. Short articles on many key figures in the missionary movement in China (as well as the rest of the world).

Campbell, Jack, W.D., and Gavin McGrath, eds., New Dictionary of Christian Apologetics. Good articles on the interaction of Christianity with other faiths.

Dyrness, William A., and Veli-Matti Karkkainen, eds., Global Dictionary of Theology. Stimulating, informative, and generally helpful, though some key articles are from the more "liberal" wing of the church.

Moreau, A. Scott, Evangelical Dictionary of World Missions. Exceptionally useful.

Sunquist, Scott W., ed., A Dictionary of Asian Christianity. Comprehensive and generally very helpful; reflects a broadly ecumenical perspective.

BIBLICAL FOUNDATIONS

Introductory

Piper, John, Let the Nations Be Glad: The Supremacy of God in Missions.

Winter, Ralph, and Steven Hawthorne, Perspectives Reader, "The Biblical Perspective."

For Further Reading

Bosch, David J., Transforming Mission: Paradigm Shifts in Theology of Mission. Discussing cross-cultural missions from biblical, historical, and theoretical perspectives, this magisterial work is often extremely helpful and informative, but is seriously flawed by a rejection of biblical inerrancy, failure to understand the overall evangelical position, and sometimes confusing parallel discussions of several contradictory points of view.

Chang, Lit-sen, Strategy for Missions in the Orient.

Jennings, J. Nelson, GOD: The Real Superpower: Rethinking Our Role in Missions. A strong challenge to American Christians.

Kostenberger, Andreas J., and Peter T. O'Brien, Salvation to the Ends of the Earth: A Biblical Theology of Missions. Very sound and illuminating. Gives a clear exposition of this key theme of the Bible, with a number of fresh insights.

Larkin, William J., Jr., and Joel F. Williams, eds., Mission in the New Testament. Extremely helpful.

McGavran, Donald A., Understanding Church Growth. A classic work, though not without its critics, including Leslie Newbigin (see below).

Newbigin, Leslie, The Open Secret. Elegantly-written, clear, biblical theology, filled with brilliant insights and trenchant criticisms of faulty positions, but reflecting a mixture of evangelical and ecumenical views, as well as a lack of commitment to biblical inerrancy. Repeated expressions of support for the overthrow of "unjust" governments are also problematic.

History of Missions and of World Christianity

Anderson, Gerald, et al., Mission Legacies: Biographical Studies of Leaders of the Modern Missionary Movement. Though the entire volume is well worth reading, Part Three deals with China.

Broomhall, A.J., The Shaping of Modern China. Originally published in seven volumes as Hudson Taylor and China's Open Century. A masterpiece.

Latourette, Kenneth Scott, A History of Christian Missions in China.

Robert, Dana L., Christian Mission: How Christianity Became a World Religion.

Sanneh, Lamin, Disciples of All Nations: Pillars of World Christianity.

Walls, Andrew F., The Cross-Cultural Process in Christian History.

———, The Missionary Movement in Christian History: Studies in the Transmission of Faith.

Practical Missiology

Bieler, Stacey, China at Your Doorstep.

Borthwick, Paul, Western Christians in Global Mission: What's the Role of the North American Church?

Choy, Leona, Touching China: Close Encounters of the Christian Kind. Dated, but still useful.

Journals

Asian Missions Advance. Official bulletin of the Asia Missions Association.

Evangelical Missions Quarterly. Essential for all who are involved in missions, including missions committee members, missions pastors, administrators, missionaries, tentmakers, and even academic missiologists.

International Bulletin for Missionary Research (IBMR). Published by the Overseas Ministries Study Center. Indispensable for advanced students of missions.

Missiology. Academic journal for professionals and students of missions theory and practice.

PRAYER

Bridge to China: China Resource and Trip Guide. Pacific Bridge, info@ pacbridge.org. CD.

Forget Not China: A beautiful calendar with inspiring essays each month and daily requests, arranged by the provinces of China. 1-888-462-5481; order@prayforchina.com.

Overseas Missionary Fellowship International. Ministry to East Asia, including China and Taiwan, as well as materials. omf.org; 10 W Dry Creek Cir., Littleton, CO 80120; 800-422-5330; info@omf.org; bookstore: omfbooks.com; 303-730-4160. Global Chinese Ministries: Free monthly prayer report with accurate articles on the current situation among Chinese and specific requests for each day. Order from OMF International by calling 1-800-4225330 (ext. 264); omf.org > US > Resources > Newsletters> Global Chinese Ministries.

Pray for China: Issued every two months, this twelve-page newsletter features excellent stories, perceptive analysis, and compelling calls to pray. pfc@ccl.org.hk.

SERVING AMONG THE CHINESE

Introduction to Serving China. servingchina.com.

Introduction to the Mainland Chinese Soul. LEAD Consulting, 919-783-0354.

CHINESE CULTURE, SOCIETY, AND RELIGION

Introductory

Doyle, G. Wright, and Peter Xiaoming Yu, China: Ancient Culture, Modern Society.

Gifford, Rob, China Road.

For Further Reading

Becker, Jasper, The Chinese.

Bloodworth, Dennis, The Chinese Looking Glass. A fascinating description of Chinese culture, customs, and character.

Bridge to China: China Resource and Trip Guide. Pacific Bridge, info@
pacbridge.org. CD.

Kristof, Nicholas D., and Sheryl Wudunn, China Wakes.

Hessler, Peter, Oracle Bones.

Hutchings, Graham, Modern China: A Guide to a Century of Change.

Ling, Samuel and Stacey Bieler, eds., Chinese Intellectuals in Crisis.

Su, Shuyang, A Reader on China: An Introduction to China's History,
Culture and Civilization. A highly laudatory survey; beautifully illus-
trated, but with poor English editing.

Wah, Sheh Seow, Chinese Leadership: Moving from Classical to Contemporary. Excellent analysis, poor English editing.

Wu, Guoguang, and Helen Landsdowne, Socialist China, Capitalist
China: Social Tension and Political Adaptation under Economic Globalization.

CHINESE HISTORY

Introductory

Doyle, G. Wright, and Peter Xiaoming Yu, China: Ancient Culture,
Modern Society.

Fairbank, John King, and Merle Goldman, China: A New History.

Spence, Jonathan, The Search for Modern China.

Wills, John E., Jr., Mountain of Fame: Portraits in Chinese History.

For Further Reading

deBary, William Theodore de, Wing-tsit Chan, and Burton Watson, eds.,
Sources of Chinese Tradition. Two volumes.

Bieler, Stacey, "Patriots" or "Traitors"? A History of American-Educated
Chinese Students.

Broomhall, A.J., The S with Paganism. haping of Modern China. Originally published in seven volumes as Hudson Taylor and China's Open
Century. A masterpiece.

Butterfield, Fox, China: Alive in the Bitter Sea.

Chang, Jung, Wild Swans: Three Daughters of China. A gripping
account of the Cultural Revolution (1966-76).

Fairbank, John King. China: Tradition and Transformation.

———, The Great Chinese Revolution: 1800-1985.

Li, Zhisui. The Private Life of Chairman Mao.

Lyall, Leslie, New Spring in China.

Spence, Jonathan D., The Gate of Heavenly Peace: The Chinese and Their Revolution, 1895-1980.

————, The Chan's Great Continent: China in Western Minds.

————, God's Chinese Son: The Taiping Heavenly Kingdom of Hong Xiuquan.

————, To Change China: Western Advisers in China.

Su, Shuyang, A Reader on China: An Introduction to China's History, Culture, and Civilization.

Taylor, Jay, The Generalissimo: Chiang Kai-shek and the Struggle for Modern China.

————, The Generalissimo's Son: Chiang Ching-kuo and the Revolutions in China and Taiwan.

Wills, John W., Jr, Mountain of Fame: Portraits in Chinese History. Perhaps the most accessible Chinese history book, since it is structured around famous people.

CHINESE BELIEF SYSTEMS

Introductory

Chang, Lit-sen, Asia's Religions: Christianity's Momentous Encounter with Paganism.

Doyle, G. Wright, and Peter Yu, China: Ancient Culture, Modern Society.

Poceski, Mario, Introducing Chinese Religions.

Names for God

Doyle, G. Wright, 聖經漢譯時的問題：God 的名稱 (Bible Translation: God's Name). http://www.chinainst.org/zh/articles/christianity/god. php. English version available at chinainst.org

Yin and Yang

Zhang, Qizhi, ed., Traditional Chinese Culture (Beijing: Foreign Languages Press, 2004) 50-60.

Buddhism

Chang, Lit-sen, Asia's Religions: Christianity's Momentous Encounter with Paganism.

Confucius and Confucianism (and other belief systems):

Bell, Daniel A., China's New Confucianism: Politics and Everyday Life in a Changing Society.

Chan, Wing-tsit, A Source Book in Chinese Philosophy.

Chen, Jingpan, Confucius as a Teacher: Philosophy of Confucius with Special Reference to Its Educational Implications.

Creel, H.G., Chinese Thought from Confucius to Mao Tse-tung.

————, Confucius and the Chinese Way.

Doyle, G. Wright,, and Peter Xiaoming Yu, China: Ancient Culture, Modern Society.

Huang, Chichung, The Analects of Confucius: A Literal Translation with an Introduction and Notes.

Ivanhoe, Philip J., and Bryan W. Van Nordern, Readings in Classical Chinese Philosophy.

Christianity and Confucianism:

Ching, Julia, Confucianism and Christianity: A Comparative Study.

Covell, Ralph R., Confucius, the Buddha, and Christ: A History of the Gospel in Chinese.

Popular Religion

Glahn, Richard von, The Sinister Way: The Divine and the Demonic in Chinese Religious Culture.

Poceski, Mario, Introducing Chinese Religions.

Su, Jennifer, Dead Women Walking.

Daoism/Taoism

Huang, Chichung, Tao Te Ching: A Literal Translation with Notes and Commentary.

HISTORY OF CHRISTIANITY IN CHINA

Introductory

Aikman, David, Jesus in Beijing.

For Further Reading

GCC Studies in Chinese Christianity, edited by Carol Lee Hamrin and G. Wright Doyle:

Cook, Richard, and David Pao, After Imperialism: Christian Identity in China and the Global Evangelical Movement.

Doyle, G. Wright, ed., Wise Man from the East: Lit-sen Chang. A Translation of Critique of Indigenous Theology (trans. by G. Wright Doyle) and of Critique of Humanism (trans. by Dr. Samuel Ling).

Hamrin, Carol Lee, with Stacey Bieler, Salt and Light: Lives of Faith that Shaped Modern China, Volumes 1-3. The three English volumes of Salt and Light make very encouraging reading while providing an enormous amount of information about twentieth-century China. Currently, a second Chinese volume of the best chapters of the last two volumes of Salt and Light is being translated.

Seitz, Jonathan, ed., The Life of Liang-Fa, China's First Evangelist.

Other Books on the History of Christianity in China

Adeney, David, China: The Church's Long March.

_____, China: Christian Students Face the Revolution.

Bays, Daniel, ed., Christianity in China: From the Eighteenth Century to the Present.

_____, A New History of Christianity in China.

Broomhall, A.J., The Shaping of Modern China: Hudson Taylor's Life and Legacy. Originally published in seven volumes as Hudson Taylor and China's Open Century. A masterpiece, worth several readings.

Cao, Nanlai, Constructing China's Jerusalem: Christians, Power, and Place in Contemporary Wenzhou.

Charbonnier, Jean-Pierre, Christians in China: A.D. 600 to 2000.

Christian History and Biography, issue #98, Spring 2008. Special issue on Chinese Christianity.

Cliff, Norman, Fierce the Conflict: Stories of Eight Chinese Christians Who Suffered for Jesus Christ and Remained Faithful.

Covell, Ralph, Confucius, the Buddha, and Christ: A History of the Gospel in Chinese.

Dunch, Ryan, Fuzhou Protestants and the Making of Modern China, 1857-1927.

Falkenstine, Mike, The Chinese Puzzle.

Hattaway, Paul, China's Book of Martyrs (AD 845-present). 600 pages of stories of brave Chinese Christians and missionaries who were willing to suffer for their faith.

Hamrin, Keating, John Craig William, A Protestant Church in Communist China: Moore Memorial Church Shanghai, 1949-1989.

Kindopp, Jason, and Carol Lee Hamrin, God and Caesar in China: Policy Implications of Church-State Tensions.

Lai, Pan-chiu, and Jason Lam, eds., Sino-Christian Theology: A Theology Qua Cultural Movement in Contemporary China.

Lambert, Tony, China's Christian Millions: The Costly Revival.

_____, The Resurrection of the Chinese Church.

Lawrence, Carl, The Church in China: How It Survives and Prospers under Communism.

Ling, Samuel and Stacey Bieler, eds., Chinese Intellectuals in Crisis.

Luo, Weihong, Christianity in China. The view of the official Chinese government-sponsored church.

Moffett, Samuel Hugh, A History of Christianity in Asia. Two volumes. A standard work.

Paterson, Ross, and Elisabeth Farrell, China: The Hidden Miracle.

Starr, Chloe, Reading Christian Scriptures in China.

Tiedemann, R. G., ed., Handbook of Christianity in China, Vol. Two: 1800-Present. An essential resource.

Uhalley, Stephen, Jr., and Xiaoxin Wu, eds., China and Christianity: Burdened Past, Hopeful Future.

Xi, Lian, Redeemed by Fire: The Rise of Popular Christianity in Modern China.

Xin, Yalin, Inside China's House Church Network: The Word of Life Movement and Its Renewing Dynamic.

Yamamori, Tetsunao, and Kim-Kwong Chan, Witnesses to Power: Stories of God's Quiet Work in a Changing China.

Yao, Kevin Xiyi, The Fundamentalist Movement among Protestant Missionaries in China, 1920-1937. An excellent treatment of a pivotal moment in Chinese Christianity; a good balance to Daniel Bays' more positive evaluation of the China Christian Council movement.

BIOGRAPHIES AND AUTOBIOGRAPHIES

Anderson, Ken, Bold as a Lamb: Pastor Samuel Lamb and the Underground Church of China.

Armitage, Carolyn, Reaching for the Goal: The Life Story of David

Adeney—Ordinary Man, Extraordinary Mission.

Biographical Dictionary of Chinese Christianity: bdcconline.net.

Broomhall, A.J., The Shaping of Modern China: Hudson Taylor's Life and Legacy. Originally published in seven volumes as Hudson Taylor and China's Open Century. A masterpiece, worth several readings.

Caughey, Ellen, Eric Liddell.

Chang, Irene, et al., Christ Alone: A Pictorial Presentation of Hudson Taylor's Life and Legacy. A Beautiful book in English and Chinese.

Goforth, Rosalind, Jonathan Goforth. The original biography, Goforth of China, retold for today's reader.

Hancock, Christopher, Robert Morrison and the Birth of Chinese Protestantism. Beautifully written and inspiring.

Harvey, Thomas Alan, Acquainted with Grief: Wang Mindao's Stand for the Persecuted Church in China.

Hamilton, Pauline, To a Different Drum. Fast-moving story of a missionary in China and Taiwan.

Kuhn, Isobel, In the Arena.

Lee, Lydia, A Living Sacrifice: The Life Story of Allen Yuan.

Lutz, Jessie Gregory, Opening China: Karl F. A. Gutzlaff and Sino-Western Relations, 1827-1852. A scholarly and well-written biography of a remarkable and controversial pioneer.

North, Barbara, Maid in Taiwan.

Pollock, John C., A Foreign Devil in China. The biography of L. Nelson Bell.

Steer, Roger, Hudson Taylor: A Man in Christ.

Taylor, Dr. and Mrs. Howard, Hudson Taylor and the China Inland Mission. Two volumes. A missionary and devotional classic.

———, Hudson Taylor's Spiritual Secret. An abridgment of the two-volume biography.

CHINESE CHRISTIANITY IN AMERICA

Ambassadors for Christ, Mainland Chinese in America: An Emerging Kinship.

Chen, Carolyn, Getting Saved in America: Taiwanese Immigration and Religious Experience.

Yang, Fenggang, Chinese Christians in America.

POINTS OF CONTACT: CHRISTIANITY AND CHINESE CULTURE

China Institute: chinainst.org.

China Source: chsource.org

Global Chinese Ministries: China Insight Newsletter. OMF International, omf.org/us. Online journal.

Marshall, David, True Son of Heaven: How Jesus Fulfills the Chinese Culture.

Ruokanen, Miika, and Paulos Huang, eds., Christianity and Chinese Culture.

ZGBriefs. zgbriefs.com. Weekly online update on many facets of Chinese society, including Christianity.

MINISTRY TO CHINESE LIVING OVERSEAS

Ambassadors for Christ. Chinese-speaking ministry and literature. afcinc. org; 21 Ambassadors Drive, Paradise, PA 17562; 717-687-8564; afc@ afcinc.org. AFC Bookstore: 800-624-3504; 888-999-7959; bookstore@ afc.org.

China Outreach Ministries. Chinese-speaking ministry. chinaoutreach. org; 555 Gettysburg Pike, Suite A-200, Mechanicsburg, PA 17055; 717-591-3500; com@chinaoutreach.net.

International Students Inc. English-speaking international ministry, materials. isionline.org; PO Box C, Colorado Springs, CO 80901; 800-ISI-TEAM; team@isiwebnet.net.

Inter-Varsity Christian Fellowship. English-speaking international ministry, materials. intervarsity.org; 6400 Schroeder Rd., PO Box 7895, Madison, WI 53707; 608-274-9001; info@intervarsity.org.

The Navigators. English-speaking ministry. navigators.org/us; PO Box 6000, Colorado Springs, CO 80934; 719-598-1212; questions@navigators.org.

Overseas Campus Ministries. Chinese- and English- speaking ministry and Overseas Campus Magazine. oc.org; 1753 Cabrillo Ave., Torrance CA 90501; 310-328-8200; info@oc.org.

Reformed University Fellowship International. English-speaking international ministry. ruf.org/ruf-international; 1700 N. Brown Rd., Suite 104, Lawrenceville, Georgia 30043; 678-825-1070.

Popular Magazines for Chinese

Behold. 舉目.For believers. Order from oc.org/web.

Blessings. 恩福雜誌. For intellectuals; discusses Christianity and Chinese culture. Order from Blessing Cultural Missions Fellowship. bf21.org.

Family Keepers Magazine. 真愛雜誌. Order from familykeepers.org. Teaching biblical family values and skills.

Life and Faith. 生命季刊 Order from smyxy.org.

Overseas Campus. 海外校園. Mostly for seekers. Order from oc.org/web.

SHORT-TERM TRIPS

Gibson, Tim, et al, eds. Stepping Out: A Guide to Short Term Missions. YWAM publishing.

Mack, J., and Leeann Stiles, Mack and Leeman's Guide to Short-Term Missions. I have not read this but it looks good.

FRIENDSHIP

Robert, Dana, "Cross-cultural Friendship in the Creation of Twentieth-Century World Christianity," International Bulletin of Missionary Research, Vol. 35, No.2, April, 2011, 100-107.

SENDING ORGANIZATIONS

Educational Resources and Referrals China. Places professors in Chinese universities. errchina.com; 1405 Arch St., Berkeley, CA 94708; 510-486-8170; errc@aol.com.

English Language Institute China. Openings for English teachers in Chinese schools and colleges. elic.org; 1629 Blue Spruce Drive, Fort Collins, CO 80524; 800-366-3542.

Jian Hua Foundation. Christian organization based in Hong Kong providing medical help and training, orphan care, and community development in China's less-developed areas. jhf-china.org; 602 Shoemaker Ave., Jenkintown, PA 19046; 215-572-0464; jhf-usa@jhf-china.org.

MSI Professional Services. Christian organization based in Hong Kong providing medical help and training in China's less-developed areas. msips.org; 513-636-9595; twelty@kumc.edu.

OMF International. Ministry to East Asia, including China and Taiwan. Materials. omf.org; 10 W Dry Creek Cir., Littleton, CO 80120; 800-422-5330; info@omf.org; bookstore: omfbooks.com; 303-730-4160. Global Chinese Ministries: Free monthly prayer report with accurate articles on the current situation among Chinese and specific requests for each day. ext. 264; omf.org > US > Resources > Newsletters> Global Chinese Ministries.

S.E.N.D. Ministry in Taiwan. send.org/taiwan; Box 513, Farmington, MI 48332; 248-477-4210; 800-SEND-808; info@send.org.

T.E.A.M. Ministry in Taiwan. team.tw; PO Box 7-460, Taipei 106 Taiwan; +886(2)2321-2879; Mission@TEAM.org.tw.

INTERNET, RADIO, AND LITERATURE

CCNTV. Broadcasts in various forms from California, featuring a wide range of programs, which are sent via Internet. CCNTV.org.

Far East Broadcasting Company. Radio broadcasting. febc.org; PO Box 1, La Mirada, CA 90637; 562-947-4651.

Third Millennium Ministries. thirdmill.org; PO Box 300769, Fern Park, FL 32730; 407-830-0222; webfeedback@thirdmill.org.

Trans World Radio. twr.org; PO Box 8700, Cary, NC 27512; 919-460-3700; 800-456-7897.

Ambassadors for Christ. Student ministries, Bibles and Christian books in Chinese, Ambassadors magazine, discipleship training, conferences. afcinc.org; 21 Ambassadors Dr., Paradise, PA 17562; 717-687-8564; afc@afcinc.org; bookstore: 1-800-624-3504; magazine ext. 218; Chinese and English: afcresources.org/bookstore. See the very helpful list of materials in Chinese available from Ambassadors for Christ: afcinc.org/mclit.htm.

STORIES OF CHINESE CHRISTIANS

Biographical Dictionary of Chinese Christianity. bdcconline.net.

Hamrin, Carol Lee, with Stacey Bieler, Salt and Light. Three volumes.

SMALL GROUP BIBLE STUDIES

Campus Evangelical Fellowship. Offers a whole range of Bible study materials as well as guides on how to lead small group Bible studies. 校園網路書房首頁. shop.campus.org.tw; estore@campus.org.tw; 傳真電話: 02-23678486 服務時間：週一～五10:00～13:00; 14:00～18:00.

International Students, Inc. (ISI). In the process of developing an inductive Bible study curriculum that incorporates the exciting chronological Bible study method developed by New Tribes Mission. When published, these materials should be considered first. They take the beginner from Genesis, through the Old Testament, and finally then to the story of the Deliverer.

TEACHING ENGLISH

Arrington, Aminta, Saving Grandmother's Face, and Other Tales from Christian Teachers in China.

Educational Resources and Referrals China. Places professors in Chinese universities. errchina.com; 1405 Arch St., Berkeley, CA 94708; 510-486-8170; errc@aol.com.

English Language Institute China. Openings for English teachers in Chinese schools and colleges. elic.org; 1629 Blue Spruce Drive, Fort Collins, CO 80524; 800-366-3542.

MERCY MINISTRIES

Jian Hua Foundation. Christian organization based in Hong Kong providing medical help and training, orphan care, and community development in China's less-developed areas. jhf-china.org; 602 Shoemaker Ave., Jenkintown, PA 19046; 215-572-0464; jhf-usa@jhf-china.org.

MSI Professional Services. Christian organization based in Hong Kong providing medical help and training in China's less-developed areas. msips.org; 513-636-9595; twelty@kumc.edu.

SPIRITUAL WARFARE

Doyle, G. Wright, "United We Stand: Unity and Spiritual Warfare." Can be found on chinainst.org.

Lowe, Chuck, Territorial Spirits and World Evangelisation: A Biblical, Historical and Missiological Critique of Strategic-Level Spiritual Warfare (Bristol, Great Britain: Christian Focus, 1998).

Moreau, A. Scott, "Gaining Perspective on Territorial Spirits." Lausanne Movement. http://www.lausanne.org./en/index2?option=com_content&do_pdf=1&id=202.

Tang, Alex, Book Review of Chuck Lowe, Territorial Spirits and World Evangelisation http://www.kairos2.com/book_review_of_chuck_lowe.htm.

SCIENCE AND THE BIBLE

Books In Chinese

Doyle, G. Wright, The Way Home: a Faith for the 21st Century

———, The Bible: Words of Men or Word of God? Tunghai University Press

Li, Cheng, Song of a Wanderer. A Chinese intellectual who moved from unbelief to faith in Christ has written an immensely popular book, which has been translated into English, and many shorter booklets on this subject published in Chinese are available from Ambassadors for Christ. .

Books in English

Berlinski, David, The Deniable Darwin and Other Essays.

Dembski, William A., Intelligent Design.

Denton, Michael, Evolution: A Theory in Crisis.

Behe, Michael, Darwin's Black Box.

Johnson, Philip, Darwin on Trial.

Wells, Jonathan, Icons of Evolution.

Wise, Kurt, Faith, Form, and Time.

HOUSE CHURCHES

Doyle, G. Wright, "A Theology for House Churches," http://www.chinainst.org/en/articles/christianity/a-theology-for-house-churches.php.

Gehring, Roger W., House Church and Mission: The Importance of Household Structures in Early Christianity.

House2House: Simple Organic Church, http://www.site.house2house.com/about-us/welcome.

House Church Network, http://housechurch.org/basics/index.html.

Zdero, Rad, "The Apostolic Strategy of House Churches for Mission Today," Evangelical Missions Quarterly, July, 2011, 346-353.

REACHING MEN

Celebrate Recovery. celebraterecovery.com.

Doyle, G. Wright, Jesus: The Complete Man; published in Chinese as Confucius and Jesus.

————, "Gender Imbalance in the Chinese Church: Causes, Consequences, and Possible Cures." http://www.chinainst.org/en/articles/christianity-in-china/gender-imbalance-in-the-chinese-church-causes-consequences-and-possible-cures.php.

————, "Real Men." chinainst.org.

Getz, Gene, The Measure of a Man.

LEADERSHIP TRAINING: THEOLOGICAL EDUCATION

Covenant Evangelical Theological Seminary. Internet-based theological training in Chinese. www.cetsedu.org.

China Horizon. Dr. Samuel Ling offers many excellent outlines and lectures on theology and leadership training: http://www.chinahorizon.org/live/.

Third Millennium Ministries. A full year of theological education in a multi-media format; some courses are for credit. A second year is being produced. thirdmill.org; PO Box 300769, Fern Park, FL 32730; 407-830-0222; webfeedback@thirdmill.org.

Strategic Asian Leadership Training (SALT). Theological training crafted especially for Chinese churches. saltpobox@gmail.com; 704-942-0438.

MENTORING AND COACHING

Coleman, Robert, The Master Plan of Evangelism.

Reese, Randy D., and Robert Loand. Deep Mentoring: Guiding Others on Their Leadership Journey.

COUNSELING

The volumes listed below have been of great help to me in my counseling. They come from a variety of theoretical and theological backgrounds; I do not necessarily agree with everything said in any one of these books, but recommend them for the amount of useful material they contain. Most of them are older; many newer treatments of this vital subject have come out in recent years.

Adams, Jay, Competent to Counsel. Polemical, challenging, path-setting.

————, Christian Counselor's Manual. Especially helpful.

————, The Christian Counselor's New Testament.

Chang, Brandon, and Martin Symonds, Counseling Dialogues. This superb textbook contains dialogues and crucial Chinese vocabulary dealing with the two dozen most common situations which Christians serving among Chinese will face.

China Horizon. A number of excellent Chinese-language counseling resources. http://www.chinahorizon.org/live/.

Christian Counseling and Educational Foundation. http://www.ccef.org. Their excellent perspective needs to be supplemented by others, however.

Crabb, Lawrence, Effective Biblical Counseling.

Hesselgrave, David, Counseling Cross-Culturally.

Lowe, Chuck, Territorial Spirits and World Evangelisation: A Biblical, Historical and Missiological Critique of Strategic-Level Spiritual Warfare.

Sandford, John and Mark, A Comprehensive Guide to Deliverance and Inner Healing. The section on deliverance must be corrected by Chuck Lowe's Territorial Spirits.

Sandford, John and Paul, The Transformation of the Inner Man. The most insightful work I have read.

In addition, David Powlison's books are highly recommended by many people. http://www.ccef.org/authors/david-powlison.

MEETING PRACTICAL NEEDS

Mercy Ministries

Agape Way. agapeway.org; 919-636-3447.

Chinese Church Support Ministries. amccsm.org.

Jian Hua Foundation. Christian organization based in Hong Kong providing medical help and training, orphan care, and community development in China's less-developed areas. jhf-china.org; 602 Shoemaker Ave., Jenkintown, PA 19046; 215-572-0464; jhf-usa@jhf-china.org.

MSI Professional Services. Christian organization based in Hong Kong providing medical help and training in China's less-developed areas. msips.org; 513-636-9595; twelty@kumc.edu.

BOOKS PRODUCED BY CHINA INSTITUTE

Books in English

Even books in English can be used, since many educated Chinese can read English, and volumes printed first in English sometimes have greater prestige than those issued in Chinese. Such works stand a good chance of being translated later; they also build credibility.

Doyle, G. Wright. Carl Henry: Theologian for All Seasons. This book tries to show why this great theologian has a message for the twenty-first century. It introduces the theology of Henry's God, Revelation and Authority and defends it against common criticisms.

————, Christ the King. Four hundred meditations on almost all of Matthew's Gospel. Suitable for personal or group devotions, mostly using Matthew itself to interpret Matthew.

————, Christianity in America: Triumph and Tragedy. Traces the history of Christian involvement in society and politics, with lessons for American and Chinese Christians today.

————, Jesus: The Complete Man. Compares and contrasts the example and teachings of Jesus and Confucius on the subject of the ideal male: his relationship to himself, to others, and to God.

————, The Lord's Healing Words. A study of what the Bible says about physical, mental, and spiritual health. An appeal to non-Christians and an aid to believers to enjoy healthier, happier lives.

Books in Chinese

Most of these can be obtained from Ambassadors for Christ in the U.S. (http://www.afcresources.org/bookstore) and Campus Bookstore in Taiwan (+886-2-2365-3665; http://www.campus.org.tw/).

These include the following books, using their English titles:

Doyle, G. Wright, The Bible: The Words of Men or the Word of God? 聖經是神的話?人的話?, A booklet on the Bible as the Word of God. Briefly presents the case for the authority of the Scriptures. In Taiwan, order from cclm.org.tw.

————, Confucius and Jesus. 孔子 & 耶穌

A comparison and contrast of the example and teaching of these two men on the subject of the ideal man (male).

————, ed., God, Revelation, and Authority. 神・啟示・權威 濃縮版（卡爾・亨利博士著). Abridged by G. Wright Doyle. The abridgment of the Chinese edition of the first four volumes of Carl Henry's 6-volume work, this book provides Christians and seekers with the rich, profound thought of perhaps the greatest American theologian in modern times. Henry makes the case for God's authoritative revelation in a way that strengthens believers and answers the main question that inquirers pose. The last two volumes of the abridgment are being translated. Order from Campus Press, Taiwan: shop.campus.org.tw.

————, ed., Greek-Chinese Lexicon of the New Testament. 新約希臘文中文辭典. G. Wright Doyle abridged and supervised the translation by his students of Gingrich and Danger's standard work. This book provides pastors and scholars with easy access to the original language of the New Testament. Order from Conservative Baptist Press; cbp@seed.net.tw.

————, Hope Deferred: Studies in Christianity and American Culture, 遲延的盼望--基督教與美國的關係 Trying to present a balanced view of this very complex relationship, this volume shows how Christians in America have affected and been affected by their society. Order from AFC Bookstore; 800-624-3504; #076030.

————, The Lord's Healing Words. 神的話語・你得健康 Offers a comprehensive examination of what the Bible teaches about physical, mental, and spiritual health.

———, Mercy All the Way (An Autobiography). 從名門到僕人-戴德理在台灣的日子 Traces God's merciful treatment of the author from birth through his leaving Taiwan in 1988. It includes the time he spent in Taiwan as a young boy. It focuses mostly on his many failures, and God's grace to him despite them. In the USA, order from AFC Bookstore; 800-624-3504; #046053. In Taiwan, order from cclm.org.tw.

———, New Testament Reference Works. 新約工具書使用簡介 Briefly and simply explains how to use Chinese-language materials for the study of the New Testament. A revised version is in preparation. CES Press. In Taiwan, order from cclm.org.tw.

———, The Switzerland of the New Testament. 新約中的瑞士-洞悉以弗所書精髓 A simple commentary on Paul's letter to the Ephesians, which has been likened to Switzerland which, though small, is rich in beauty. Because of the scope of Ephesians, this volume serves as a survey of basic Christian doctrinal and ethical teaching. In the USA, order from AFC Bookstore: 800-624-3504; #05531081. In Taiwan, order from cclm.org.tw.

———, The Way Home: A Faith for the 21st Century. 歸家之道　第21 世紀的信仰。The Luce Theological Lectures at Tunghai University in 2009. A simple yet comprehensive introduction to Christian faith and practice, with comparison to alternatives. Includes book and CD recording. Based on John 14:6, it seeks to present the essence of the Christian faith for both believers and seekers. Order from chaplain@thu.edu.tw. The English version is available at http://www.chinainst.org/en/articles/christianity/requirements-for-a-21st-century-faith-lecture-one.php

Hamrin, Carol Lee, with Stacey Bieler, eds., Salt and Light: Lives of Faith that Shaped Modern China. 光与盐

WEBSITES

The Biographical Dictionary of Chinese Christianity Website (bdcconline.net)

This site seeks to portray the rich heritage of Chinese Christianity. An online repository of brief biographies of Chinese Christians and Western missionaries to China, it features English and Chinese pages, both in traditional and simplified characters. Our aims are (1) to encourage Chinese believers; (2) to change the perception of non-Christian Chinese, especially intellectuals, who have been taught that Christianity is a noxious foreign imposition; and (3) to create a network of people around the world, including within China, who are pondering the past, present, and potential role of Christianity in Chinese society. You can find stories according to time period, organizational affiliation, geographical region, and author (by last name).

China Institute (chinainst.org)

This site features both English and Chinese pages. On it you will find a variety of material, including:

- Hundreds of devotional messages, including Worship and Wisdom (meditations upon the Psalms and Proverbs) and Following Jesus the King (meditations on Matthew's Gospel).

- Reviews of books about China, Christianity in China, and Christianity in general.

- Articles about various subjects, including Chinese history and culture, missions theory and practice, serving God among the Chinese, religion in China, theology, Christian living, and more.

- Outlines of seminary courses in the Bible and theology, in English and Chinese.

- Suggested readings and links to a number of other sites with a wide range of information, including Chinese-language resources.

Global China Center (www.globalchinacenter.org)

This is a more "academic" page, containing many of the book reviews and articles to be found on the China Institute site, but much more as well. This site includes analyses of Chinese history and culture, Chinese society and politics, and Christianity in China by various writers, including our advisers and associates. It also includes suggested readings, resources, and links to other sources of information about China.

WHO WE ARE
AND WHAT WE DO

VISION

We envision a time when many educated Chinese grasp and follow the truths of the Gospel; when non-Christian Chinese influencers acknowledge the contributions which Christianity has made and will make to their country; when Chinese church leaders communicate the Word of God by word and deed even more effectively than they do now; when Chinese Christians are not only aware of their heritage, but able to apply its lessons to today's church and society and grow into greater maturity as witnesses of Christ in a dark and dying world; and when their words and deeds serve as salt and light, bringing substantial change to the entire society.

OUR PURPOSE AND CHARACTER

China Institute has associates in the United States, England, and Taiwan, who seek to understand the deepest aspirations and assumptions of the Chinese people, so that we might forge strong friendships with them, earning trust before we presume to speak. On our travels, we seek to strengthen existing ties and forge new ones.

We attempt also to share with our non-Chinese friends what little we ourselves have begun to learn, so as to help them love the Chinese more effectively. We seek to be, and to prepare, a small group of dedicated students of both Chinese culture and of Christian thought and history, including Chinese Christian history for ministry. Furnished with the language, we are able to engage in meaningful conversations with educated seekers of the truth. Backed by prayer and empowered by the Spirit, we strive to evince the love of God and express his truth in a winsome fashion as occasions arise.

China Institute Partners

- Preach, teach, and counsel in North America, Taiwan, and England.
- Produce and distribute literature in English and/or Chinese, including books, the China Institute website, and regular prayer letters.
- Provide consulting for Christian organizations and advise individuals.

Global China Center

Global China Center was formed in 2004. GCC associates seek to encourage genuine academic exchange, to deepen the knowledge of Christianity and of its role in society, especially Chinese society. In a spirit of appreciative inquiry, our associates have, or are seeking to attain, advanced familiarity both with Chinese culture and with Christianity, and to share what they have learned with Chinese and Western scholars with similar interests.

- Participate in seminars and conferences that highlight the contributions of Christianity in China.
- Lecture on Christianity at Chinese universities—not only do these lectures (to undergraduates, graduate students, and faculty) offer a platform for expressing Christian ideas, but they also afford informal occasions for conversation.
- Produce and distribute popular and scholarly materials by GCC associates and others, in English and/or Chinese, which address issues of Chinese culture, religion (especially Christianity), and society, including the Biographical Dictionary of Chinese Christianity, Studies in Chinese Christianity, the Salt and Light series, and the Global China Center website.
- Host Chinese scholars in our homes, engage in correspondence with them, and seek, in a variety of ways, to build lasting friendships with both Chinese and non-Chinese believers and promote collaboration with Chinese scholars and nonprofit-sector practitioners in China, North America, Europe, and Asia.
- Inform, advise, and train those who desire to interact with Chinese on issues of Chinese culture, society, and history, building networks of Christian professionals in academia, nonprofit service, and business who can relate as peers to their Chinese counterparts.

PRAY FOR US

Prayer Updates

We send a monthly prayer letter to several hundred people and organizations. Each letter focuses on one theme, and the "Reaching Chinese Worldwide" series forms the basis of this book.

Weekly prayer updates go to a smaller number of committed prayer partners and include the most recent reports on what God has done, as well as requests for intercession.

SUPPORT US

China Institute and Global China Center are nonprofit organizations registered in Albemarle County, Virginia, and governed by a Board of Directors. Tax-deductible contributions may be sent to China Institute or Global China Center at the addresses listed in the "Contact Us" section. Please specify in the memo if you would like your donation to go toward a specific project or person.

CONTACT US

Please visit our websites or contact us for more information and resources. We would love to hear from you!

CHINA INSTITUTE

PO Box 7312
Charlottesville, VA 22906
chinainst.org
Telephone/fax: 434-974-1996
civirginia@nexet.net

GLOBAL CHINA CENTER

PMB 201, 977 Seminole Trail
Charlottesville, VA 22901
globalchinacenter.org
Telephone/fax: 434-974-1996
office@globalchina.org

CPSIA information can be obtained at www.ICGtesting.com
Printed in the USA
BVOW07s0457111213

338769BV00001B/77/P